Dimensions of Inequality

Dimensions of Inequality

Impacts on Growth, Governance and Human Development

Ines A. Ferreira, Rachel M. Gisselquist and Finn Tarp

BLOOMSBURY ACADEMIC
LONDON • NEW YORK • OXFORD • NEW DELHI • SYDNEY

BLOOMSBURY ACADEMIC

Bloomsbury Publishing Plc, 50 Bedford Square, London, WC1B 3DP, UK
Bloomsbury Publishing Inc, 1359 Broadway, New York, NY 10018, USA
Bloomsbury Publishing Ireland, 29 Earlsfort Terrace, Dublin 2, D02 AY28, Ireland

BLOOMSBURY, BLOOMSBURY ACADEMIC and the Diana logo are trademarks of Bloomsbury Publishing Plc

First published in Great Britain 2026

Copyright © Ines A. Ferreira, Rachel M. Gisselquist and Finn Tarp, 2026

Ines A. Ferreira, Rachel M. Gisselquist and Finn Tarp have asserted their right under the Copyright, Designs and Patents Act, 1988, to be identified as Authors of this work.

For legal purposes the Acknowledgements on pp. xiv–xvi constitute an extension of this copyright page.

Cover images: dMz via Pixabay and Frank Wagner and fotograzia via Getty Images

This work is published open access subject to a Creative Commons Attribution-NonCommercial-NoDerivatives 4.0 International licence (CC BY-NC-ND 4.0, https://creativecommons.org/licenses/by-nc-nd/4.0/). You may re-use, distribute, and reproduce this work in any medium for non-commercial purposes, provided you give attribution to the copyright holder and the publisher and provide a link to the Creative Commons licence.

No part of this publication may be used or reproduced in any way for the training, development or operation of artificial intelligence (AI) technologies, including generative AI technologies. The rights holders expressly reserve this publication from the text and data mining exception as per Article 4(3) of the Digital Single Market Directive (EU) 2019/790.

Bloomsbury Publishing Plc does not have any control over, or responsibility for, any third-party websites referred to or in this book. All internet addresses given in this book were correct at the time of going to press. The author and publisher regret any inconvenience caused if addresses have changed or sites have ceased to exist, but can accept no responsibility for any such changes.

A catalogue record for this book is available from the British Library.

Library of Congress Cataloging-in-Publication Data available

ISBN: HB: 978-1-350-51691-5
PB: 978-1-350-51690-8
ePDF: 978-1-350-51694-6
eBook: 978-1-350-51692-2

Typeset by Newgen KnowledgeWorks Pvt. Ltd., Chennai, India
Printed and bound in Great Britain

For product safety related questions contact productsafety@bloomsbury.com.

To find out more about our authors and books visit www.bloomsbury.com and sign up for our newsletters.

Contents

List of Figures	vi
List of Tables	ix
Notes on Authors	x
Preface	xii
Acknowledgements	xiv
1 Introduction: Inequality matters	1
2 Inequality of what?	21
3 Rising inequality?	53
4 How do people understand, perceive and act on inequality?	99
5 Inequality, economic growth and well-being	135
6 Inequality, governance and conflict	173
7 What should be done? What can be done?	203
Index	233

Figures

1.1	The evolution of global inequality	9
1.2	Growth incidence curve, 1988–2022	10
1.3	Global absolute income gains, 1988–2022	11
2.1	Lake Michelle, Masiphumelele Township, Cape Town, South Africa	23
2.2a	The Political Inequality Index for Colombia and South Africa	26
2.2b	Political inequality in Colombia	27
2.2c	Political inequality in South Africa	27
2.3	Proportion of seats held by women in national parliaments 2000–23	28
2.4	Human Development Index, 1990–2022	32
2.5	Evolution of the HDI at the departmental level in Colombia, 2011 and 2022	33
3.1	Evolution of Gini index in Colombia considering different measures of income	55
3.2	Simplified example of the different properties of inequality measures	62
3.3	Trends in inequality considering percentiles and the Palma ratio in Colombia and South Africa	64
3.4	Lorenz curves for Ethiopia, 1996–2016	67
3.5	Trends in inequality considering the Gini index and the mean log deviation (or M-Theil), South Africa and Vietnam	68
3.6	Different measures of inequality as different 'filters' of the empirical reality	74
3.7	Trends in global inequality using different relative measures	74

3.8	Decomposition of global inequality into within- and between-countries components based on the mean log deviation, 1950–2022	76
3.9	Income shares and ratios of different percentiles, 1950–2022	77
3.10	The updated 'elephant curve' (growth incidence curve), 1988–2022	79
3.11	Comparison between the relative and the absolute Gini coefficients, 1950–2022	80
3.12	The updated 'serpent curve' (global absolute income gain), 1980–2022	81
3.13	Absolute and relative Gini coefficients in countries with similar income levels, 1950–2022	84
3.14	Absolute and relative Gini coefficients in different regions, 1950–2022	86
3.15	Absolute and relative Gini coefficients in our five country cases, 1950–2022	89
4.1	Thinking about inequality in relative versus absolute terms	103
4.2	Inequality perceived as a problem versus actual level of inequality in Mozambique, 2001–22	107
4.3	Perceptions of inequality	109
4.4	Amount allocated to the other player in a modified dictator game	119
4.5	Share of participants agreeing that the source of inequality is fair	123
5.1	Stylized representation of the Kuznets curve	138
5.2	Evolution of the Gini coefficient in Colombia, 1964–2020	139
5.3	Trends in inequality and income in four countries	141
5.4	Human Development Index and the Gini coefficients over time for our five countries	155

5.5	Life satisfaction over time in Colombia, Ethiopia, Vietnam and South Africa	158
5.6	Subjective well-being and different measures of inequality over time in Colombia	159
6.1	Political party positioning in South Africa, 1994–9, according to the Comparative Manifestos Project	176
6.2	Political party positioning in South Africa 2014–19, according to the Comparative Manifestos Project	177
6.3	Interpersonal trust versus income inequality	180
7.1	Visual representation of Okun's 'leaky bucket' metaphor	205

Tables

2.1	Lifespan disparities	25
2.2	Multidimensional Inequality Framework (MIF): Domains	34
2.3	Intersectional inequalities in Colombia (%)	36
3.1	Gini coefficients according to the WIID and the WID databases	60
3.2	Examples of measures of inequality in 2020 using data from Ethiopia	69
5.1	Schematic representation of different mechanisms through which inequality leads to lower growth	144
5.2	References for empirical studies on the link between inequality and growth	148
6.1	Key mechanisms through which inequality impacts political and governance outcomes	191
7.1	Datt-Ravallion decomposition: illustration from Ethiopia, 2011–16	208
7.2	Policies affecting inequality: a framework of options	212

Notes on Authors

Ines A. Ferreira, a development economist, is an independent researcher. She was assistant professor with the University of Copenhagen (UCPH) Development Economics Research Group (DERG) until 2024. She works on different topics related to inequality and institutions, both from a cross-country perspective and with a particular focus on Mozambique and Vietnam. She has previously engaged in projects on the determinants of individual behaviour and preferences, poverty measurement, state fragility and aid effectiveness. Her publications include articles in various journals, such as *International Studies Review* and *Review of Development Economics*, alongside several book chapters and an edited book volume. Ines holds a PhD in International Development from the University of East Anglia and a master's degree in Political Economy of Late Development from the London School of Economics.

Rachel M. Gisselquist, a political scientist, is Professor in Governance and Development, and Director of the Governance and Social Development Resource Centre (GSDRC), University of Birmingham (UK). She is also a non-resident senior research fellow with the United Nations University World Institute for Development Economics Research (UNU-WIDER), where she was based during 2011–24. Previously, she was a research director at Harvard University, where she co-authored the first several editions of the Ibrahim Index of African Governance, now a standard reference on governance. Her research examines inequality, ethnic and identity politics, state capacity, aid and development cooperation, governance and democracy. She is the editor of *How States Respond to Crisis: Pandemic Governance across the Global South* (with A. Vaccaro) and *Fragile Aid: Development Cooperation in Weak States and Conflict Contexts* (with P. Justino and

A. Vaccaro), both published in 2025. Her publications include over thirty articles and chapters and fourteen edited special issues/sections in internationally refereed journals such as *World Development, Journal of Development Studies, Oxford Development Studies, Annals of the American Academy of Political and Social Science* and *Journal of Ethnic and Migration Studies*. She holds a PhD in Political Science from the Massachusetts Institute of Technology and an MPP from Harvard.

Finn Tarp, a development economist, is a University of Copenhagen (UCPH) Professor and Coordinator of the UCPH Development Economics Research Group (DERG). Formerly the Director of UNU-WIDER (2009–18) he is a leading international academic and policy expert on issues of development strategy and foreign aid, with extensive research in poverty, inequality, agricultural sector policy and planning, household and enterprise development, and climate change, sustainability and natural resources. His publications include more than 140 articles in internationally refereed academic journals, including top journals such as *The Economic Journal, Journal of Development Economics, World Bank Economic Review, European Economic Review, American Journal of Agricultural Economics, World Development, Oxford Bulletin of Economics and Statistics, Land Economics, Food Policy, Review of Income and Wealth, Journal of Economic Geography, Feminist Economics, Economic Development and Cultural Change, Journal of Development Studies,* and *Climatic Change* as well as regional journals including for example *Journal of African Economies, South African Journal of Economics, Journal of Asian Economics* and *China Economic Review* – alongside six books, thirty edited book volumes/special journal issues, seventy-three book chapters with leading international academic publishers plus a very large number of research reports and other studies and publications. He has extensive research and policy advisory background in countries such as Mozambique, Vietnam, South Africa, Tanzania, Kenya, Ethiopia, and Myanmar. His h-index is 71.

Preface

This book is the capstone presentation of the results of a multi-year, international and cross-disciplinary project, *The Impact of Inequality on Growth, Human Development, and Governance – @EQUAL*. Supported by the Novo Nordisk Foundation (Grant NNF19SA0060072), the project was carried out as a collaboration coordinated by researchers based in Denmark, Finland, Vietnam and Mozambique; at the University of Copenhagen's Development Economics Research Group (UCPH-DERG); United Nations University World Institute for Development Economics Research (UNU-WIDER) in Helsinki; Central Institute for Economic Management (CIEM) in Hanoi; and Eduardo Mondlane University in Maputo.

In the early stage of the project, we took stock of the research literature on inequality and its impact, with particular attention to work from economics and political science and decided to adopt a three-pronged approach to addressing gaps in the literature. First, we revisited findings at the cross-country level, drawing on new and existing datasets – in particular, but not only, UNU-WIDER's World Income Inequality Dataset (WIID). We explored for instance how core findings about inequality's impact may shift when different inequality measures are relied on.

Second, we conducted original field research in two low/lower-middle-income countries, Mozambique and Vietnam, to better understand how inequality is understood, perceived and acted upon in diverse contexts – outside the Global North. We used experimental approaches and collected survey data in both urban and rural areas across several parts of each country. We also conducted new econometric analysis of data for each country, considering several key hypotheses on the impact of inequality. Third, we brought the cross-country and in-country findings together, exploring how well the findings from our within-country work carried elsewhere, and how well cross-country findings applied in Mozambique and Vietnam.

In writing this book, we have drawn both on findings from our own original research and on our review of and reflection on the broader research literature. While based in scholarly research, it is written for a general audience and thus necessarily abbreviates and simplifies discussion of some topics.

Readers wishing to delve more deeply into the topics and studies discussed here may wish to consult the publications we reference throughout. In our view, this is always simpler to do when the works cited are close at hand – thus, we have kept reference lists at the end of each chapter, rather than at the end of the entire book as is more customary.

We have also highlighted a handful of key suggestions for further reading within each reference list, marked with bold text. We hope that students, for instance, might find these suggestions useful.

For those readers who may wish to read more about the research prepared under our @EQUAL project, we have marked these studies in each reference list with an asterisk. To date, the project has produced several dozen research studies, which are available as peer-reviewed journal articles, as working papers, or both. All this work is freely available. Journal articles and this volume are open access.

Acknowledgements

The idea for this book grew out of our work together over the past five years in the context of a project entitled *The Impact of Inequality on Growth, Human Development, and Governance – @EQUAL*. We are grateful to the Novo Nordisk Foundation (Grant NNF19SA0060072) for supporting the @EQUAL project, including Senior Vice-President for Impact, Dr Thomas Alslev Christensen, who guided us all along the process, and to our project research colleagues for their excellent collaboration, in particular Dr Thi Thu Hoai Dang and Mr Fernando Lichucha, who served as co-PIs along with Finn and Rachel.

Research conducted under the @EQUAL project is referenced throughout this volume. It has been a pleasure to engage with the researchers involved, as colleagues and (in many cases) co-authors. We have learned from and been inspired by their research and our discussions. These researchers include Sanghamitra Bandyopadhyay, Giulia Barletta, Enea Baselgia, Rute Martins Caeiro, David Castells-Quintana, Matthew Easterbrook, Shakeba Foster, Reto Foellmi, Carlos Gradin, Thu K. Hoang, Vanesa Jorda, Thomas Markussen, Miguel Niño-Zarazúa, Cuong Viet Nguyen, Annalena Oppel, Klarizze Puzon, Laurence Roope, Vincenzo Salvucci, Saurabh Singhal, Smriti Sharma and Andrea Vaccaro.

Antonio Diaz Caycedo provided excellent research assistance in the preparation of this volume, including sharing insight from his own research on inequality and conflict in Colombia. Antti Pelantari graciously lent his expertise on the World Income Inequality Database (WIID) and helped us to tease out and visualize key relationships in the data. He produced Figures 3.13–3.15 and numerous others that have informed this and related work. Anustup Kundu provided key research assistance in the early stages of the project. The data collection described in Chapter 4 was only possible thanks to the great work of the field coordinators in Mozambique – Giulia Barletta, Francesca Gioia, Agustina Lopez and Stefano Tarroni – and in Vietnam, Nghiêm Dinh Xuân, as well as the teams of enumerators in both countries. The data collection would not have been possible without the participants, who accepted to take part.

Discussion and feedback from colleagues in presentations on several key components of this book are greatly appreciated – at the Development Economics Research Group (UCPH-DERG); Nordic Conference in Development Economics; symposium on 'Perspectives on wealth and social inequality', organized by the Volkswagen Foundation; CEEG Seminar Series (University Eduardo Mondlane); UNU-WIDER Seminar Series; UNU-WIDER Development Conference on 'Reducing Inequality'; German Institute of Development and Sustainability (IDOS) conference, 'Perils and Promises: Social Cohesion Amidst the Global Polycrisis'; Bertelsmann Foundation's Symposium, 'Countering Democratic Erosion'; and a workshop hosted by the United Nations Office of the High Commissioner for Human Rights (OHCHR). We have also benefited from discussions with Tony Addison, Sam Jones, Omar McDoom, Ricardo Santos and numerous collaborators in Mozambique and Vietnam.

We are grateful for the institutional support provided by the Department of Economics, University of Copenhagen (UCPH) and UNU-WIDER throughout the @EQUAL project, with special thanks to Dominik Etienne, Christel Brink Hansen, Aino Hiltunen, Patricia Justino, Iina Kuuttila, Dorthe Mejlsted, Siméon Rapin, Mauricio Roa, Tim Shipp, Lumi Young and Vu Hong Nhung. The International Development Department and School of Government, University of Birmingham, provided a welcoming (new) institutional home for Rachel during the final stages of writing.

Our warmest gratitude to Lorraine Telfer-Taivainen for her expert editorial guidance and shepherding of this book from proposal to publication. At Bloomsbury, we thank Nick Wolterman and his colleagues for their support and encouragement, including expert editorial guidance.

Finally, we thank our families and partners. Writing a book, even a short one, takes much time and attention – and we have been lucky in their patience, support and engagement.

The usual caveats apply.

Ines A. Ferreira, Copenhagen
Rachel M. Gisselquist, Birmingham
Finn Tarp, Copenhagen
November 2025

1

Introduction: Inequality matters

Inequality matters. It matters for normative reasons, because people and societies care about fairness and social justice. And it matters because of its potential implications for major societal outcomes, from economic prosperity and well-being to good governance and peace. The UN Sustainable Development Goals (SDG)[1] underscore global commitment to addressing inequality, both in Goal 10: Reduce Inequality Within and Among Countries, and in the central, transformative promise of 'Leave No One Behind'.

In recent years, inequality has once again shifted to the centre of much public and international academic debate. Events such as the global financial crisis of 2008 and the Covid-19 pandemic have been held responsible for causing rising inequality, prompting renewed calls for solutions. 'Inequality Kills' is the attention-grabbing title of a 2022 Oxfam report. 'The wealth of the world's 10 richest men has doubled since the pandemic began. The incomes of 99% of humanity are worse off because of COVID-19' (Ahmed et al. 2022).

Many observers argue that rising inequality, in turn, is a cause of increasing political polarization, support for the far-right, vulnerability to crises, and violent conflicts. Indeed, reports underline, inequality 'hurts everyone, even the rich' (Ingraham 2018). Inequality means that 'social tensions will continue to rise in this century, fuelling populist nationalism and the erosion of democracy and public trust around the world' (Dixson-Decleve 2024). And it has been argued that rising inequality may fuel a new wave of populism (*The Economist* 2022).

Yet, is inequality actually rising? If it is, what are its precise trends? Experts disagree, sometimes sharply. 'Why economists are at war over inequality', *The Economist* explained in November 2023, reviewing debate over empirical trends in inequality in the United States between economists Thomas Piketty, Emmanuel Saez and Gabriel Zucman on the one hand, and Gerald Auten and David Splinter on the other. While Piketty et al. claimed rising inequality, Auten and Splinter found stability – 'the idea that inequality is rising is very far from a self-evident truth', concluded *The Economist*. In *The Atlantic*, Yascha Mounk considered updated findings from what he described as 'three former prophets of [economic] doom' – Piketty along with Branko Milanović and David Autor. 'It would be premature to put worries about stagnating incomes or rising inequality to rest', Mounk argued, but updated findings suggest these outcomes are not inevitable. Social and political factors play a significant role in shaping economic outcomes (Mounk 2023). The debate continues. In a 2024 working paper, Piketty, Saez and Zucman (2024) responded again to Auten and Splinter, arguing that 'correcting for errors' in their analysis, inequality is indeed rising.

In brief, even with respect to what might seem to be simple facts, discussions about inequality are themselves often polarized. Experts on inequality present multiple views, backed by sophisticated analysis – but how is the layperson to navigate the evidence and engage in informed conversation and reflection? Debates also are often skewed to focus on the experiences of those in predominantly Western, high-income countries – but what about the troubling inequality in low- and middle-income countries in Africa, Asia and Latin America?

This book speaks to these gaps and contrasting understandings. Grounded both in our own research and findings, as well as the broader research literature, we aim to offer a balanced, readable introduction to what is happening to inequality and its impact – with examples from across the Global South. In so doing, we advance two central points that push beyond current characteristics in the literature and public debates.

First, there is no single 'best' indicator or measure of inequality. Inequality is multidimensional. Measures of inequality often relate to economic inequality between individuals or households, but indicators of its other aspects – social, political, spatial, cultural and so on – and of inequalities between groups, can also be highly relevant. Even with a narrow focus on economic inequality, and specifically – like much of the economics literature – income inequality, understanding income inequality and how to address it requires consideration of the whole distribution and a range of measures. The Gini coefficient tends to be the 'go-to' measure of inequality, but it is alone insufficient. In particular, it is a measure of *relative* inequality only. Different measures reflect different values and different empirical realities, and give rise to conflicting popular narratives around inequality trends.

Second, individuals around the world understand, perceive and act on 'unequal' distributions sometimes in similar, and sometimes in dramatically different ways. It is not surprising then that links between measured inequality and individual and group behaviour can vary considerably across contexts. Inequality is a global challenge, but both global and local knowledge are essential to understand and address it.

In this introductory chapter we consider these two arguments in more depth, situating them within broader conversations on inequality and its impact. We also introduce the five countries to which we pay special attention throughout this book: Colombia, Ethiopia, Mozambique, South Africa and Vietnam. While our arguments and evidence extend beyond these countries, they serve here as empirical touchpoints and illustrations. This book was developed under a multi-year project entitled *The Impact of Inequality on Growth, Human Development, and Governance – @EQUAL*, funded by the

Novo Nordisk Foundation; the preface provides further details on this project.

Each of the following six chapters addresses a key question or set of questions. Chapters 2 and 3 speak to how inequality is conceptualized and measured, and what we know about its trends and patterns across and within countries. Chapter 4 turns to how inequality is perceived and understood by individuals around the world. Chapters 5 and 6 discuss the impact of inequality on economic growth and well-being, and governance and conflict, respectively. Bringing the threads of our discussion together, Chapter 7 considers what can be done to address inequality with a focus on government policies.

This book is written specifically for an interested general audience. Our academic publications provide more in-depth and formal presentation of core arguments and evidence. For readers who wish to delve more deeply into the topics introduced here, we have included details in notes and reference lists at the end of each chapter. We have highlighted in bold in these lists a handful – and no more than a handful – of readings that we recommend as good places to continue. In addition, we have marked with an asterisk work from our @EQUAL project.

What's new?

Over the past decade, scholars have released a number of popular books on inequality. These include, for instance, Thomas Piketty's *Capital in the Twenty-First Century* (2014); Anthony Atkinson's *Inequality: What Can Be Done?* (2015); Keith Payne's *The Broken Ladder: How Inequality Affects the Way We Think, Live, and Die* (2017); Branko Milanovic's *Global Inequality: A New Approach for the Age of Globalization* (2018) and *Visions of Inequality: From the French Revolution to the End of the Cold War* (2023); Richard Wilkinson and Kate Pickett's

The Spirit Level: Why More Equal Societies Almost Always Do Better (2009) and *The Inner Level: How More Equal Societies Reduce Stress, Restore Sanity and Improve Everyone's Wellbeing* (2018); and Marcos González Hernando and Gerry Mitchell's *Uncomfortably Off: Why Inequality Matters for High Earners* (2023). Nobel laureates Joseph Stiglitz and Angus Deaton have also weighed in with *The Price of Inequality: How Today's Divided Society Endangers our Future* (2012) and *The Great Escape: Health, Wealth, and the Origins of Inequality* (2013), respectively. For a more academic audience, Deaton's 2024 edited collection *Dimensions of Inequality: the IFS Deaton Review*, published by Oxford Open Economics, provides encyclopaedic coverage with seventeen topical chapters, from the history of inequality to gender. Some of our own work fits here as well – in particular, *Inequality in the Developing World*, edited by Carlos Gradín, Murray Leibbrandt and Finn Tarp (2021).

This book is different in several ways. First, previous studies have focused a lot on trends in inequality and the factors that cause or drive these trends. Piketty, for instance, argues for an inevitable link from market capitalism to rising inequality. Milanovic shows how inequality has evolved over hundreds of years across and within countries in cycles. And Deaton finds that uneven global progress over the past 250 years has set the stage for major inequalities today. This book, in contrast, concentrates on what inequality means and its impact – that is, on how inequality is understood, perceived and acted upon by people, communities and countries. This is not because understanding the causes of inequality is unimportant, but because discussing both inequality's causes and its impact would be at least two volumes, not one. And the former is already well covered in other works, in our view.

Second, the existing literature on inequality tends to offer highly focused (and sometimes highly technical) discussion of specific arguments or topics, while our book aims for a broader synthesis to help readers navigate the major debates. This makes our book very different to one like Piketty's *Capital in the Twenty-First Century*, which advances the important and provocative argument – over almost 700 pages – that market capitalism leads inevitably to economies dominated by inherited wealth, and a rising wealth-to-income ratio absent of major interventions.[2] Or to a book like *The Price of Inequality*, in which Stiglitz spotlights the vicious cycle of inequality in the United States, shaped by the ways in which 'politics have shaped the market, and shaped it in ways that advantage the top at the expense of the rest' – with negative consequences for growth, political polarization, and democracy. There are several volumes that provide brief introductions to specific topics in inequality[3] but broad introductions are in short supply.

Third, much of the literature focuses on Western, high-income countries, when inequality is also concerning in low- and middle-income countries, in Africa, Asia and Latin America. Stiglitz in his *The Price of Inequality* is concerned with the United States, and Wilkinson and Pickett with wealthy countries. Piketty draws on data primarily from Europe and the United States, while Gonzales Hernando and Mitchell focus on data primarily from the UK, as does Deaton's 2024 IFS review. Academic research, including some of our own, does study inequality extensively in developing countries and we draw on that here in putting together this book.

Finally, we advance two central points that push beyond current characteristics in popular debate and the research literature:

Dimensions of inequality: A dashboard approach

The Gini coefficient is the go-to measure of inequality in both popular and policy research discussion (see Box 1.1). When comparing inequality across countries it is often the Gini coefficient that is used to rank them – for instance, in CNN's reporting that South Africa was the most unequal country in the world (Scott 2019). In a recent review of the literature, we counted that sixty-nine of ninety-eight studies used the Gini as a key measure of inequality (sometimes along with other measures) (Ferreira, Gisselquist and Tarp 2022).

Box 1.1: The Gini coefficient

The Gini coefficient, developed by the Italian statistician Corrado Gini (1884–1965), is the most commonly used measure of inequality. It is typically used for income inequality but can be used to measure the inequality of any distribution – such as wealth.

The Gini coefficient measures inequality on a scale 0–1, where higher values indicate higher inequality. A value of 0 indicates perfect equality: everyone has the same income. A value of 1 indicates perfect inequality where one person receives all the income: everyone else receives nothing. This is often shown as a percentage 0–100 per cent, known as the Gini index.

The Gini coefficient provides important information, but is alone insufficient and can be misleading. Research literature provides extensive discussion of diverse measures of inequality, including their conceptual foundations, relative merits and empirical comparisons. There is a large body of work advocating for or adopting different measurement approaches. For instance, Piketty and colleagues associated with the World Inequality Lab argue for focus on top and bottom welfare shares, with attention to different dimensions of inequality, such as wealth, income and carbon emissions. Alternatively, UNU-WIDER's World Income Inequality Database (WIID)[4] focuses on income inequality, and covers a variety of measures, including the Gini as well as various absolute measures, such as the absolute Gini and the coefficient of variation of incomes, and relative measures, such as the Theil and Atkinson index families.

We do not take sides in the measurement debates. Instead we favour a dashboard approach with consideration of the whole distribution and a range of indicators, including both relative approaches (like the Gini) and 'absolute' and 'mixed' approaches. We see a dashboard approach as essential for diagnosing inequality trends and challenges, as well as for designing appropriate policy interventions and evaluating their impact.

Of course, few of us have the time to compile and reflect on such comprehensive information whenever we read about or discuss inequality in everyday life. But, even when we rely by necessity on a few selected indicators, we can still benefit from deeper understanding of how they compare theoretically and empirically with other indicators. This can help us to ask good questions and to evaluate claims critically.

Let's think about the Gini coefficient. The Gini is a relative measure, which means that if the relative relationship remains the same there is no recorded change in inequality, even if the absolute gap between the poorest and richest widens dramatically.[5]

For instance: suppose that ten years ago Mahmoud earned $1 a day and his neighbour earned $10 a day, while today Mahmoud earns $10 a day and his neighbour earns $100 a day. A relative measure of inequality, like the Gini, will record inequality as unchanged. Ten years ago, Mahmoud's neighbour earned ten times more than him per day, and today he also earns ten times more.

Such a measure of inequality is not 'incorrect', but it obscures an important fact: ten years ago Mahmoud's neighbour earned $9 more than him, but today the neighbour earns $90 more. The income gap has widened, and Mahmoud is now far behind his neighbour in absolute terms. Many of us intuitively see the situation today as more unequal and less fair than the situation ten years ago, but this intuition is not captured in the Gini. By extension, if we look only at the Gini coefficient when considering inequality in Mahmoud's community we would miss an inequality rise in this latter sense.

As we will see in Chapters 2 and 3, different types of inequality measures sometimes reveal dramatically different patterns and trends – as the example of Mahmoud and his neighbour suggests. This is the case for instance with *global* inequality over the past decades: relative measures suggest a general decline in global inequality, while absolute measures show an increase. The former has been the dominant view in the economics literature, while the latter characterization is more consistent with civil society narratives around inequality – that the world is becoming less equal.

This is illustrated in Figure 1.1 drawn from WIID data on global income inequality. The graph indicates a steep decline in the Gini (i.e., relative global income inequality) from the 1990s to the 2020s, but in terms of absolute inequality (as measured here by the 'absolute Gini') there has been a consistent increase since the 1950s linked directly to global economic growth. The latter is a function of how it is calculated. In brief, the absolute Gini, which is obtained by multiplying the

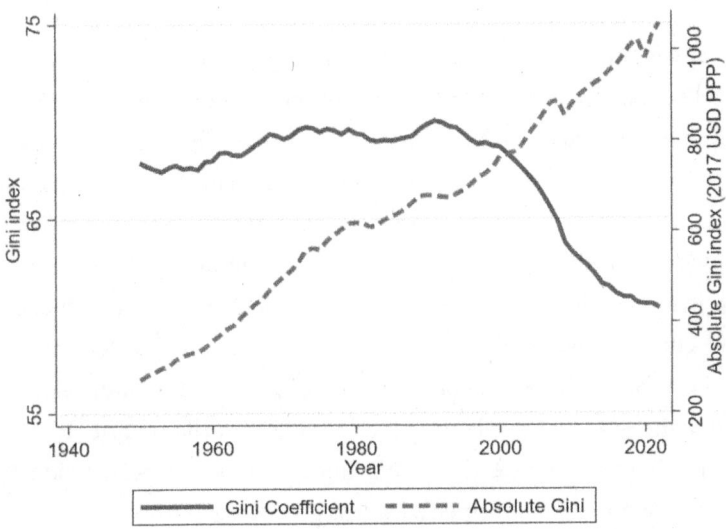

Figure 1.1 The evolution of global inequality.

Source: Authors' illustration based on UNU-WIDER, World Income Inequality Database (WIID) Companion Dataset data.

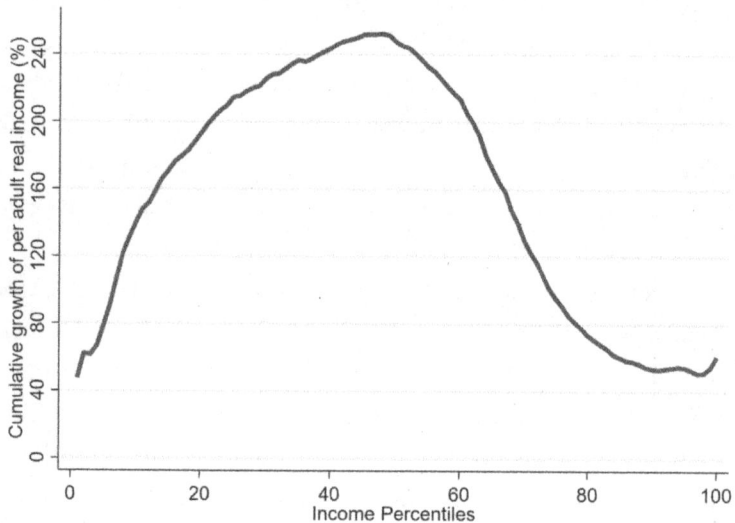

Figure 1.2 Growth incidence curve, 1988–2022.

Source: Authors' illustration based on UNU-WIDER, World Income Inequality Database (WIID) Companion Dataset data.

(relative) Gini by the mean income, can capture the widening income gap between Mahmoud and his neighbour in the example above, but it also has drawbacks – as we discuss further in Chapter 3. Figures 1.2 and 1.3 reflect two other ways of representing change in global incomes and inequality. Figure 1.2 is known as a growth incidence curve, which shows cumulative growth rates of average incomes of different parts of the income distribution over the years 1988–2022. This graph shows that cumulative growth in real income has been lowest for the very poorest (at the lowest income percentiles) and the wealthiest (those above the 80th percentile or so), and highest in the middle. In other words, it suggests that the global middle class has been rising the fastest – a possible movement towards greater equality.

Figure 1.3 shows global absolute income gains over the same period. While Figure 1.2 shows growth rates of average incomes on the y-axis (a relative measure), Figure 1.3 shows absolute changes in

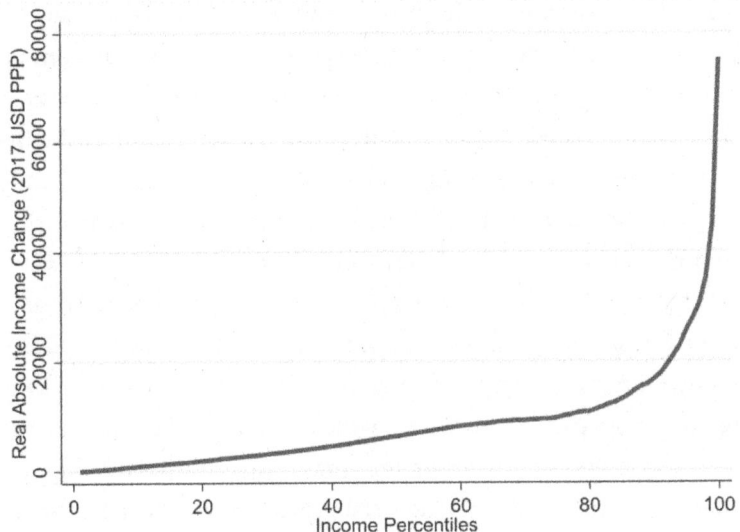

Figure 1.3 Global absolute income gains, 1988–2022.

Source: Authors' illustration based on UNU-WIDER, World Income Inequality Database (WIID) Companion Dataset data.

average incomes. Figure 1.3 shows dramatic increase in the incomes of the wealthiest 90+ per cent during 1988–2022, spotlighting a more concerning picture of rising inequality. Both figures *are* correct but each point towards different possible concerns – considering both together is worthwhile.

Inequality's impact: Similarities and differences in how inequality is understood and how it matters around the world

A common theme in best-selling books on inequality is that inequality is concerning, not only for moral reasons but also because it has negative implications for many other outcomes that we care about. In *The Spirit Level* and *The Inner Level*, for instance, Wilkinson and Pickett (2009, 2018) present a powerful argument that inequality has wide-ranging negative consequences for health and well-being.

But does everyone understand 'inequality' in the same way? And is 'inequality's' impact the same everywhere? How well do common understandings across diverse contexts match up with the measures and indicators used in academic research? We look in more depth at these perceptual issues in Chapter 4, as well as in Chapters 5 and 6, showing that there can be both striking differences across and within countries, as well as some notable similarities.

What this means is that while we are deeply concerned about inequality and its potential harms, we also caution against universal claims. Our own research demonstrates that, while the literature shows support in specific contexts for a wide range of hypotheses about the impact of inequality on economic prosperity, human development, good governance and democratic stability, systematic support in cross-country analyses is in fact slim (Ferreira, Gisselquist and Tarp 2022). In other words, there seems to be evidence for particular hypotheses in some contexts, but not across all countries. In our view, this is not that surprising precisely because there is so much variation in how individuals around the world understand, perceive and act on 'unequal' distributions. Because of this, measured inequality likely has different impacts on individual and group behaviour in different circumstances.

Consider again the situation of Mahmoud and his neighbour. Let's suppose that, like many of us, Mahmoud sees the situation today where he earns $90 per day less than his neighbour as fundamentally more unequal and far less fair than the situation ten years ago. This may influence both his views – how he feels about the economy, government policy and his neighbours in general – and his actions – how he votes, how much he is willing to cooperate with his neighbour and others in his community and whether he joins a social movement that pushes for change. While a Gini measure of inequality would be unchanged, Mahmoud, influenced by (his perception of) inequality, may change his behaviour. In Chapters 5 and 6 we look at such linkages in more depth.

Universal claims about inequality's impact are not only problematic for understanding such relationships, they are also problematic for action to address inequality because they lead us towards one-size-fits-all thinking. Chapter 7 explores these issues.

Five countries

The core arguments of this book build on a wide range of research, both theoretical and empirical, both cross-country and within country. In the rest of this volume, however, we provide empirical examples principally from five Global South countries – Colombia, Ethiopia, Mozambique, South Africa and Vietnam. Collectively we have long-standing research experience and multiple publications on four of these countries (Ethiopia, Mozambique, South Africa and Vietnam), and long-standing research interest on the fifth. These are not formal case studies from which our core arguments in this book are generated or tested. Rather we selected them to illustrate a range of issues and dilemmas we consider in this volume.

Three of these countries are in Africa, a region of global concern in terms of both inequality and poverty trends, as well as a region which often receives comparatively little attention. Ethiopia is the second most populous country in the region. In 2024, it had 127 million people and the fifth largest economy with a nominal gross domestic product (GDP) of $163.70 billion.[6] Its nominal GDP per capita of $1,293 is like that of Senegal, Haiti, and Kenya. South Africa, with roughly half the population of Ethiopia (60.4 million) and twice the nominal GDP ($377.78 billion), is the fourth most populous country in the region and the largest economy. Its GDP per capita ($6,253) is the seventh highest in the region, just under that of Equatorial Guinea. Mozambique by contrast has the ninth lowest GDP per capita ($608) in the region. Its GDP of $20.62 million is mid-range in the region, and its population (33.90 million) is less than a third of Ethiopia's.

Latin America has been described as the world's most unequal region, but also one where inequality is falling.[7] From Latin America, we offer examples from Colombia, the third most populous country in the region (52.10 million) and fourth largest economy (nominal GDP of $363.54 billion). Its GDP per capita ($6,979), which exceeds South Africa's by almost a thousand dollars, is on the mid-low side compared to other countries in the region.

In contrast to Latin America, Asia in recent years has been noted for rising income inequality, a shift from the past 'growth with equity' performance in many Asian countries.[8] From Asia, we consider here Vietnam, the sixteenth most populous country in the world (about 98.9 million people). Its GDP of $429.71 billion and GDP per capita of $4,347 are broadly mid-range in comparison to other Asian and Southeast Asian countries.

As explored further below, across these five countries, there is deep diversity not only in size and economic structure, but also in history, society and politics. Several (South Africa and Colombia) are electoral or 'flawed' democracies (see Nord et al. 2024; Economist Intelligence Unit 2024).[9] Vietnam, by contrast, is a one-party authoritarian system dominated by the Communist Party of Vietnam. Also an authoritarian state, Ethiopia has been considerably more unstable in recent years with ongoing conflict since 2018. Mozambique, which has been considered a flawed electoral democracy, held its first multiparty elections in 1994, although the opposition has disputed the results of recent elections.

The experiences of these five countries are not presented to be representative, even of their regions. Nor are they necessarily generalizable – as we argue in this volume, inequality and its impact vary sometimes considerably across contexts. That said, as we also argue, they are not necessarily unique. Some similarities are apparent in how individuals around the world understand, perceive and act on 'unequal' distributions across diverse contexts.

Looking ahead

The next chapter of this book provides an empirical starting point, addressing the question: Inequality of what? It defines inequality and considers the diverse dimensions and indicators of inequality and how they relate to each other. It explores the relationship between income and wealth inequality and considers economic, social and political dimensions of inequality and the multiple indicators that can be used to measure such dimensions. It considers group-based (horizontal) versus individual (vertical) approaches to inequality, with attention to ethnicity and to gender, and discusses inequality of opportunity versus inequality of outcome.

Chapter 3 delves more deeply into questions about the concept and measurement of economic inequality, especially income inequality; its empirical patterns and trends; and how we can make sense of the diverse numbers reported in the press and social media, by civil society groups and in academic research – which often seem to conflict. It introduces key definitions of income inequality and conceptual approaches, as well as discussing data and data challenges with particular attention to income and consumption inequality. Through this discussion, we illustrate how different measures are linked to varying value judgements and reflect different empirical realities. While the Gini coefficient has long been the go-to measure of inequality, it is insufficient in capturing this diversity.

Chapter 4 considers how beliefs and perceptions of economic inequality compare with the sorts of numbers presented in Chapters 2 and 3. That is: How do individuals perceive inequality, what are some key ways this varies across countries and contexts, and what factors influence such perceptions? How 'accurately' do individuals identify inequality in their societies and their own position compared to others? It explores whether individuals think about inequality in relative versus absolute terms, and how their behaviour may be influenced by available information and by the framing of information – as well as the match between understandings and measures including the Gini. It considers also the closely linked concept of fairness and how it relates to preferences for redistribution. While underscoring variation across diverse cultures and contexts, discussion also points to evidence for some commonalities in response to perceived fair and unfair situations.

Chapters 5 and 6 examine evidence on the impact of economic inequality on key outcomes. Chapter 5 focuses on economic prosperity and well-being. It begins with consideration of economic growth and inequality, and the classic question of whether increases in inequality are inevitable with growth, alongside several illustrative examples. It then considers in turn inequality's impact on growth and on key indicators of human development and well-being, and concludes by reflecting on arguably inherent tensions between growth and inequality.

Chapter 6 speaks to questions on the relationship between economic inequality and political stability and institutions, with diverse country examples. It begins with consideration of the (imperfect) linkages between inequality and political polarization, social cohesion and trust, and the relationship between economic inequality and political inequality – all of which may in turn have implications for conflict and good governance. It considers multiple channels through which the level of inequality may influence democracy and political stability, in linear as well as non-linear ways.

Chapter 7 concludes with consideration of what should and can be done? It reflects on divergent perspectives on potential trade-offs between inequality and other key objectives, and maps diverse governmental strategies to address inequality. It presents selected examples of promising interventions from around the world, and considers both constraints and opportunities for action.

Notes

1 United Nations Sustainable Development Goals. https://sdgs.un.org/goals
2 https://mpra.ub.uni-muenchen.de/52384/1/MPRA_paper_52384.pdf
3 For instance, Beramendi and Rogers's *Geography, Capacity, and Inequality: Spatial Inequality,* or Tanninen, Tuomala and Tuominen's *Inequality and Optimal Redistribution*, both published by Cambridge Elements.
4 https://www.wider.unu.edu/project/wiid-%E2%80%93-world-income-inequality-database
5 If a doubling of income takes place everywhere in the income distribution then there is no change in inequality as measured by the Gini, even if the absolute gap between the poorest and richest widens drastically (scale neutrality).
6 Figures in this section are drawn from the World Bank's World Development Indicators (WDI) database, last accessed 22 August 2024. We use nominal GDP in current US$, which measures economic activity based on current market prices. This means that comparisons between countries are difficult, as the same US$ can buy different amounts of goods in different countries, with sometimes striking differences. To overcome this limitation, economists often adjust currency exchange rates to the amount of goods the currency can buy. When GDP is adjusted for local prices, economists use the term purchasing power parity, or PPP.
7 See, e.g., https://www.imf.org/external/pubs/ft/fandd/2015/09/pdf/lustig.pdf
8 See, e.g., https://www.adb.org/publications/demystifying-rising-inequality-asia
9 In its 2024 Democracy Report, the Varieties of Democracy (V-Dem) institute rated South Africa and Colombia 0.69 and 0.70 respectively in

terms of electoral democracy, while Vietnam was rated 0.15. Scores in the 2024 report describe 2023; see Nord et al. 2024.

References

Ahmed, N., A. Marriott, N. Dabi, M. Lowthers, M. Lawson and L. Mugehera (2022). *Inequality Kills: The Unparalleled Action Needed to Combat Unprecedented Inequality in the Wake of COVID-19*. Oxfam Report. Oxford: Oxfam House.

Dixson-Decleve, S. (2024). 'Growing Income Inequality is Driving Public Mistrust'. *The Financial Times*. 15 January.

Economist Intelligence Unit (2024). *Democracy Index 2023: Age of Conflict*. London: Economist Intelligence Unit.

Economist, The (2022). 'Inequality in Latin America is Fuelling a New Wave of Populism: The Jet Set and the Rest.' 6 August.

*Ferreira, I. A., R. M. Gisselquist and F. Tarp (2022). 'On the Impact of Inequality on Growth, Human Development, and Governance'. *International Studies Review*, 24(1). https://doi.org/10.1093/isr/viab 058. Accessed: 9 September 2025.

Hernando, M. G. and G. Mitchell (2023) *Uncomfortably Off: Why Addressing Inequality Matters, Even for High Earners*. Bristol: Policy Press.

Ingraham, C. (2018). 'How Rising Inequality Hurts Everyone, Even the Rich'. *The Washington Post*. 6 February. https://www.washingtonpost.com/news/wonk/wp/2018/02/06/how-rising-inequality-hurts-every one-even-the-rich/.

Mounk, Y. (2023). 'Goodbye to the Prophets of Doom'. *The Atlantic*. http://archive.today/2023.07.17-142925/https://www.theatlantic.com/ideas/archive/2023/07/economics-inequality-piketty-milanovic/674702/. Accessed: 9 September 2025.

Nord, M., M. Lundstedt, D. Altman, F. Angiolillo, C. Borella, T. Fernandes, L. Gastaldi, A. Good God, N. Natsika and S. I. Lindberg (2024). *Democracy Report 2024: Democracy Winning and Losing at the Ballot*. Gothenburg: V-Dem Institute, University of Gothenburg. https://

www.v-dem.net/documents/44/v-dem_dr2024_highres.pdf. Accessed: 9 September 2025.

Piketty, T., E. Saez and G. Zucman (2024). 'Income Inequality in the United States: A comment'. World Inequality Lab Technical Note 04/2024. Paris: Paris School of Economics.

Scott, K. (2019). 'South Africa is the World's Most Unequal Country. 25 years of Freedom Have Failed to Bridge the Divide'. *CNN*. https://edition.cnn.com/2019/05/07/africa/south-africa-elections-inequality-intl/index.html. Accessed: 9 September 2025.

Wilkinson, R., and K. Pickett (2009). *The Spirit Level: Why Greater Equality Makes Societies Stronger*. London: Bloomsbury Press.

Wilkinson, R., and K. Pickett (2018). *The Inner Level: How More Equal Societies Reduce Stress, Restore Sanity and Improve Everyone's Wellbeing*. London: Penguin Books.

2

Inequality of what?

Now we delve more deeply into the nature of inequality and its patterns and trends, with attention to inequality as a multidimensional concept. We consider inequality in economic, social and political dimensions, and how multiple dimensions intersect. We explore different indicators and how they compare. We also consider how inequality can be observed not only among individuals, or across households, but also between groups in society – for instance, among countries, regions, or ethnic groups, or across genders – and we address the concept of inequality of opportunity.

Dimensions of inequality

Inequality is commonly defined as 'the difference' or 'unfair difference' in social status, wealth or opportunities between people or groups of people.[1] While sometimes discussed in terms of disparities in income, assets or education for instance, inequality as a concept is far broader. Consideration of its multiple dimensions is important for understanding both the nature of inequality and its impact. The literature considers this multidimensionality from many different perspectives. Amartya Sen's seminal and influential 'capability approach' spotlights inequality, as well as poverty and development, as multidimensional concepts linked to capabilities and freedoms (see Box 2.1). The approach 'concentrates on our capability to achieve

> **Box 2.1: Sen's capability approach**
>
> Sen's capability approach advises us not to make misleading judgements about a person's well-being by merely focusing on their choices and not the opportunities open to them. Sen's classic example is of a fasting saint vis-à-vis a starving peasant. Focusing on the chosen functioning, the saint and peasant appear to have the same level of nourishment, or lack thereof. The saint has chosen to fast but could avoid hunger, whereas the peasant does not have that choice.
>
> For his contributions to welfare economics, Amartya Sen won the Nobel Prize in economics in 1998.

valuable functionings that make up our lives, and more generally, our freedom to promote objectives we have reasons to value' (Sen 1992).[2]

Sen introduced the concept of capability in his 1979 Tanner Lecture *Equality of What?* Considering different approaches to equality, he argued that each had major limitations and that an alternative formulation was needed that goes beyond the then conventional focus on utility, income or primary goods. According to Sen, to address disparities in well-being, (non-)exploitation, entitlements and needs, it is necessary to consider 'some notion of "basic capabilities": a person being able to do certain basic things' – for instance, the ability to move around, 'to meet one's nutritional requirements, the wherewithal to be clothed and sheltered, the power to participate in the social life of the community' (p. 218). This notion, he argued, is not captured in approaches focusing on utility or primary goods.[3] Sen's capability approach has had wide-ranging influence on thinking and policy in international development and has served as the foundation for multiple measurement projects – as we discuss more in the next section.

Another example of a multidimensional approach to inequality is that of sociologist Göran Therborn. He distinguishes among three core dimensions: *vital inequality* of life expectancy and health; *existential inequality* of human dignity and autonomy; and *material and resources inequality* including access to natural resources (Therborn 2007, 2012).

A third example can be seen in economist Frances Stewart's work on horizontal inequality (which we return to later) in its definition of horizontal inequalities as 'inequalities in economic, social or political dimensions or cultural status between culturally defined groups' (Stewart and Langer 2008). In the economic dimension, inequality can be observed for instance in disparities in wages or income, spending and consumption, or ownership of land and other assets.

Some economic inequalities may be highly visible, evident for instance when walking through different neighbourhoods in the same city (see Figure 2.1). Or they may be less readily apparent – unless we have access to private information such as savings balances.

Figure 2.1 Lake Michelle, Masiphumelele Township, Cape Town, South Africa.

Source: Photo by permission of Johnny Miller @Unequal Scenes.

Inequalities in the social dimension often intersect with the economic – but are also distinct. Educational attainment, occupation, and social class are common indicators of social (or socioeconomic) inequalities. The distinction between the social and economic dimensions can be seen with each of these indicators. There is of course a relationship between inequalities in educational opportunity and inequalities in wealth and income (Pfeffer 2018), but it is not one-to-one. Primary, secondary and tertiary education completion rates capture different information to wealth or income. The poorest generally have the lowest levels of educational attainment, but factors such as the quality of state-funded education may mediate this relationship. In higher education, various policy measures around outreach and financial aid can facilitate stronger educational attainment for economically disadvantaged students (Herbaut and Geven 2020).

Likewise, social class identifiers are generally more than a reference to where an individual fits in income or wealth brackets, or to their position in the economic structure more broadly. They also imply something about social status, cultural norms and practice, and possibly collective class consciousness (Kraus, Piff and Keltner 2011). Indicators of social class in turn may be revealing of inequalities in cultural status among groups. Accent or native fluency in a national language, for instance, are common indicators of social class, reflecting also disparities in cultural status between dominant and subordinate cultural groups (Langer and Brown 2008).

Many indicators of social inequality, such as educational attainment, are ordinal; they have a clear ordering, such as the number of years of schooling completed, or completion of various levels or degrees from primary school to post-graduate. Other indicators are more categorical. For instance, occupations are routinely ranked in classification from lower to higher skilled, or lower to higher status, but such ranking is not intrinsic in the same way as years of schooling, or annual income. Still inequality implies ranking, even if contested.

As Therborn argues, inequality is distinct from difference, for one because it implies a hierarchical ranking (Therborn 2007, 2012).

Health inequalities might also be considered under the social dimension – just as healthcare policy is a core component of social policy. For Therborn these fall under 'vital inequalities' – in life expectancy and health.

One way to measure inequality in life expectancy is to calculate the 'Lifespan Disparity', which is the average remaining life expectancy at death within a population. As such, it is an absolute measure of lifespan inequality. Recent work by Jorda, Niño-Zarazúa and Tejería-Martínez (2024) has compiled lifespan disparity statistics for 258 countries for the period 1950–2021. Table 2.1 provides lifespan disparity numbers for our five example countries, showing in all cases decreases in inequality according to this measure.

Inequalities in the political dimension, closely related to existential inequalities in Therborn's terms, often speak to disparities in representation and access, reflected in indicators of whether individuals have equal voice or opportunity for participation in politics. Political equality in turn is closely bound to democratic theory. In Dahl (1971)'s conceptualization, for instance, democracy[4] requires eight institutional guarantees ensuring that citizens may formulate and signify their preferences, and that government will equally weigh those preferences in its rule. Free and fair elections are important, but so are freedom of

Table 2.1 Lifespan disparities

Country	Lifespan Disparity	
	1950	2021
Colombia	23.7	12.9
Ethiopia	26.3	15.8
Mozambique	26.3	16.5
Vietnam	23.4	13.2
South Africa	24.5	16.1

Source: Based on Jorda, Niño-Zarazúa and Tejería-Martínez (2024).

expression and freedom to form and join associations and institutions, such as legislatures, that tie government policy to citizen preferences.

Choi (2019), for instance, is one effort to quantify political inequalities in a manner that can be compared across countries and over time. Covering sixty-seven countries during 1990–2016, the Political Inequality Index (PII) is based on indicators of equality in democratic participation and representation.[5] The aggregated values are then normalised on a scale of 0–100, with 0 corresponding to the lowest value in the data and 100 the highest.

Using the PII we can compare Colombia and South Africa for instance and consider changes in their political inequality over time. As Figure 2.2a illustrates, according to this measure, both countries show a generally downward trend in political inequality over 1990–2016, while Colombia is slightly less unequal (more equal) than South Africa in the final year (a value of 39.5 versus 41.7). Figures 2.2b and 2.2c show how the index and its subcomponents evolved over time in each country.

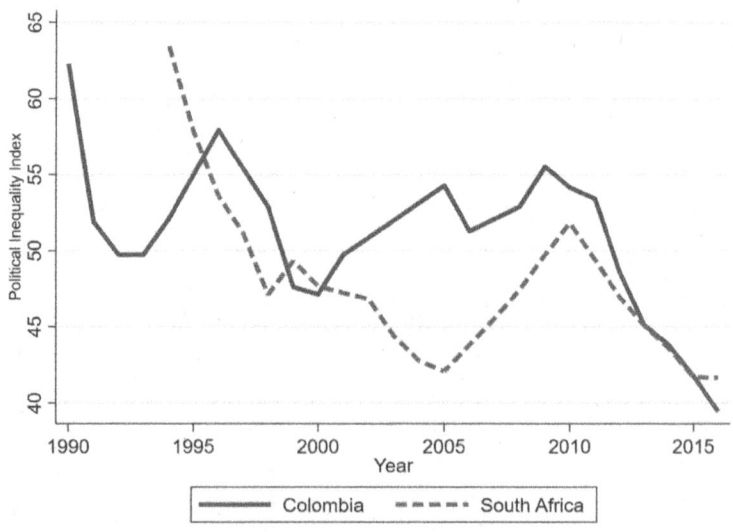

Figure 2.2a The Political Inequality Index for Colombia and South Africa.

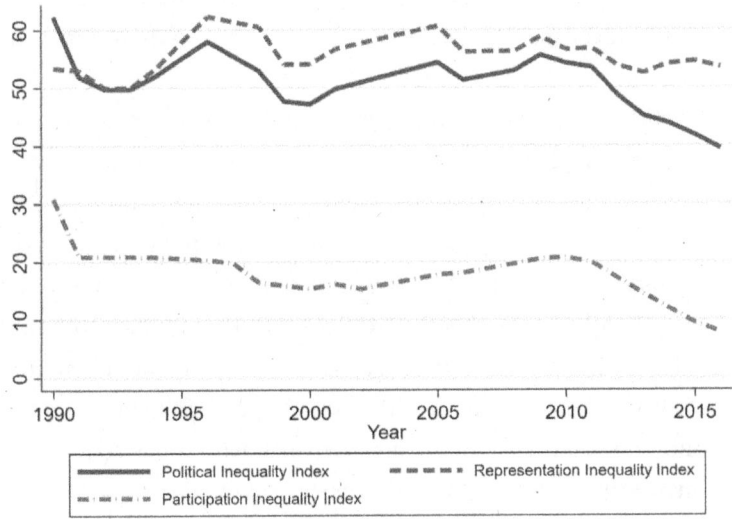

Figure 2.2b Political inequality in Colombia.

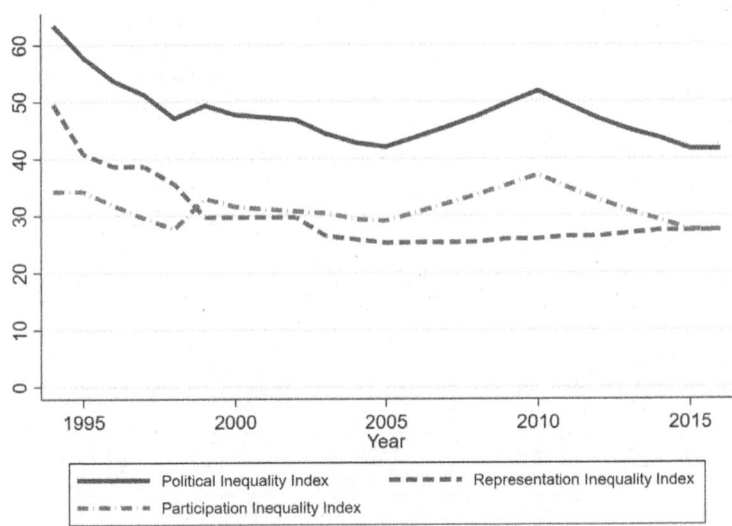

Figure 2.2c Political inequality in South Africa.

Source: Authors' illustration based on data by Choi (2021).

The number or percentage of members of different groups in executive office, the legislature, the civil service or the military are other common indicators of political inequality. Such measures reflect stark political inequalities linked with gender, for instance, in many contexts: although half of the adult population in most countries are women, the percentage of women occupying senior political positions is well below 50 per cent in most countries. Figure 2.3 shows the proportion of seats held by women in national parliaments for our five focus countries. By this metric, South Africa was the most equal in 2023 – with almost half the seats held by women – and Colombia and Vietnam the least – both with about 30 per cent held by women. Ethiopia showed the greatest improvements, with 2 per cent of seats held by women in 1999 and about 40 per cent in 2023.

Other indicators of political inequality reflect access to elected officials, state institutions and public services. This may be assessed,

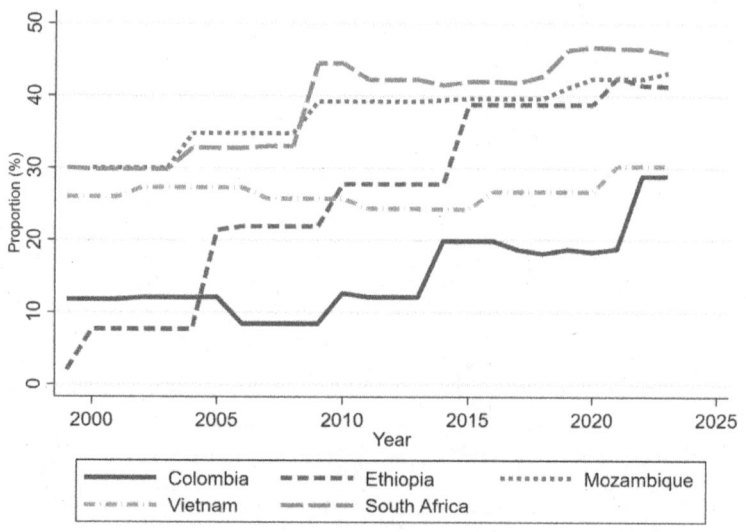

Figure 2.3 Proportion of seats held by women in national parliaments 2000–23.

Source: International Parliamentary Union (2024).

for instance, through individual reporting on such experience in public opinion surveys, such as the Afrobarometer and Latinobarometro (see Osei, Konte and Avenyo 2024). Responses in many countries are suggestive of significant inequalities in access to public officials and services – which may intersect also with economic and social inequalities. In Ethiopia, of the people that said they had accessed a public clinic or hospital in the last year, 32.3 per cent said it was 'difficult' or 'very difficult' to access the medical care they needed.

Another way to approach inequality in access to state and public services is to consider institutions or conditions that explicitly or implicitly facilitate or impede that access. For instance, requirements to operate in an official state language, or to travel to regional centres to access public facilities such as civil registries, may place remote, linguistic minority populations (for instance, indigenous peoples) on an unequal footing in their interactions with the state (Gisselquist 2019). Rates of birth registration are another indicator. To go to school, to receive public health services, or to apply for a job requires in many countries some form of legal identity such as a birth certificate. Underscored in the UN's Sustainable Development Goals under Target 16.9[6] as essential for peace, inclusive societies and access to justice for all, legal identity has also been recognized since the 1989 UN Convention of the Rights of the Child (Article 7) as 'the foundation for the fulfilment of other rights'.

South Africa offers one example of how improvements in civil registration post-apartheid facilitated improvement in the coverage of its social protection services, including the Child Support Grant (Lund 2012). With levels of birth registration today near 90 per cent, South Africa is considered a model in this area for how improvements can be achieved (Van der Straaten and Metz 2019).

Inequalities in political dimensions regularly intersect with economic and social inequalities. Money can buy political influence in many contexts – not only through illegal activities, but also through normal channels such as campaign finance. However, the dimensions are far from a perfect match. Indeed, cross-nationally, looking at income inequality and political inequality, measured using the PII introduced earlier, Choi (2021) finds only weak correlation.

Measuring inequality as a multidimensional concept: Composite indexes

The capability approach has had wide-ranging influence on thinking and policy in international development, directing global attention beyond development as growth in income or GDP to broader consideration of human development and quality of life. Since 1990, the UNDP's Human Development Index (HDI)[7] has provided empirical comparison based on this approach across countries. Many countries also produce national human development reports and subnational HDIs offering within-country empirical comparisons.

The HDI speaks to three core dimensions of human development: a long and healthy life, knowledge, and a decent standard of living (see Box 2.2).

In measuring human development this way, the HDI evidences disparities, inequalities in other words, in human development across countries. Figure 2.4 summarizes the HDI for our five countries over time, pointing to significant disparities among them. Colombia, South Africa, and Vietnam show substantially higher levels of human development than Ethiopia and Mozambique. All show a general increase over time, although South Africa experienced a notable period of decline in human development starting in the mid-1990s.

Likewise, HDIs calculated for subnational groupings demonstrate in many contexts significant subnational inequalities. Figure 2.5, based

Inequality of What? 31

> ## Box 2.2: The UNDP's Human Development Index
>
> The HDI is calculated based on four indicators across three dimensions. The first dimension, a long and healthy life, is measured based on life expectancy at birth; the second with mean years of schooling for adults 25 years old and above, and expected years of schooling for children entering school age; and the third dimension by gross national income[8] per capita.
>
>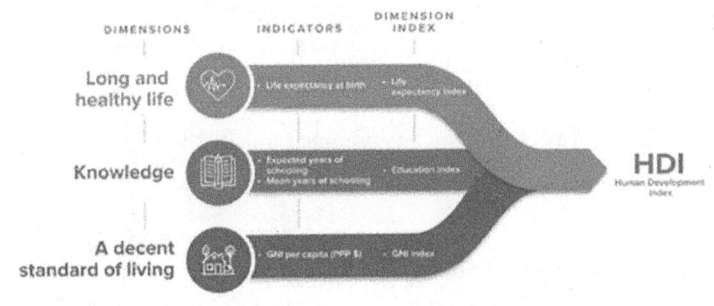
>
> Source: United Nations Development Programme: reproduced under Creative Commons Attribution 3.0 IGO license.

on the Colombian National Human Development Report, illustrates such disparities at the departmental level[9] during the period 2011–22. HDIs have been consistently highest in the capital, Bogotá DC, while other departments – such as Vaupés, Guainía, and Vichada along the eastern border – have had consistently the lowest HDIs.

Other projects also have sought to map inequalities directly within a capability approach. The inequality-adjusted HDI (IHDI) in particular considers inequality in the distribution of each HDI dimension across the population. The IHDI can be compared to the HDI as a way of

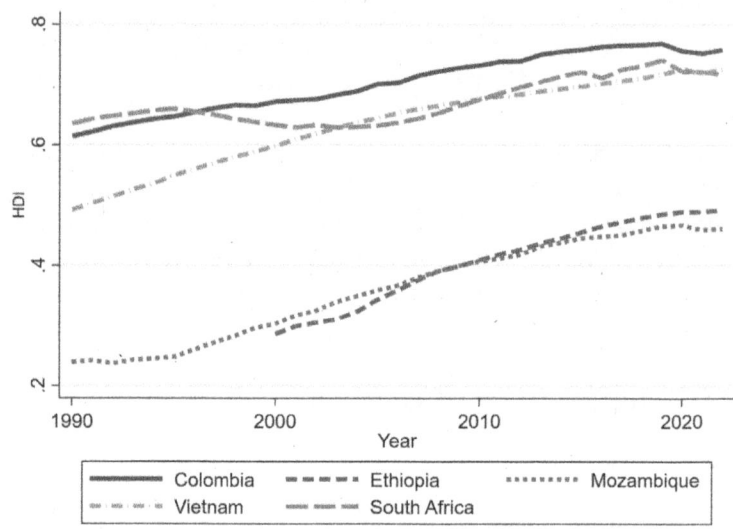

Figure 2.4 Human Development Index, 1990–2022.
Source: UNDP (2024).

measuring the costs of inequality. In the most equal countries, the loss when comparing the IHDI to the HDI is small (e.g., Iceland at 5.1 per cent in 2022), while in others it can be upwards of 40 per cent. In Mozambique, the loss in 2022 is 41.4 per cent, with IHDI of 0.27 and HDI of 0.46.[10]

The Multidimensional Inequality Framework (MIF) is another example of a capability-based effort to capture inequality.[11] The MIF considers seven domains (see Table 2.2), each of which is assessed with sub-domains, indicators, and measures.

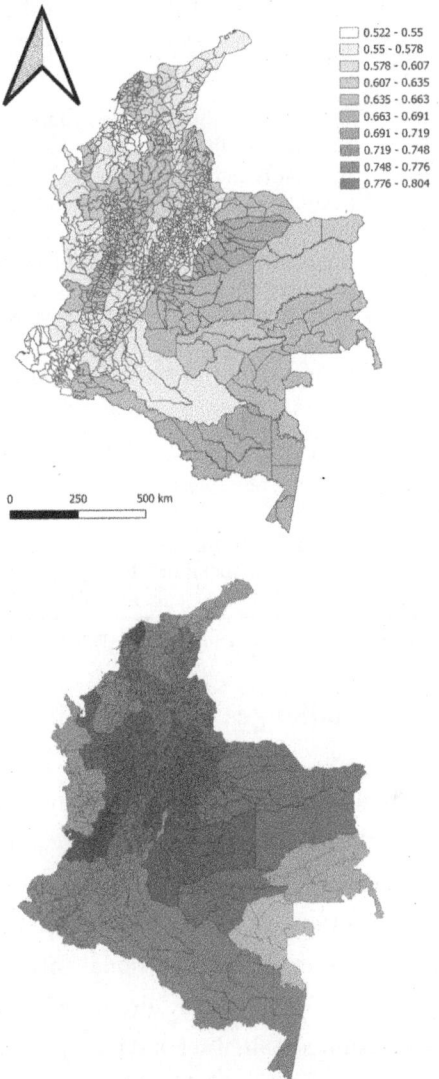

Figure 2.5 Evolution of the HDI at the departmental level in Colombia, 2011 (top) and 2022 (bottom).

Source: Authors' illustration based on data by Global Data Lab (2024).

Table 2.2 Multidimensional Inequality Framework (MIF): Domains

1	Life and health	Inequality in the capability to be alive and to live a healthy life
2	Physical and legal security	Inequality in the capability to live in physical safety and legal security
3	Education and learning	Inequality in the capability to be knowledgeable, to understand and reason, and to have the skills to participate in society
4	Financial security and dignified work	Inequality in the capability to achieve financial independence and security, enjoy dignified and fair work, and recognition of unpaid work and care
5	Comfortable, independent and secure living conditions	Inequality in the capability to enjoy comfortable, independent and secure living conditions
6	Participation, influence and voice	Inequality in the capability to participate in decision-making, have a voice and influence
7	Individual, family and social life	Inequality in the capability to enjoy individual, family and social life, to express yourself and to have self-respect

Source: Atlantic Fellows for Social and Economic Equity (AFSEE) (2019).

Challenges of aggregation

Multidimensional indexes aim to shed light on inequality beyond what can be captured with traditional one-dimensional indicators such as those based on income alone, whether using the Gini coefficient or another measure. They are useful in providing snapshot comparisons and views into trends in multidimensional inequality (Gisselquist 2014; OECD and JRC 2008), but they also have limitations.

For one, they rely on a limited set of data – even if a wider set than the traditional measures. The HDI, for instance, has contributed to broader consideration of human development and capabilities, but does not include any direct assessment of, for example, the ability to move around or to participate in social life, both of which are basic capabilities in Sen's framework.

Composite indexes can always include additional measures, but the 'correct' way to aggregate these measures is another challenge. Many composite indexes are constructed by averaging across the values of their underlying dimensions. This effectively treats those dimensions as equally important and substitutable, which does not necessarily fit our theories and commitments. For instance, Arndt, Mahrt, Hussain and Tarp (2018) analyse the well-regarded Alkire-Foster multidimensional poverty index, finding that its methodology of construction is in fact inconsistent with the Universal Declaration of Human Rights principles of indivisibility, inalienability, and equality (see Alkire and Foster 2007).

They further present an alternative approach to multidimensional comparison based on first-order stochastic dominance – that in essence applies the criterion that Individual A is only better off than Individual B if he/she is doing at least as well, or better, along *all* dimensions. In Mozambique, this approach has been applied to comparison of poverty over time and across districts based on five welfare indicators (safe water, sanitation, education, electricity and a functioning ratio) (Arndt, Hussain, Salvucci, Tarp and Østerdal 2016). In sum, indexes of multidimensional inequality can be useful, but so too is careful consideration of diverse indicators. The best analyses take a dashboard approach, with attention to multiple indicators and composite approaches.

Intersectionality and interactions

Intersectional approaches to inequality implicitly spotlight another critique of composite measures – the multiple dimensions are not that distinct. For instance, to understand the experience, impact and causes of inequality, intersectional approaches suggest, it is necessary to consider how multiple dimensions overlap and reinforce each other (see Hancock 2007). Coined by legal scholar Kimberlé

Table 2.3 Intersectional inequalities in Colombia (%)

	Monetary Poverty Rate (2021)	
Men compared to women	38.2	40.3
Indigenous compared to overall population	61.6	39.7
Woman and indigenous compared to men	63.6	38.2

Source: DANE (2022).

Crenshaw in 1989 to describe the intersection of race and gender in the marginalization of African American women, intersectionality also has been applied widely in other contexts (see Crenshaw 1989). Table 2.3 offers an example of such intersectional inequalities from Colombia: poverty rates are higher for women than for men, and for the indigenous versus the general population, and higher still among indigenous women.

Intersectional approaches today are widely applied, often referring to a broader range of social categories, including class, ethnicity, nation, age, sexuality and gender, among others. Considerable attention also is paid to the way in which other dimensions and types of inequality may relate to and reinforce each other. Indeed, economist Francisco Ferreira argues there is a 'new policy consensus' on inequality, that 'multiple, interrelated and mutually reinforcing inequalities exist – in income, wealth, education, health, power and recognition – and that these inequalities are generally "too high"' (Ferreira 2023). A key example of the former, he notes, is the so-called 'wealth gradient of health', the association between better health and higher incomes or wealth.

Vital, existential and resource inequalities, Therborn (2012) finds, 'are interrelated and interacting, but irreducible to each other, and have had different historical trajectories, within and between nations'. From a very different angle, Piketty (2020) identifies 'inequality regimes', economic, social and political mechanisms that together sustain inequalities in a society. In *Capital and Ideology*, Piketty argues that elites in many societies throughout history have sought to 'naturalize' inequality, claiming that social disparities benefit society and that changes to the existing order would be costly. Today, the discourse to justify inequality is centred around property, entrepreneurship and meritocracy. Inequality in premodern societies, by contrast, was based more on rigid and often arbitrary differences in status.

While Piketty aims to step away from Eurocentric models of development, some scholars have noted that his analysis could be enriched with more attention to developing countries. For instance, Díaz Pabón et al. (2021) argue that the case of South Africa both aligns with and complicates Piketty's framework of inequality regimes. They argue that while the end of apartheid came with a dramatic ideological and political shift towards equality, this has not translated into a strong redistribution of income and wealth. The South African experience, they find, both shows that history matters for understanding inequality, and that extreme wealth and racial inequities can undermine well-intentioned policies.

Income, wealth and economic inequality

In the rest of this book, we ground our discussion to focus on economic inequality and in particular on *income* inequality. We do discuss other types of inequality selectively when relevant – but income inequality is central to the way in which we proceed.

Our focus on income inequality reflects similar focus in much of the research literature on inequality, especially in economics. It allows us thus to speak to core conversations in the literature and to synthesize them for a general audience.

One key reason that the literature focuses on income is that it is a useful indicator of inequality – even if it is by no means a perfect indicator. Income is highly correlated with several other key indicators. Income disparities are linked with disparities in health, education and access to services. For instance, using data from the United States for 1999–2014, Chetty et al. (2016) estimated the gap in life expectancy between individuals in the top and bottom 1 per cent at 14.6 years for men and 10.1 years for women. Improvements also may be linked with changes in income. For instance, studying a series of welfare programme experiments from the United States and Canada from the 1990s, Duncan, Morris and Rodrigues (2011) find that a $1000 increase in parental income increases children's school performance by 5–6 per cent of a standard deviation.

We also adopt this focus for precision so that we can more clearly consider core theoretical and empirical claims. Theory suggests that different types of inequality may influence key outcomes differently. For instance, the distinction between land inequality and income inequality in democratization is central to the work of political scientists Ben Ansell and David Samuels. In their contractarian approach, equality in land distribution supports democratization, while income inequality promotes it.

There are evident limitations to this focus. As Sen (1997) reminds us, economic inequality and income inequality are often 'effectively synonymous' in the economics literature, but there are meaningful differences from a capabilities approach. A focus on income inequality also may obscure important empirical realities. South Africa, for instance, is among the most unequal countries in the world in terms of income inequality, but its wealth inequality is even worse (see Leibbrandt, Ranchhod and Green 2021). Chatterjee, Czajka and Gethin (2020) calculate that the top 0.01 per cent (3,500 individuals) own more than the bottom 90 per cent – about 15 per cent of household net worth – and the top 10 per cent about 86 per cent. Such extreme concentration of wealth is an important part of the story when we reflect on inequality in South Africa, its drivers and its implications.

Units of analysis and levels of aggregation: Individuals, households, groups, countries

An additional question we may pose is: Inequality between whom? Not only are there multiple dimensions and indicators of inequality, but inequality can also be observed across multiple levels of analysis and aggregation, both across and within countries – as SDG10 underscores. Many of our most common measures of inequality capture differences at the individual or household level, with reference to other individuals or households within the same country. Commonly cited Gini coefficients are one example; recent WIID data, for instance, gives us Gini values of 70.0 in South Africa, 62.5 in Mozambique, 54.1 in Colombia, 50.9 in Ethiopia, and 37.5 in Vietnam.[12]

The same measures can be calculated for smaller subsets, in terms of individuals living within a particular province, state or municipality for instance. Or, as we return to later, among other groupings, such as rural or urban populations, members of particular ethnic groups, men or women, etc.

For example, Gradín (2024) analyses spatial inequality dynamics across provinces in Mozambique, and finds that the surge in consumption inequality in the decade of the 2010s was largely driven by differences between provinces – especially the poor performance of the rural north and central regions of the country, hit hard by natural disasters and conflict. Such an analysis highlights the importance of going beyond national aggregate indicators to understand inequality dynamics.

Likewise, inequality measures can be calculated for larger groupings, such as for individuals within a region, or globally. Using the WIID dataset, regional interpersonal inequality in 2022 measured with the Gini index is 61.3 in sub-Saharan Africa and 50.6 in Latin America and the Caribbean, compared with 60.4 globally.

Group-based inequalities

A growing body of research considers inequalities between social groups, sometimes called 'horizontal inequalities' in contrast to 'vertical inequalities' between individuals or households (Stewart 2002). Whether linked with race, ethnicity, language, caste or another social category, group-based inequalities may be highly influential to a variety of economic, political and social outcomes. They are in the research literature especially linked with conflict. The influential *Pathways for Peace* report identified that 'some of the greatest risks of violence today stem from the mobilization of perceptions of exclusion and injustice, rooted in inequalities across groups' (United Nations and World Bank 2018).

The idea that ethnic and other social divisions undermine economic progress has been called one of the most powerful hypotheses in political economy (Banerjee, Iyer and Somanathan 2005). Ethnic inequalities, multiple studies suggest, may be even more important than ethnic divisions per se in undermining economic outcomes. Alesina, Michalopoulos and Papaioannou (2016) find that 'ethnic differences in economic performance rather than the degree of ethnic diversity or the overall level of inequality are negatively correlated with economic development', while Baldwin and Huber (2010) 'find a strong and robust relationship between the level of public goods provision and between-group inequality' but they do not find the same for traditional measures of ethno-linguistic fractionalization or cultural differences between groups.

Ethnic and other group-based inequalities likewise may be deeply pronounced and slow to change, even over generations and even with targeted policy effort (Canelas and Gisselquist 2018). Using the World Inequality Database on Education (UNESCO), for instance, Canelas and Gisselquist (2018) considered estimates of average years of schooling across 'most deprived' and 'least deprived' ethnic groups for various countries. In Nigeria the most deprived ethnic group had just one year of schooling on average, while the least deprived group had about twelve years on average. Imagine the negative impact of this eleven-year difference in educational opportunity and attainment not only on the average person's lifetime earnings, but also on their children's education and earnings.

Group-based inequalities can also manifest geographically thus creating regional disparities. For example, Colombia has a higher education attendance rate of 46 per cent in the capital of Bogotá, compared with 20 per cent in the Orinoquia-Amazonia region (UNESCO 2015).

Extending from a capabilities approach, Stewart (2009) argues that persistent horizontal inequality results from two 'traps', which are closely related and mutually reinforcing making them likely more persistent than individual inequalities. The first is a 'capability inequality trap' related to how different capabilities (education, health, nutrition) each promote other capabilities, and in turn influence productivity and income. The second is a 'capital poverty trap' related to how access to each type of capital (human capital, social capital, cultural capital and physical capital) affects returns to other types. Inequalities in capabilities and assets exist across groups due not only to group-based discrimination, but also to asymmetries in social capital and cultural capital.

To illustrate, consider evidence from Ethiopia. Since 1994, women's rights and gender equality are enshrined in the country's constitution (Amahazion 2023). Laws promoting equality have been passed, and the country's Gender Inequality Index (GII) moved from 0.599 in 2010 to 0.494 in 2022 (UNDP 2024). Nonetheless, Amahazion (2023) notes that 'gender inequality continues to be a major national challenge in Ethiopia, and it manifests itself in every dimension of life, community, and society'. Traditional cultural views of women as caretakers and child-bearers contribute to their structural disadvantage, particularly in rural areas. As a result, one study found, young women aged 18–19 years spent around 4.1 hours per day doing domestic tasks compared to only 1.5 hours for men of the same age (Pankhurst, Crivello and Tiumelissan 2016). This disparity in workload not only leads to less leisure time, but also takes time away from education and the development of professional skills.

Similarly in Colombia, rural women face disproportionate barriers to access agricultural land (see Cronkleton and Enokenwa 2024). Despite laws and policies guaranteeing land rights, in practice these are not always socially acknowledged, limiting the autonomy of rural women – since their rights are often tied to a male head of the household. Out of fear of being attacked, women also often do not exercise their land rights. Moreover, due to the complex legal formalities related to land registration, many poor women, largely due to their low levels of education, are not comfortable with the application procedure (CIFOR-ICRAF 2024).

Vietnam offers a more optimistic picture concerning women's land rights. Since 2003, land titles can be held by two people at once if both operate the land. This gives women more autonomy and bargaining power within the household since they are economically less dependent on their husbands. Land titling in general is seen to support tenure security, incentivizing investment and improving land productivity, and when compared to single land titling there is no evidence that jointly held titles make the land any less productive (Newman, Tarp and van den Broeck 2015).

Inequality of opportunity

Inequalities between groups link closely with the concept of inequality of opportunity, emphasizing the role of circumstances on socioeconomic disparities (Ferreira and Peragine 2015). In *Equality of Opportunity*, Roemer posits that two types of factors influence individuals' outcomes: those over which they have control (effort) and those over which they do not have control (circumstances). The latter circumstances include all factors individuals cannot control, from their parents' education and where they grew up, to their gender, race or ethnicity.

Like group-based inequalities, inequality of opportunity can be difficult to measure not least because of practical and financial constraints in compiling information on all relevant circumstances. There may also be political constraints in compiling information, for instance when ethnic divisions are contentious. Atamanov et al. (2024) use nationally representative household survey data to measure inequality of opportunity across eighteen sub-Saharan African countries, in some cases for the first time. Using consumption per capita as the outcome, their analysis suggests that inherited circumstances – in particular birthplace, parental education, and ethnicity – explain more than half the inequality in the region, ranging from a high of 74 per cent in South Africa to a low of 26 per cent in Ethiopia.[13] Which circumstances are most important in turn varies substantially across countries. In South Africa it is ethnicity that accounts for a whopping 90 per cent, while place of birth accounts for 34 per cent in Ethiopia.

Using substantially different methods, Brunori, Ferreira and Peragine (2013) similarly find that almost three-quarters of South Africa's current inequality is inherited from predetermined circumstances. Race (ethnicity), they find, plays the largest role, but parents' education levels and occupations are also important.

Inequality of opportunity in turn offers a link between the concepts of income inequality and social mobility. As Brunori, Ferreira and Peragine (2013) note 'if higher inequality makes intergenerational mobility more difficult, it is likely because opportunities for economic advancement are more unequally distributed among children'. Roemer and Trannoy (2015) propose that economic development be conceived of as the equalization of opportunities for income in a country.

Indeed, identifying and implementing the interventions and reforms that best facilitate greater equality of opportunity is a central challenge for policymakers around the globe.

Key takeaways

- Inequality has multiple dimensions and can be observed at many levels of aggregation. Economic, social, and political dimensions of inequality, for instance, can be usefully considered and compared, across both individuals and groups. Nobel Laureate Amartya Sen's influential capability approach reminds us also to consider, beyond income, inequalities in basic capabilities and freedoms.
- Multiple measurement projects seek to capture such multidimensional approaches. The Human Development Index is a key effort inspired by the capabilities approach. Multidimensional measures usefully draw attention to inequality's multiple aspects, but are not necessarily more appropriate, depending on our aims.
- In this book, income inequality across individuals and households is central to the way in which we proceed because it is often a useful indicator of other aspects and because it allows us to reflect on much of the research literature, especially in economics, which also adopts this approach.

Notes

1 See https://www.collinsdictionary.com/dictionary/english/inequality#:~:text=Inequality%20is%20the%20difference%20in,bias%20M

ore%20Synonyms%20of%20inequality and https://www.oxfordlearn ersdictionaries.com/definition/english/inequality
2. See https://plato.stanford.edu/entries/capability-approach/ and https://iep.utm.edu/sen-cap/
3. The latter 'is concerned with good things rather than what these good things do to human beings' while the former 'is concerned with what these good things do to human beings but uses a metric that focusses not only on the person's capabilities but on his mental reaction'. See Sen (1979: 218).
4. More precisely, 'polyarchy'.
5. For fuller description of the indicators and index methodology, see Choi (2021: 38–41).
6. SDG16 Target 9: By 2030, provide legal identity for all, including birth registration. https://sdgs.un.org/goals
7. https://hdr.undp.org/data-center/human-development-index#/indicies/HDI
8. Gross national income (GNI) is the aggregate value of the gross balances of primary incomes for all sectors.
9. Colombia has 32 administrative divisions, referred to as 'departments' (*departamentos* in Spanish). Each department has an elected governor and a representative assembly.
10. https://hdr.undp.org/inequality-adjusted-human-development-index#/indicies/IHDI
11. Developed through collaboration between the Centre for Analysis of Social Exclusion (CASE) at the London School of Economics, School of Oriental and African Studies (SOAS), and Oxfam. See https://sticerd.lse.ac.uk/inequality/the-framework/media/mif-framework.pdf
12. https://www4.wider.unu.edu/?ind=1&type=ChoroplethSeq&year=70&byCountry=false&slider=buttons).
13. Mozambique is not included in the sample.

References

Alesina, A., S. Michalopoulos and E. Papaioannou (2016). 'Ethnic Inequality'. *Journal of Political Economy*, 124(2): 428–88. https://

www.journals.uchicago.edu/doi/abs/10.1086/685300. Accessed: 10 September 2025.

Alkire, S., and J. Foster (2007). 'Counting and Multidimensional Poverty Measurement'. OPHI Working Paper 7. Oxford: Oxford Poverty and Human Development Initiative, University of Oxford.

Amahazion, F. (2023). 'Gender Inequality in Ethiopia'. In *The Palgrave Handbook of Global Social Problems*. Cham: Palgrave Macmillan. https://doi.org/10.1007/978-3-030-68127-2-400-1. Accessed: 10 September 2025.

Arndt, C., A. M. Hussain, V. Salvucci, F. Tarp and L. P. Østerdal (2016). 'Poverty Mapping Based on First-Order Dominance with an Example from Mozambique'. *Journal of International Development*, 28(1): 3–21. https://doi.org/10.1002/jid.3200

Arndt, C., K. Mahrt, M. A. Hussain and F. Tarp (2018). 'A Human Rights-Consistent Approach to Multidimensional Welfare Measurement Applied to Sub-Saharan Africa'. *World Development*, 108: 181–96. https://www.sciencedirect.com/science/article/pii/S0305750X18301049. Accessed: 10 September 2025.

Atamanov, A., P. F. Cuevas, J. Lebow and D. G. Mahler (2024). 'New Evidence on Inequality of Opportunity in Sub-Saharan Africa: More Unequal Than We Thought'. World Bank Policy Research Working Paper, 10723. Washington, DC: World Bank. http://hdl.handle.net/10986/41208

Atlantic Fellows for Social and Economic Equity (AFSEE) (2019). 'The Multidimensional Inequality Framework'. Centre for Analysis of Social Exclusion, SOAS Univeristy of London and Oxfam. https://sticerd.lse.ac.uk/inequality/the-framework/media/mif-framework-0719.pdf. Accessed: 10 September 2025.

Baldwin, K., and J. D. Huber (2010). 'Economic versus Cultural Differences: Forms of Ethnic Diversity and Public Goods Provision'. *American Political Science Review*, 104(4): 644–62. http://dx.doi.org/10.1017/S0003055410000419. Accessed: 10 September 2025.

Banerjee, A., L. Iyer and R. Somanathan (2005). 'History, Social Divisions, and Public Goods in Rural India'. *Journal of the European Economic Association*, 3(2–3): 639–47. https://doi.org/10.1162/jeea.2005.3.2-3.639. Accessed: 10 September 2025.

Brunori, P., F. H. G. Ferreira and V. Peragine (2013). 'Inequality of Opportunity, Income Inequality, and Economic Mobility: Some International Comparisons'. In E. Paus (ed.), *Getting Development Right* (pp. 85–115). Basingstoke: Palgrave Macmillan.

Canelas, C., and R. M. Gisselquist (2018). 'Horizontal Inequality as an Outcome'. *Oxford Development Studies*, 46(3): 305–24. https://doi.org/10.1080/13600818.2018.1508565

Chatterjee, A., L. Czajka, and A. Gethin (2020). 'Estimating the distribution of household wealth in South Africa'. WIDER working paper 2020/45. Helsinki: UNU-WIDER.

Chetty, R, M. Stepner, S. Abraham, S. Lin, B. Scuderi, N. Turner, A. Bergeron and D. Cutler. (2016). 'The Association Between Income and Life Expectancy in the United States, 2001–2014'. *JAMA*, 315(16): 1750–66. doi:10.1001/jama.2016.4226. Accessed: 10 September 2025.

Choi, G. (2019). Political Inequality Index. Ann Arbor, MI: Inter-university Consortium for Political and Social Research [distributor]. https://doi.org/10.3886/E101268V3. Accessed: 10 September 2025.

Choi, G. (2021). 'Conceptualizing and Measuring Political Inequality in a Cross-National Perspective'. *Comparative Sociology*, 20(1): 1–44. https://doi.org/https://doi.org/10.1163/15691330-BJA10027. Accessed: 10 September 2025.

Crenshaw, K. (1989). 'Demarginalizing the Intersection of Race and Sex: A Black Feminist Critique of Antidiscrimination Doctrine, Feminist Theory and Antiracist Politics'. *University of Chicago Legal Forum*, 1(8). Available at: http://chicagounbound.uchicago.edu/uclf/vol1989/iss1/8. Accessed: 10 September 2025.

Cronkleton, P., and O. Enokenwa (CIFOR-ICRAF) (2024). Women's Land Rights in Colombia. *Global Initiative for Gender Transformative Approaches for Securing Women's Resource Rights (WRR) (report)*. Bogor and Nairobi: Center for International Forestry Research (CIFOR) and World Agroforestry (ICRAF). https://www.cifor-icraf.org/publications/pdf_files/Books/Socio-legal-review-Colombia.pdf. Accessed: 10 September 2025.

Dahl, R. (1971). *Polyarchy: Participation and Opposition*. New Haven: Yale University Press.

DANE (2022). *Pobreza monetaria con enfoque diferencial año 2021.* Bogota: Departamento Administrativo Nacional de Estadistica – DANE. 2 June. Available at https://www.dane.gov.co/index.php/estadisticas-por-tema/enfoque-diferencial-e-interseccional. Accessed: 10 September 2025.

Díaz Pabón, F. A., M. Leibbrandt, V. Ranchhod and M. Savage (2021). 'Piketty Comes to South Africa'. *British Journal of Sociology*, 72(1): 106–24. https://doi.org/https://doi.org/10.1111/1468-4446.12808. Accessed: 10 September 2025.

Duncan, G. J., P. A. Morris and C. Rodrigues (2011). 'Does Money Really Matter? Estimating Impacts of Family Income on Young Children's Achievement with Data from Random-Assignment Experiments'. *Developmental Psychology*, 47(5), 1263–79. https://doi.org/10.1037/a0023875. Accessed: 10 September 2025.

Ferreira, F. H. (2023). 'Is There a "New Consensus" on Inequality?', III Working Paper 101 and IZA Discussion Paper 16422. London and Bonn: International Inequalities Institute, LSE, and IZA Institute of Labor Economics. https://eprints.lse.ac.uk/120113/. Accessed: 10 September 2025. https://docs.iza.org/dp16422.pdf. Accessed: 10 September 2025.

Ferreira, F. H. G., and V. Peragine (2015). 'Equality of Opportunity: Theory and Evidence'. IZA Discussion Paper 8994. https://docs.iza.org/dp8994.pdf. Accessed: 10 September 2025.

Gisselquist, R. M. (2014). 'Developing and Evaluating Governance Indexes: 10 Questions'. *Policy Studies*, 1–19. https://doi.org/10.1080/01442872.2014.946484. Accessed: 10 September 2025.

Gisselquist, R. M. (2019). 'Legal Empowerment and Group-Based Inequality'. *Journal of Development Studies*, 55(3): 333–47. https://doi.org/10.1080/00220388.2018.1451636. Accessed: 10 September 2025.

Global Data Lab (2024). Subnational HDI (version 8.1). https://globaldatalab.org/shdi/table/shdi/COL/?levels=1+4&interpolation=0&extrapolation=0. Accessed: 10 September 2025.

*Gradín, C. (2024). 'Spatial Consumption Inequality in Mozambique'. WIDER Working Paper 2024/63. Helsinki: UNU-WIDER. https://onlinelibrary.wiley.com/doi/10.1111/saje.12225. Accessed: 10 September 2025.

Hancock, A. M. (2007). 'When Multiplication Doesn't Equal Quick Addition: Examining Intersectionality as a Research Paradigm'. *Perspectives on Politics*, 5(1): 63–79. http://dx.doi.org/10.1017/S1537592707070065. Accessed: 10 September 2025.

Herbaut, E., and K. Geven (2020). 'What Works to Reduce Inequalities in Higher Education? A Systematic Review of the (Quasi-)Experimental Literature on Outreach and Financial Aid'. *Research in Social Stratification and Mobility*, 65: art. 100442. https://doi.org/10.1016/j.rssm.2019.100442. Accessed: 10 September 2025.

International Parliamentary Union (2024). Proportion of women in national parliaments. https://data.ipu.org/women-ranking/?date_year=2024&date_month=10. Accessed: 10 September 2025.

*Jorda, V., M. Niño-Zarazúa and M. Tejería-Martínez (2024). 'The Lifespan Disparity Dataset: An Open Repository on Inequality and Polarization in Length of Life (1950–2021)'. *Scientific Data*, 11(1): 650. https://doi.org/10.1038/s41597-024-03426-6. Accessed: 10 September 2025.

Kraus, M. W., P. K. Piff and D. Keltner (2011). 'Social Class as Culture: The Convergence of Resources and Rank in the Social Realm'. *Current Directions in Psychological Science*, 20(4): 246–50. https://doi.org/10.1177/0963721411414654. Accessed: 10 September 2025.

Langer, A., and G. K. Brown (2008). 'Cultural Status Inequalities: An Important Dimension of Group Mobilization'. In F. Stewart (ed.), *Horizontal Inequalities and Conflict: Understanding Group Violence in Multiethnic Societies* (pp. 41–53). Basingstoke: Palgrave Macmillan. https://doi.org/10.1057/9780230582729_3. Accessed: 10 September 2025.

Leibbrandt, M., V. Ranchhod and P. Green (2021). 'South Africa: The Top End, Labour Markets, Fiscal Redistribution, and the Persistence of Very High Inequality'. In C. Gradín, M. Leibbrandt and F. Tarp (eds), *Inequality in the Developing World* (pp. 205–30). Oxford: Oxford University Press. https://doi.org/10.1093/oso/9780198863960.003.0009. Accessed: 10 September 2025.

Lund, F. (2012). 'Children, Citizenship and Child Support: The Child Support Grant in Post-Apartheid South Africa'. In K. Breckenridge and S. Szreter (eds), *Registration and Recognition: Documenting the Person* in *World History* (pp. 475–94). https://doi.org/10.5871/bacad/978019 7265314.003.0019. Accessed: 10 September 2025.

Newman, C., F. Tarp and K. van den Broeck (2016). 'Property Rights and Productivity: The Case of Joint Land Titling in Vietnam'. *Land Economics*, 91(1): 91–105. https://doi.org/10.3368/le.91.1.91. Accessed: 10 September 2025.

OECD and JRC (2008). *Handbook on Constructing Composite Indicators: Methodology and User Guide*. Paris: OECD Publishing.

Osei, D., M. Konte and E. K. Avenyo (2024). 'Escaping Corruption in the Demand for Public Services in Africa: The Dual Nature of Civic Networks'. *World Development*, 177: 106541. https://doi.org/https://doi.org/10.1016/j.worlddev.2024.106541. Accessed: 10 September 2025.

Pankhurst, A., G. Crivello and A. Tiumelissan (2016). 'Children's Work in Family and Community Contexts: Examples from Young Lives Ethiopia', Young Lives Working Paper 147. Oxford: Oxford Department of International Development, University of Oxford. https://ora.ox.ac.uk/objects/uuid:21aa8d96-d24c-4833-a498-fbe184504076/files/ma941c31c1da121404c126a21047348dc. Accessed: 10 September 2025.

Pfeffer, F. T. (2018). 'Growing Wealth Gaps in Education'. *Demography*, 55(3): 1033–68. https://doi.org/10.1007/s13524-018-0666-7. Accessed: 10 September 2025.

Piketty, T. (2020). *Capital and ideology*. Cambridge MA: Harvard University Press.

Roemer, J. E., and A. Trannoy (2015). 'Equality of Opportunity'. In A. B. Atkinson and F. Bourguignon (eds), *Handbook of Income Distribution* (Vol. 2: 217–300). Elsevier. https://doi.org/https://doi.org/10.1016/B978-0-444-59428-0.00005-9. Accessed: 10 September 2025.

Sen, A. (1979). *Equality of What?*. **The Tanner Lecture on Human Values. Stanford University. 22 May. https://ophi.org.uk/sites/default/files/Sen-1979_Equality-of-What.pdf**

Sen, A. (1992). *Inequality Re-examined*. Cambridge MA: Harvard University Press.

Sen, A (1997). 'From Income Inequality to Economic Inequality'. *Southern Economic Journal*, 64(2): 384–401. Distinguished Guest Lecture.

Stewart, F. (2002). *Horizontal Inequality: A Neglected Dimension of Development*. WIDER Annual Lecture 5. Helsinki: UNU-WIDER.

Stewart, F. (2009). 'Horizontal Inequality: Two Types of Trap'. *Journal of Human Development and Capabilities*, 10(3): 315–40. https://doi.org/10.1080/19452820903041824. Accessed: 10 September 2025.

Stewart, F., and A. Langer (2008). 'Horizontal Inequalities: Explaining Persistence and Change'. In F. Stewart (ed.), *Horizontal Inequalities and Conflict: Understanding Group Violence in Multiethnic Societies* (pp. 54–82). Basingstoke: Palgrave Macmillan. https://doi.org/10.1057/9780230582729_4. Accessed: 10 September 2025.

Therborn, G. (2007). *Inequalities of the World: New theoretical frameworks, multiple empirical approaches*. Los Angeles: Sage Publications, CA.

Therborn, G. (2012). 'The Killing Fields of Inequality'. *International Journal of Health Services*, 42(4): 579–89. http://www.jstor.org/stable/45140301. Accessed: 10 September 2025.

UNDP (2024). *Human Development Report* (https://hdr.undp.org/data-center/human-development-index#/indicies/HDI. Accessed: 10 September 2025.

UNESCO (2015). *World Inequality Database in Education* (https://www.education-inequalities.org/countries/colombia. Accessed: 10 September 2025.

United Nations and World Bank (2018). *Pathways for Peace: Inclusive Approaches to Preventing Violent Conflict*. New York and Washington DC: United Nations and World Bank https://hdl.handle.net/10986/28337. Accessed: 10 September 2025.

Van der Straaten, J., and A. Z. Metz (2019). South Africa ID Case Study (English). World Bank Working Paper 137142. Washington, DC: World Bank.

3
Rising inequality?

In Chapter 2, we considered the concept of inequality and its multiple dimensions and indicators. For the rest of this book we focus on economic inequality measured in terms of income and consumption, and sometimes wealth. Addressing the question 'Is inequality rising?' requires deeper consideration of the concept of inequality and the specifics of its measurement. Without such understanding, debates on inequality levels and trends can be ineffective, often confusing. This chapter provides an empirical starting point reviewing core issues in the *measurement* of income inequality, in particular, and considers its patterns and trends. It aims to shed light on how to make sense of the diverse numbers reported in the press and social media, by civil society groups and in academic research – which often seem to conflict.

We start by briefly revisiting the conceptual approaches taken in this book and then turn to issues of measurement. We first consider the challenges of measuring income inequality and then introduce commonly used measures. Through this discussion, we illustrate how different measures are linked to varying value judgements.

We then turn to empirical patterns and trends showing how different data and, especially, different measures also reflect different realities. This is the core of the third section, which describes global trends and illustrates how measures that capture more 'absolute' approaches to inequality bring out concerning upward trends in global inequality. While the Gini coefficient has long been the go-to measure of inequality, it does not capture these trends.

What is inequality? An economics approach

We can think about inequality in simple terms as the distribution of a certain welfare indicator – frequently income, or alternative dimensions such as consumption or wealth[1] – among individuals or groups within a country or, at the global level, among countries.

Household incomes, individual earnings, or consumption expenditures are frequently used as welfare indicators. Still, they come with additional choices, namely how comprehensive the definition should be (e.g., income with or without consumption of own production), the scale to use (e.g., total, per capita, or using other equivalence scales[2]) and the tax treatment of income (gross or net of taxes and transfers) (Alvaredo et al. 2023: 5). Figure 3.1 illustrates the differences between the levels of the Gini obtained when using different scales and when including or excluding tax payments, drawing on data from Colombia. While the trends remain the same, one notices the differences in levels when using the different measures of income.

While in OECD countries the preferred measure of well-being is disposable income, consumption expenditure is regularly favoured in relation to the Global South. In many contexts it can be hard to measure income, namely where there is prevalence of subsistence farming as the main economic activity. Consumption can be a more stable, and thus more reliable indicator of welfare and less susceptible to measurement error (Ravallion 2004). This focus on income and consumption is the conceptual approach we adopt throughout the rest of this book.

An additional question we pose is: Inequality between whom? First, one can consider as the unit of analysis the individual or the household. The latter means, for instance, that gender issues within the household are not captured. Additionally, one can

Rising Inequality? 55

(a) Different scales

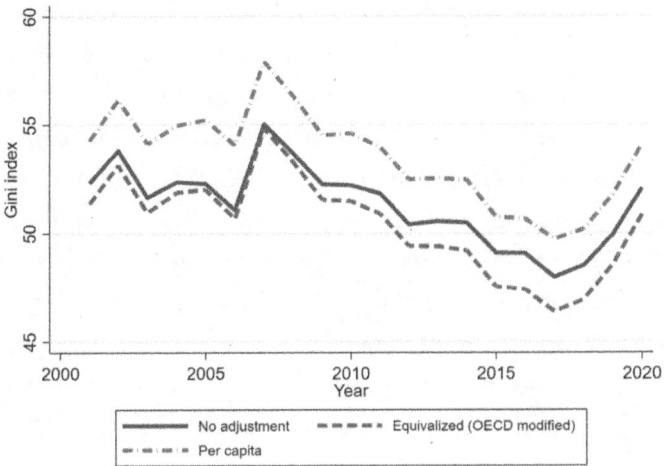

(b) Different tax treatments

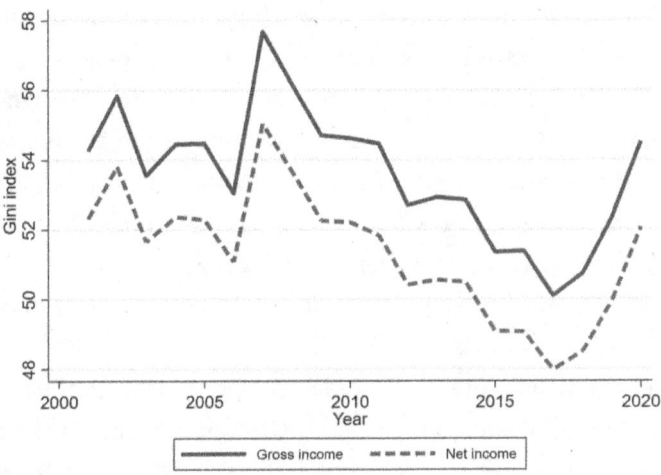

Figure 3.1 Evolution of Gini index in Colombia considering different measures of income.

Source: Authors' illustration using World Income Inequality Database (WIID) data.
Note: Figure (a) shows the trends over time of the Gini varying the equivalence scale, which reflects how income in the economic unit (e.g., household) is converted into income of the population unit (e.g., individual) assuming that there is equal sharing. 'No adjustment' means that the economic and the population units are the same. If income is measure at the household level and is divided by the number of household members, then the scale is 'per capita'. Instead of dividing equally between the different members of the household, the 'equivalised (OECD modified)' scale gives different weights to adults and children.

compare differences between individuals of a specific country (*within-country inequality*) or differences between countries (*between-country inequality*). When computing the latter, the comparison may consider countries as equal single units in the world (unweighted inequality) or assign them weights depending on the size of their populations (weighted inequality). Finally, one can consider differences between all individuals in the world independent of where they live (*global inequality*). We return to these definitions later and illustrate how they show differing trends and lead to different interpretations.

Closely tied to the concept of (economic) inequality is *poverty*, which relates to the means necessary to satisfy basic needs (Ferreira, Salvucci and Tarp 2023: 5). To clarify the distinction between inequality and poverty, consider Colombia and Ethiopia in 2016. The share of income going to the bottom 20 per cent of the population was 4 per cent in Ethiopia and 3.5 per cent in Colombia (UNU-WIDER 2023). According to this measure of inequality (and ignoring everything else) the living situation of those at the bottom of the distribution seems more favourable in Ethiopia than in Colombia. However, when looking at the mean incomes of the bottom 20 per cent in the same year, in Colombia this corresponded to US$2,492 dollars (2017 purchasing power parity – PPP),[3] whereas in Ethiopia it was much lower at US$381 (2017 PPP).

Looking at our three case studies in the African continent also offers a useful illustration. During the last decade they had similar high inequality levels,[4] with Gini indices roughly around 40–50 (Ethiopia and Mozambique) and 65 (South Africa), according to data from the WIID (UNU-WIDER 2023). Still, the latest poverty rates available indicate that poverty is much higher in Mozambique where in 2014, more than 60 per cent of the population lived with an income below US$2.15 a day (2017 PPP),[5] compared to 20 per cent and

27 per cent in 2015 for South Africa and Ethiopia, respectively (World Bank 2024a, 2024b).

As illustrated in this example, poverty is measured with the use of *poverty lines*. These can be *absolute*, when they specify a certain monetary amount below which an individual is considered poor (US$2.15 a day in the example), or *relative*, when they are set as a constant proportion of the mean or median income. The former is more common when discussing poverty in the Global South, whereas the latter is the standard in the discussions regarding OECD countries. Though some of the issues discussed here also apply to poverty measures, we focus on inequality measurement in this chapter and return to the links between inequality, poverty and growth in Chapter 5.

The challenges of measuring inequality

The *quality* and *availability* of data are also extremely important in inequality measurement. Box 3.1 highlights the challenges of collecting consumption data in the period after the war in Mozambique ended in 1992. It illustrates how logistical constraints and other external factors can make it dangerous and difficult for enumerator teams to collect household data. Moreover, in this example, they also led to choices that later challenged consistency between the first and subsequent survey rounds.

Not only the conditions under which data are collected, but also the types of questions asked affect the quality of the data. To give an example, the standard questionnaires on consumption used in household surveys across sub-Saharan Africa are the same for both poor and wealthier households, even if their consumption patterns are very distinct (see more details in Arndt et al. 2016).

> **Box 3.1: Challenges in data collection for household consumption surveys in Mozambique**
>
> The 1996/7 household consumption survey, which would later be the basis for the first national poverty assessment in Mozambique, was carried out in the field only four years after the end of the war in 1992. Arndt et al. (2016) highlight some of the main challenges, including destroyed infrastructure, the prevalence of landmines which required additional safety procedures and a major flood in one of the provinces.
>
> A few years later, when the 2002/3 survey began, many of these challenges had been resolved. Given the high standard that had been set for the 1996/7 survey (despite logistical difficulties) the team decided to maintain the same structure of data collection to maintain coherence. However, it was not possible to reproduce the analysis of the 1996/7 raw data, which made it difficult to implement the same choices as before and led to a series of additional decisions. Better documentation of the choices and the adoption of more systematic procedures in the 2002/3 data collection led to a more established approach in the following round in 2008/9, which allowed for comparability between the rounds.
>
> Source: Based on Arndt et al. (2016).

The data used in the measurement of inequality are usually drawn from surveys or administrative (tax/fiscal) sources.[6] Survey data consist of self-reported information collected from a sample of the population for statistical purposes, whereas administrative data refer to information collected by the government or other organizations for non-statistical reasons, such as record-keeping, when people interact with public services (e.g., schools, hospitals or tax authorities). One of the main shortcomings of survey data is the fact that frequently one does not have satisfactory information about the distribution at the top. On the one hand, this could be due to the lower probability that people with higher incomes are included in the survey sample. On the other hand, it can be caused by misreporting, for instance, of self-employed income, or by under-reporting of income by rich people (Ravallion 2021; Cowell and Flachaire 2021: 36–7). Returning to our example of Mozambique, the analysis of well-being has mostly relied on household surveys. Still, they have also been tested by this missing or incorrect information about the very rich, which is aggravated by the fact that there are big differences in consumption patterns between the rural poor and the urban elite (Arndt and Mahrt 2017). Moreover, and related to the bottom of the distribution, in recent surveys the problem of under-reporting of food consumption extended from the urban areas in the south to also affect rural areas, stemming from sporadic purchases of basic goods, such as rice and corn flour (Gradín and Tarp 2019: 113).[7]

While administrative data are sometimes more reliable, larger and better at covering the top of the distribution, there is some missing information as well. For instance, these data do not consider those who are not required to file tax returns and may not include specific household characteristics that are commonly employed to adjust the data (Cowell and Flachaire 2021: 37). The first of these points is particularly important in the Global South, where the informal sector is large (Ferreira 2023). Importantly, neither surveys nor administrative data account for intra-household inequality, that is, the fact that there is no perfect sharing of income within the household.[8]

As illustrated in Table 3.1, which lists the Gini coefficients for our focus countries, using data from two different sources – the World Income Inequality Database (WIID) and the World Inequality Database (WID) – can lead to quite disparate indicators. Notice, for instance, that while for South Africa and Ethiopia the Gini coefficients are similar, there is a difference of fourteen units between the Gini coefficients reported for Vietnam. The differences are also noticeable for Colombia and Mozambique. Behind this variation are differences

Table 3.1 Gini coefficients according to the WIID and the WID databases

	WIID (latest year available)	WID (same year as WIID)
Vietnam	36 (2018)	50 (2018)
Ethiopia	51 (2016)	53 (2016)
Colombia	54 (2020)	66 (2020)
Mozambique	59 (2015)	69 (2015)
South Africa	67 (2017)	63 (2017)

Note: Data from WID based on post-tax national income.
Source: https://wid.world/data/ and https://www4.wider.unu.edu/.

in the *type of data* used, namely the fact that the Gini coefficients reported by the WIID are based mostly on survey data, whereas the WID combines survey with administrative data and uses imputations of missing values (Ferreira 2023).

Another point we note is that the latest available data points are between four and nine years old at the time of writing. This highlights how scarce data on inequality is, especially in African countries – Mozambique and South Africa being cases in point. Given these difficulties, it is necessary to exercise caution when using existing datasets for the analysis of inequality. While most of us do not have a chance to always dig into how data was assembled and to assess their quality, one should bear in mind that their underlying approaches may be different, which undermines their comparability and can lead to diverging conclusions about inequality levels.

Inequality measurement

Let us start with the intuition behind measures of inequality. Simply comparing disparities in income[9] between countries can evidence inequality. For instance, in 2020 the average income in Colombia (US$13,448.93, 2017 PPP) and South Africa (US$12,665.83, 2017

PPP) was roughly ten times higher than the average income of US$1,229.94 (2017 PPP) in Mozambique (UNU-WIDER 2023). Several measures of inequality have been proposed over time and with different degrees of complexity. To guarantee that there is a common understanding of the criteria underlying inequality comparisons (Amiel and Cowell 1992), there are some basic properties that indicators of inequality should satisfy (see Cowell 2016 for more details).

To help illustrate these properties, we use Figure 3.2. Consider the population presented, which has four individuals, A, B, C and D. In the column 'baseline distribution', we order these individuals according to their income, from lowest ($) to highest ($$$$). In each row we use this population and its distribution as an example to illustrate the different properties. The 'comparison distribution' column represents the change, and 'inequality comparison' indicates whether inequality remained the same (=) or decreased (>).

First, shifting individuals should not change the distribution – that is, the identity of the individuals should not matter ('anonymity'). Second, if we simply replicate the distribution, the level of inequality should not change ('population principle'). Third, if there is a transfer from someone rich to someone poorer, but the rich person is still richer than the poorer, then inequality decreases ('transfer principle'). Fourth, considering two distributions with the same population size and mean, where distribution Alpha is more unequal than distribution Beta, if we merge Alpha and Beta with a third distribution, Delta, with the same mean (though not necessarily the same population size), then Alpha merged with Delta is more unequal than Beta merged with Delta ('decomposability'). Fifth, inequality remains unchanged if we multiply all incomes by a certain value ('scale invariance').

These properties guarantee that the measures are sensible from the point of view of economic intuition, but do not identify a particular measure or group of measures (and, as mentioned, this list of axioms is not exhaustive). Despite its usefulness, some of these axioms

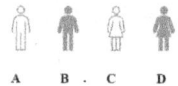

Principle	Baseline distribution $ $$ $$$ $$$$	Inequality comparison	Comparison distribution $ $$ $$$ $$$$
Anonymity	A B C D	=	A C B D
Population	A B C D	=	A E B F C G D H
Transfer	A B C D	>	A B C D (↑ $)
Decomposability	Alpha: A B C D Alpha + Delta: A E B F C G D H	> >	Beta: A C B D Beta + Delta: E A C F B D G H
Scale invariance	A B C D	=	A B C D ↑ ↑ ↑ ↑ $ x 2 $$ x 2 $$$ x 2 $$$$ x 2

Figure 3.2 Simplified example of the different properties of inequality measures.

Source: Authors' illustration.

have also been challenged. This is the case, for instance of the scale invariance, a principle that underlies the popular Gini coefficient. We return to this discussion in more detail later, but before that, we now describe the most used measures.[10]

The *variance* and the *coefficient of variation* are measures of dispersion – that is, the spread of different income levels around their average value. The coefficient of variation is obtained by taking the square root of the variance and dividing by the mean income level.

Given their simplicity, *percentiles* are also commonly used. They represent the income captured by selected groups of the distribution (e.g., top 10 per cent of the income distribution). Moreover, some measures are based on the ratios of these percentiles. For example, the *Palma ratio* is the ratio between the incomes in the top 10 per cent and the bottom 40 per cent of the income distribution.

Figure 3.3 plots the income shares of the bottom 40 per cent and top 10 per cent of Colombia's and South Africa's population, together with the Palma ratio. In Colombia, while there was a general declining trend from the mid-1990s in the Palma ratio, which corresponds to a decline in inequality, since 2018 there has been a reversal in this trend. Comparing the lines for the top 10 per cent and the bottom 40 per cent, we can see that this increase in inequality was driven by both an increase in the share of the top 10 per cent and a decline in the share of the bottom 40 per cent. In the case of South Africa, the Palma ratio highlights how the fluctuations in the share of the top 10 per cent together with a virtually unchanged share of the bottom 40 per cent have affected the level of inequality since the beginning of the 2000s.

While looking at these two shares simultaneously allows us to see whether inequality increases/reductions are driven by the top or the bottom of the population, they disregard the incomes in between. A similar argument was made recently in reference to SDG 10 (reducing inequalities within and among countries), the progress of which is

(a) Colombia

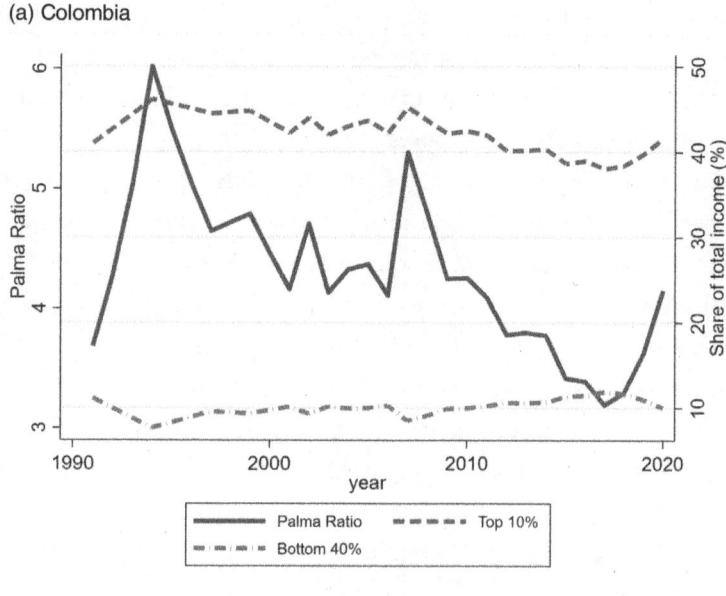

(b) South Africa

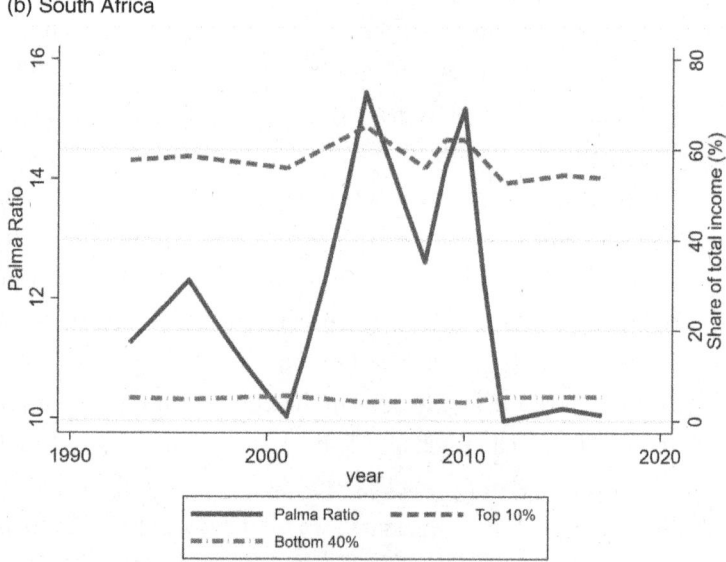

Figure 3.3 Trends in inequality considering percentiles and the Palma ratio in Colombia and South Africa.

Source: Authors' illustration using World Income Inequality Database (WIID) data.

partly based on an indicator of shared prosperity. The shared prosperity premium compares the growth rates of income or expenditure among the bottom 40 per cent and of the total population.[11] Box 3.2 provides more detail on this target and on the recent critique.

> ## Box 3.2: Shared prosperity and the Palma ratio
>
> To measure progress against the SDG Target 10.1 'by 2030, progressively achieve and sustain income growth of the bottom 40 per cent of the population at a rate higher than the national average', the United Nations use the concepts of shared prosperity and shared prosperity premium. The former refers to the annual growth of the income or consumption of the poorest 40 per cent, whereas the latter computes the difference between this and the annual growth of the income or consumption of the total population. To illustrate, here is an example using data for Vietnam:
>
> | | Shared prosperity, %[a] | Shared prosperity premium[a] | Palma ratio[b] |
> | --- | --- | --- | --- |
> | 2010–15 | 4.82 | 2.52 pp | 1.46 |
> | 2012–17 | 4.91 | -0.11 pp | 1.58 |
> | 2016–21 | 2.61 | -017 pp | NA |
>
> Notes: [a]Data for 2010–15 and 2012–17 from World Bank (2020) (Poverty and shared prosperity 2020: Reversals of Fortune) and data for 2016–21 from the latest report (World Bank 2024a, 2024b). [b]Data points correspond to the years 2014 and 2018 obtained from WIID (2023).
>
> However, this measure was not without criticism. In an open letter to the UN Secretary-General and the President of the World Bank, a group of economists and leaders warned about the potential pitfalls of considering exclusively the bottom 40 per cent instead of the whole distribution, and of not considering wealth in addition to income. Moreover, the statements on progress for this target sometimes conflate the indicators of shared prosperity and shared prosperity premium.
>
> Source: *The Guardian*, 17 July 2023, 'Top economists call for action on runaway global inequality', https://www.theguardian.com/inequality/2023/jul/17/top-economists-call-for-action-global-inequality-rich-poor-poverty-climate-breakdown-un-world-bank.

The most frequently used measure of income inequality is the *Gini index*, which measures the overall dispersion of income. It varies from 0 (perfect equality) to 1 (or 100 per cent) (perfect inequality), with higher levels corresponding to higher inequality.[12] It can be calculated based on the Lorenz curve, a line that shows the proportion of total income belonging to the bottom X per cent of the population. The bigger the distance between the Lorenz curve and the line of perfect equality, the higher the level of inequality. The Gini coefficient is the ratio of the area between the Lorenz curve and the line of perfect equality to the area between the lines of perfect equality and perfect inequality. Figure 3.4 provides an illustration of the Lorenz curve for Ethiopia in two different years. The distance between the Lorenz curve and the line of perfect equality decreased between 1996 and 2016 (the dashed line is closer than the full line), which indicates a reduction in inequality during this period.

Finally, a group of *generalized entropy (GE) indices* measure the redundancy, or compression, in the data and can be used to measure inequality. These indices have useful and desirable properties, including the possibility of expressing them as a weighted sum of a within-group and a between-group component. They are defined by a parameter α that indicates the sensitivity of the index to different parts of the distribution. Special cases of the GE inequality indices include the *Theil index* ($\alpha = 1$) and the *mean log deviation* ($\alpha = 0$). The index is more sensitive to the upper (lower) tail of the distribution, the higher (lower) α is.

Figure 3.5 compares the trends for the Gini index and the mean log deviation (also designated as M-Theil) in South Africa and Vietnam. We observe that they provide similar information about the evolution of inequality in these countries. Despite a decline from the mid-1990s to the early 2000s, inequality maintained a high level in South Africa

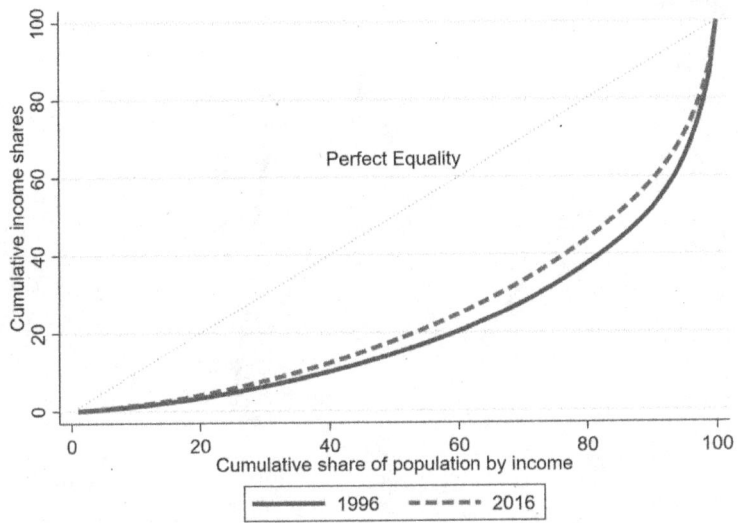

Figure 3.4 Lorenz curves for Ethiopia, 1996–2016.

Source: Authors' illustration using World Income Inequality Database (WIID) data.

until 2010, after which there was some improvement. Inequality has remained more constant in Vietnam and also saw an improvement after 2010.

To recap, Table 3.2 summarizes these measures and includes examples based on data from Ethiopia.

Different measures, varying value judgments

Given the multitude of measurement tools, one can ask what the criteria for selection should be. One element to consider is that different measures reflect different value judgements. We provide two illustrations, inspired by Ravallion (2004).

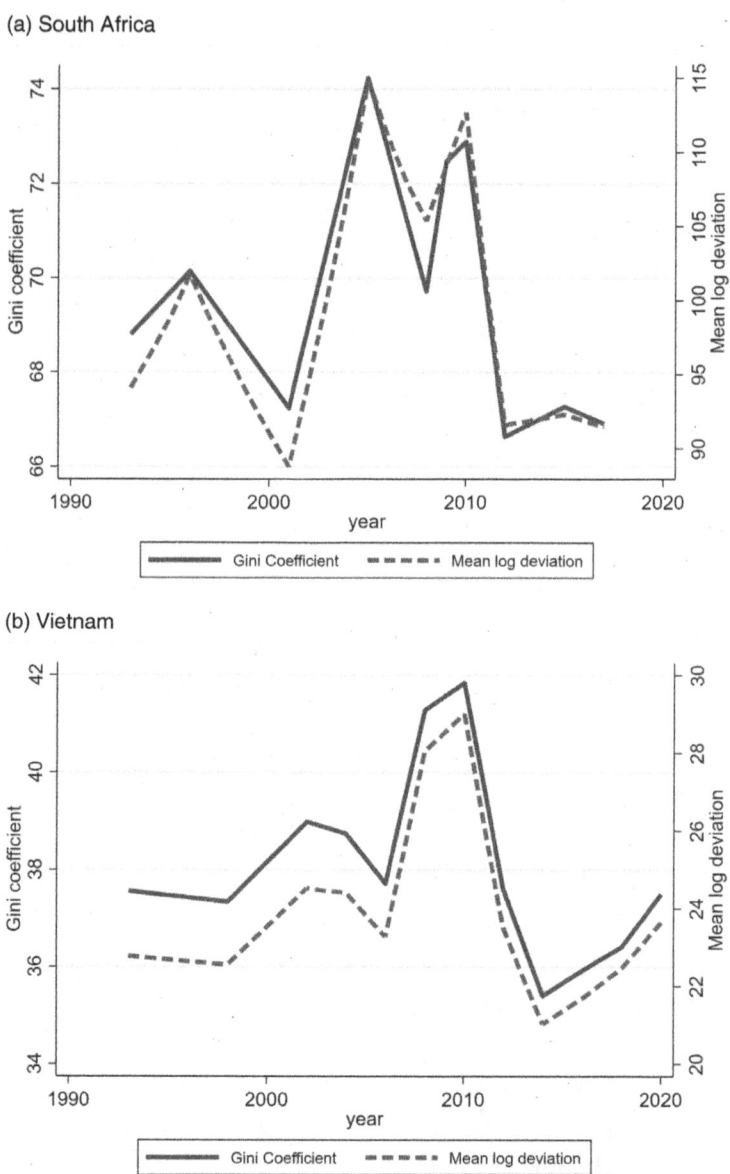

Figure 3.5 Trends in inequality considering the Gini index and the mean log deviation (or M-Theil), South Africa and Vietnam.

Source: Authors' illustration using World Income Inequality Database (WIID) data.

Table 3.2 Examples of measures of inequality in 2020 using data from Ethiopia

Measure	Definition	Ethiopia	Interpretation
Percentiles	Percentiles represent the income captured by selected groups of the distribution.	Top 10%: 41.3 Bottom 40%: 12.2	The 10% of the population with the highest income captures 41.3% of total income. In contrast, the 40% of those with the lowest income capture only 12.2%.
Percentile ratios	Compare how much bigger the share of income captured by one part of the population is compared to another part of the population.	Palma ratio: 3.4	The share of total income captured by the 10% of the population with the highest income is more than three times the share of income captured by the poorest 40% of the population.
Gini index	Measures the overall dispersion of income.	Gini (2010): 49.0 Gini (2020): 50.9	The Gini ranges between 0–100% (or 1), and higher levels correspond to higher inequality. There was an increase in inequality between 2010 and 2020.
Generalized entropy (GE) indices	Measure the redundancy in the data and can be decomposed as a weighted sum of a within-group and a between-group component.	Mean log deviation: 45.4 Theil index: 51.7	A value of 0 means perfect equality. The Theil index and the Mean log deviation represent how far away the country is from that.

Source: Data from WIID (2023).

First, consider the difference between relative and absolute measures of inequality that we discussed in Chapter 1. While there are some prominent exceptions (including Atkinson and Brandolini 2009 Ravallion 2004, 2014, 2018; Niño-Zarazúa, Roope and Tarp 2017), most of the empirical evidence on global inequality trends relies on relative measures. Relative measures satisfy the 'scale invariance' axiom mentioned earlier, meaning that if we increase all incomes by the same proportion inequality will stay the same. Still, there is evidence suggesting that there may not be consensus on this principle. In our work, described in more detail in Chapter 4, we find that some may think about inequality in absolute terms. In that case, one should use a measure that satisfies a different property. Inequality should instead remain the same when we add a constant value to all incomes.

Using a simplified example, consider two villages, A and B, with two residents each. In village A, the poor person has one chicken, and the rich person has two chickens; whereas in village B, the poor person has two chickens, and the rich person has four chickens. Thinking in relative terms, one would argue that inequality is the same in the two villages, as in both villages, the rich person has two times more chickens than the poor person. However, thinking in absolute terms, one would argue that inequality in village B is higher, given that while in village A, the rich person has one more chicken than the poor person, in village B the rich person has two more chickens than the poor person. Thus, measures that fulfil one or the other requirement reflect different value judgements and lead to different perceptions about which contexts experience inequality that is higher or lower. Drawing a link with political ideologies, absolute measures tend to be associated with 'leftist' or 'radical' thinking, whereas relative measures are associated with 'rightist' or 'conservative' ideological views.

Moreover, this distinction also entails different answers to a question that occupies a great part of the inequality discourse: do the poor benefit from aggregate economic growth? Consider again village B in the example above and imagine a growth in income that doubles the income of the population. The poor person would now have four chickens, and the rich person would have eight chickens. The share of income going to the poor remained the same, that is, relative inequality was stable. However, the absolute gains of the rich (four chickens) are greater than the absolute gains for the poor. In relative terms the answer would be 'yes', but in absolute terms the answer would be 'no'. Anthropologist Jason Hickel has conveyed a related point, making a stronger critique for the inadequacy of relative inequality measures.[13]

A second illustration stems from different units of analysis used in inequality measures (Ravallion 2004, 2018). Some may believe that the focus should be on within-country rather than between-country inequality, as people care more about the inequality they experience or see around them. More broadly, it may be argued that everyone matters and thus global inequality, which disregards where people live, should be the focus – a perspective that has been coined as the 'cosmopolitan view' (Brandolini and Carta 2016). Still, others with a different normative basis may refute this view and advocate for taking national differences into account, given that redistributive policies are implemented mostly at the national level. Yet, others might contend that inequality between groups (horizontal inequality) rather than vertical inequality is the crux of the matter (see more in Ravallion 2004).

What are the patterns and trends?

Having clarified the concept of inequality and discussed the challenges underlying its measurement, we now return to the question of this chapter: Is inequality rising? The non-governmental organization Oxfam International says 'yes' and calls it an 'inequality explosion':

> *In recent decades, economic inequality has soared to extreme and dangerous levels. It has become an existential threat to our societies, crippling our ability to end poverty, corroding politics and putting the future of our planet in peril.*
>
> Source: Oxfam International (2023: 15).

On a more nuanced statement, *The Economist* (2022) suggests 'probably'. They argue that the decreasing trend in inequality since the 1990s is ending because of the growth in China and India. Once they reach the global average GDP per capita, the world's two most populous countries will contribute to increasing (rather than decreasing) inequality:

> *[The] long decline in global inequality that began around 1990 has come to an end – and gaps between rich and poor now look likely to widen, as poor countries take longer to recover from Covid. Yet the causes of inequality's resurgence are not universally bleak. Paradoxically, part of the explanation lies in increasing incomes among the formerly impoverished.*
>
> Source: *The Economist* (2022: 1).

The World Bank concurs with this view, but highlights the distinction between the trends in within- and between-country inequality:[14]

> *Despite this convergence between countries, inequality between – rather than within – countries continues to account for the bulk of global inequality. Two-thirds of global inequality is due to differences in average incomes between countries. As a consequence, where*

someone is born is substantially more important in determining their income than their own efforts.'

Source: World Bank (2019).

The discussion in the previous sections gives some suggestions about how conceptual and measurement choices can lead to different interpretations of the underlying empirical realities and therefore to disparate statements like the ones above. Now we delve more deeply into this in the next paragraphs.

Different interpretations of empirical realities

To make sense of the differing statements above, think about the following simplified example. The picture on the top of two giraffes in Figure 3.6 is a snapshot of reality. If you look at it with a filter that blurs the background (the bottom left picture), your eyes will focus on the details of the giraffes rather than on the South African savanna background. Then, applying yet another filter (the bottom right picture) gives you an overall idea of the shapes but much of the detail is lost. We can draw a comparison between these filters and the different measures of inequality: they all depict an empirical reality, but they look at it through filters that put focus on different aspects and provide a more (or less) nuanced view of the empirical reality. Therefore, the interpretations of reality based on these different measures will vary.

Let us see how this applies to the trends on global income inequality. Figure 3.7 portrays the trend of global inequality weighted by population using the Gini index between 1950 and 2019, and compares this trend with that obtained with other relative measures, namely the mean log deviation and the Theil index. It shows that, at the global level, relative inequality across the different measures was at a steady level with a slight increase until the 1990s, when it started

Figure 3.6 Different measures of inequality as different 'filters' of the empirical reality.

Source: Public domain image, edited here for illustrative purposes. (https://www.flickr.com/photos/82995800@N06/49192938312).

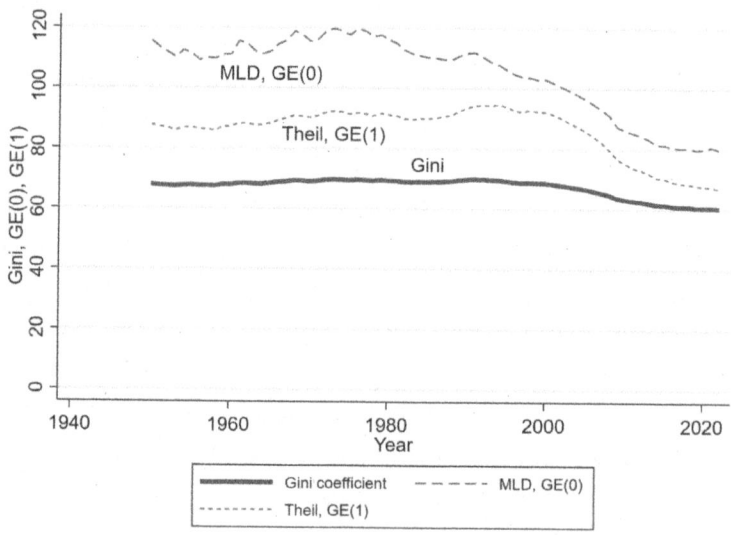

Figure 3.7 Trends in global inequality using different relative measures.

Source: Authors' illustration using World Income Inequality Database (WIID) data.

declining until the Covid-19 pandemic (see Box 3.3 for more on the impact of Covid-19).

Box 3.3: Covid-19 and inequality

While the Covid-19 pandemic posed different challenges across the world, existing evidence indicates that global income inequality (i.e., considering differences in income among everyone around the world) may have increased during this period (Garcia Rojas, Yonzan and Lakner 2025). This was driven by an increase in inequality between countries, in particular due to India's loss of income (Deaton 2021; Milanovic 2024), while inequality within countries played a moderating role. Moreover, despite widespread concern, currently available data in fact point to a more complex overall picture for within-country inequality for low- and lower-middle-income countries.

Let us take Mozambique as an example. While initial projections suggested that the increasing trend in inequality (Barletta et al. 2022, 2024) would be further aggravated by the Covid-19 shock, more recent estimates point to a decrease in the relative Gini index resulting from a reduction in the income gap between the poorer and the richer segments of the population (Salvucci and Tarp 2024b).

Overall, while projections exist based on different possible scenarios (Garcia Rojas, Yonzan and Lakner 2025), it is yet too early to know how the different effects will play out over the next couple of decades (Milanovic 2024).

Reflecting on the statements just discussed, the data concur with *The Economist* and the World Bank. Nevertheless, as highlighted by the latter, these trends are driven by underlying trends in both within- and between-country inequality. These are presented in Figure 3.8. The graph illustrates that the flat or slightly increasing trend up until the 1990s was the combined result of increasing inequalities between countries and decreasing inequality within countries. Still,

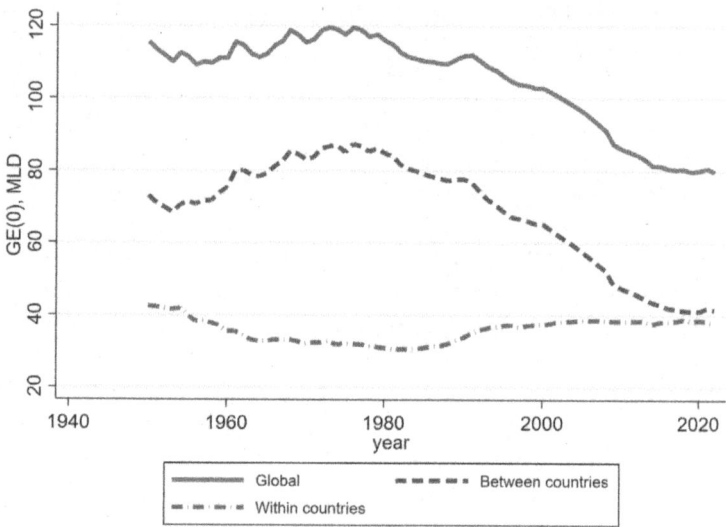

Figure 3.8 Decomposition of global inequality into within- and between-countries components based on the mean log deviation, 1950–2022.

Source: Authors' illustration using World Income Inequality Database (WIID) data.

the consistent decline from then onwards[15] was driven by the steep decline in between-country inequality, mainly due to the growth of the emerging economies India and China (Milanovic 2024), whereas within-country inequality stagnated or increased marginally. While it is not always clear from Oxfam's report which concept of inequality is being used, our discussion suggests that Oxfam refers to the increase in inequality within countries. Thus, opposing statements about increasing or decreasing inequality may not be necessarily wrong, but instead referring to different *concepts* of inequality.[16]

An additional element that may bring clarity to the diverging statements is the perspective taken. Instead of focusing on the entire population, an alternative approach to get a sense of differences across income groups is to compare income shares. Figure 3.9 presents the evolution of the income share of the top 10 per cent, the middle 50 per cent and the bottom 40 per cent. It shows a

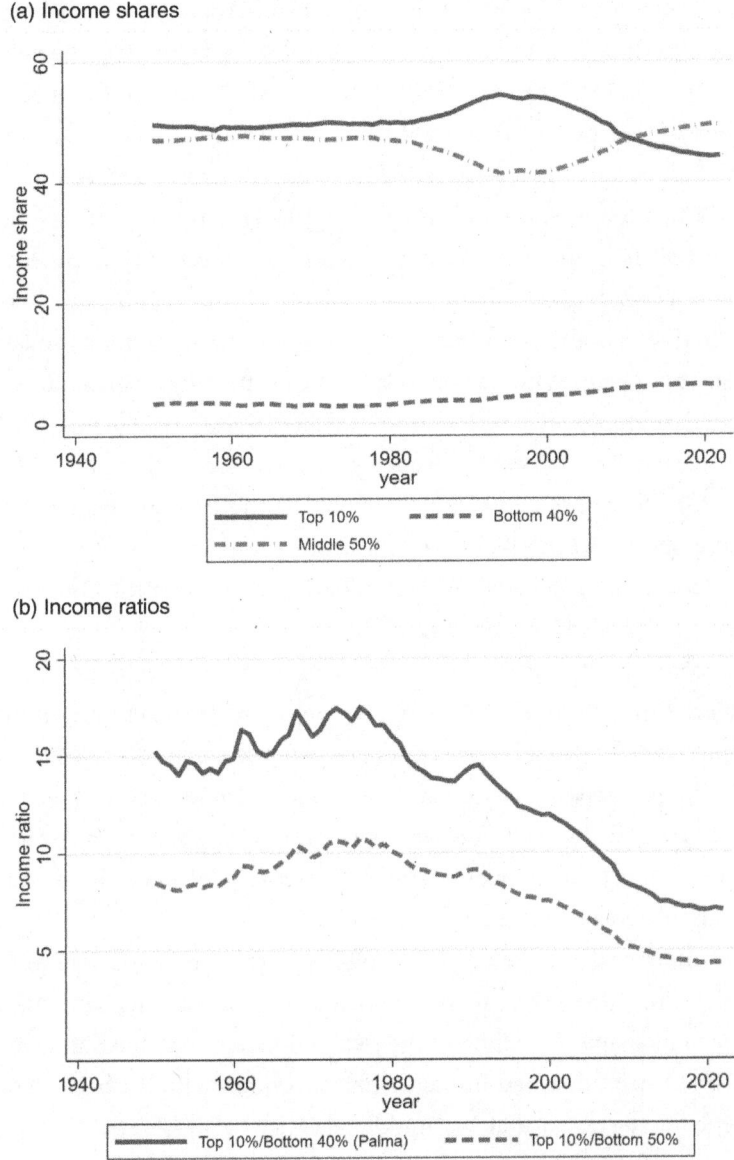

Figure 3.9 Income shares and ratios of different percentiles, 1950–2022.
Source: Authors' illustration using World Income Inequality Database (WIID) data.

decreasing trend in the income share of the top 10 per cent in the last two decades, contrasting with an increase in the income share of the middle 50 per cent and a slight upward trend of the income share of the bottom 40 per cent since the 1980s.[17] Furthermore, both the Palma ratio (that we introduced earlier in this chapter) and the ratio of the income share of the top 10 per cent over the income share of the middle 50 per cent suggest that inequality declined in the last two decades.

Still, this does certainly not mean that inequality is not a pressing issue that requires immediate action. It is. Especially when looking at the very top of the distribution, available data do concur that there are reasons for concern, as argued by Oxfam. According to the WID (2023), the household wealth[18] owned by the 0.01 per cent richest increased between 1995 and 2022 from 8 per cent to 12 per cent. Moreover, the gap between the top 0.01 per cent and the bottom 50 per cent has also been increasing.

From another perspective, one can examine the accumulated income growth rates for each income share (for example, decile or percentile) to see how the gains from economic growth[19] are distributed across the (global) population. These are portrayed in what are called *growth incidence curves* (GICs). They can be relative if depicting proportionate gains in income or absolute if showing accumulated absolute gains.

Lakner and Milanovic (2016) plotted a relative growth curve for the period 1988–2008, which became known as the 'elephant curve' due to its shape. The trunk of the elephant meant that those at the top of the distribution had immense gains from growth, the back of the elephant suggested that the middle class saw a substantial increase, while its tail indicated that for the poorest there were no big changes. They interpreted this as suggesting that the global rich and the middle class in developing countries were the main winners from growth, which did not benefit the middle class in developed countries and the

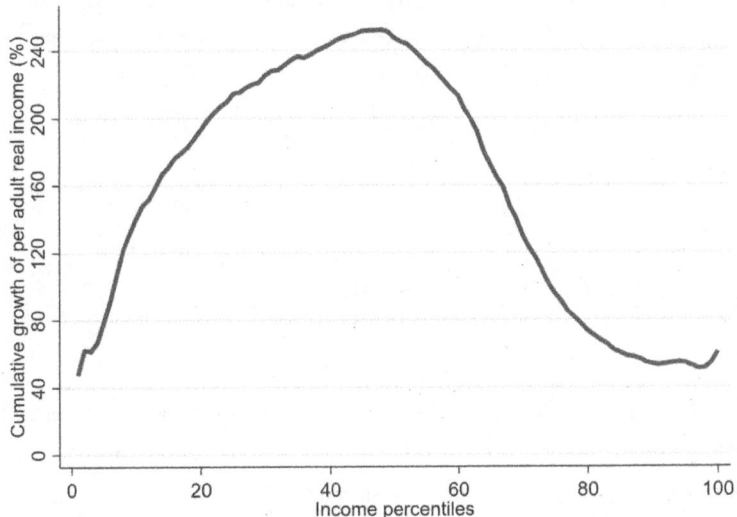

Figure 3.10 The updated 'elephant curve' (growth incidence curve), 1988–2022.

Source: Authors' illustration using World Income Inequality Database (WIID) data.

global poor. This helps to give more nuance to the trends of falling inequality that we presented earlier.

This influential picture of inequality was later questioned by Milanovic (2020), who showed that the elephant no longer has a trunk as the period after 2008 benefited the global poor and the global middle class, but less so the Western middle classes and the global top 1 per cent. Moreover, while the Western middle classes are still much richer than the middle classes in Asian countries, according to Milanovic's (2020) observations, the gap will continue to reduce progressively. Figure 3.10 shows an updated 'elephant curve' using data from WIID and extending to the latest period, which suggests that despite the growth in the bottom 50 per cent, the gains from the top 30 per cent of the population were larger (Ferreira, Salvucci and Tarp 2023: 27).

So far we have focused only on *relative* measures. Still, as we described at the beginning of the chapter, inequality can also be measured in *absolute* terms. We will show in the following paragraphs that this distinction can also help explain the disparities in the discourse around inequality.

Absolute approaches highlight concerning upward trends

Recall from earlier in this chapter that absolute measures of inequality satisfy the condition that if all incomes are increased by the same amount, then inequality remains the same. As we will discuss in more detail in Chapter 4, while most of the debate on inequality focuses on relative measures, evidence suggests that a meaningful portion of

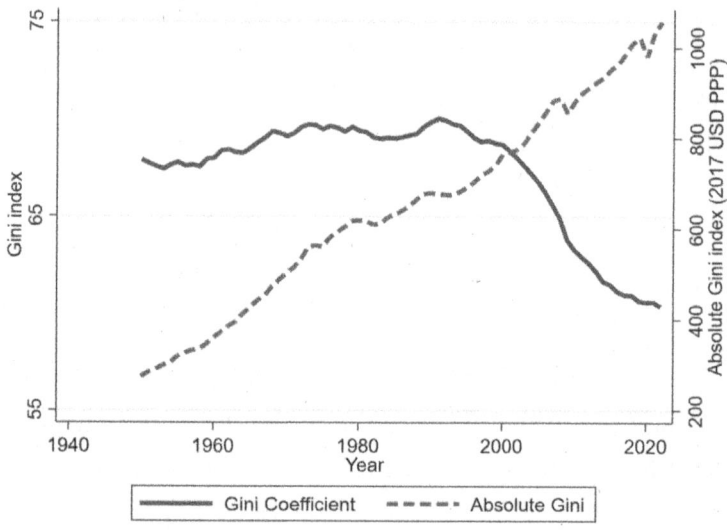

Figure 3.11 Comparison between the relative and the absolute Gini coefficients, 1950–2022.

Source: Authors' illustration based on population-weighted data from WIID (2023).

people think about inequality in an absolute way. So, looking at the recent trends in inequality in absolute terms, is inequality rising?

The answer is a definite 'yes'. Figure 3.11 compares the trends in global inequality using the relative Gini (which we showed already in the previous subsection) with those obtained when considering the absolute Gini instead. The absolute Gini satisfies the axiom underlying absolute measures (recall the example of the villages and the chickens described earlier in the chapter). In terms of the mathematical formula, it is obtained by multiplying the relative Gini by the mean income of the income distribution. The absolute Gini shows a consistent increase from 1950 until the recent period (see also Niño-Zarazúa, Roope and Tarp 2017). Gradín (2024: 10) highlights that one should expect this upward trend to happen since we have seen sustained growth in global income, which is unlikely to reduce absolute differences in income between people.

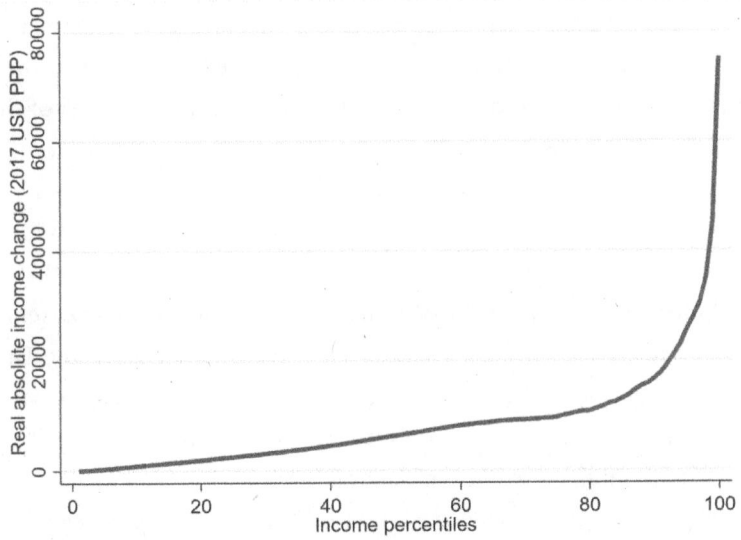

Figure 3.12 The updated 'serpent curve' (global absolute income gain), 1980–2022.

Source: Authors' illustration using World Income Inequality Database (WIID) data.

This view is reinforced by looking at the GICs in absolute rather than relative terms, that is, looking at accumulated growth. Ravallion (2018) did this exercise and, instead of an elephant, he found a 'serpent'. The high-raised head of the serpent meant that the top income distribution had experienced greater absolute gains than the bottom. Figure 3.12 shows the same curve, updated with the latest available data from the WIID and confirms this increasing trend in inequality, which contrasts with what we described in the previous subsection. According to this absolute measure, growth has barely benefited the poor and the middle class in the developing world, contrary to the richest percentiles, who gained immensely (Ferreira, Salvucci and Tarp 2023). Moreover, excluding China, there is still a substantial income gap between the 'core' and the poor 'periphery' (Milanovic 2024).

Still, it is interesting to note that the differences in the trends using the absolute and relative Gini coefficients are more pronounced in countries with higher levels of income. Figure 3.13 compares the two indices across four groups of countries, divided according to their income level. We can observe that the lower the income level of the group of countries, the less clear are the differences in the trends between absolute and relative inequality.

We derive similar conclusions when we look at groups obtained according to the regional location of countries (Figure 3.14). For instance, there is a clear difference between the inequality trends suggested by the absolute and relative Gini coefficients in the East Asia and Pacific and in the Latin America and the Caribbean regions. However, it is harder to observe clear differences when looking at the trends for South Asia and sub-Saharan Africa.

Before we conclude, we should add that these differences in perspective can also happen at the country level.[20] Figure 3.15 illustrates this by portraying trends in absolute and relative Ginis in our five countries of interest. In Colombia, it shows how opposite

(a) High-income countries

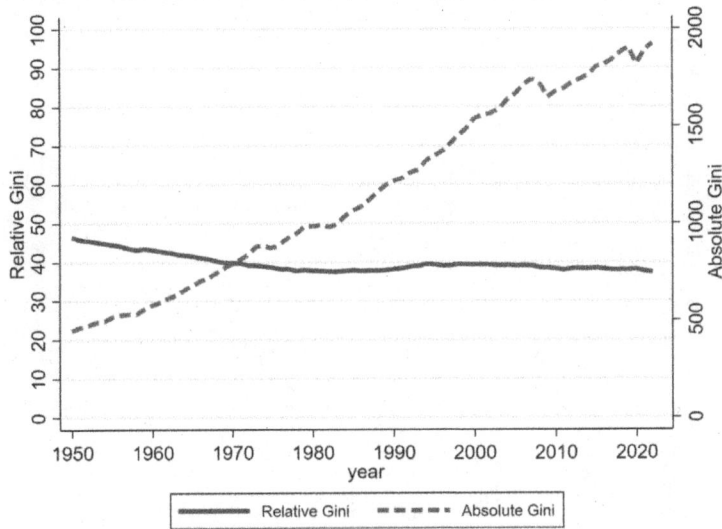

(b) Upper-middle-income countries

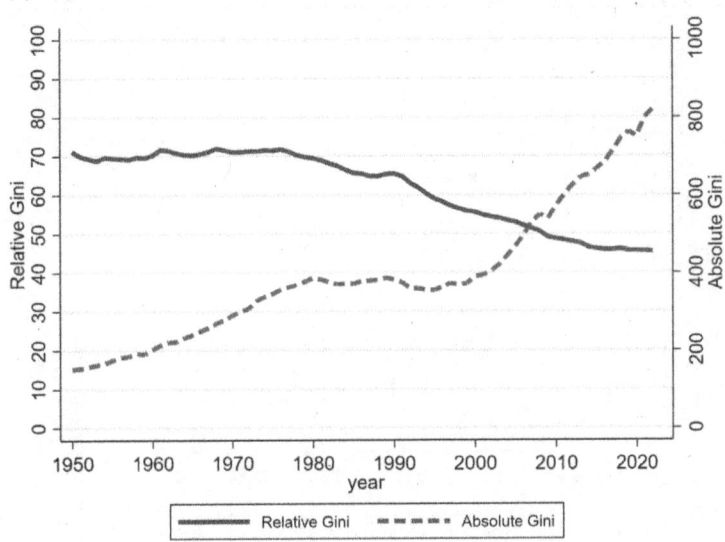

(c) Lower-middle-income countries

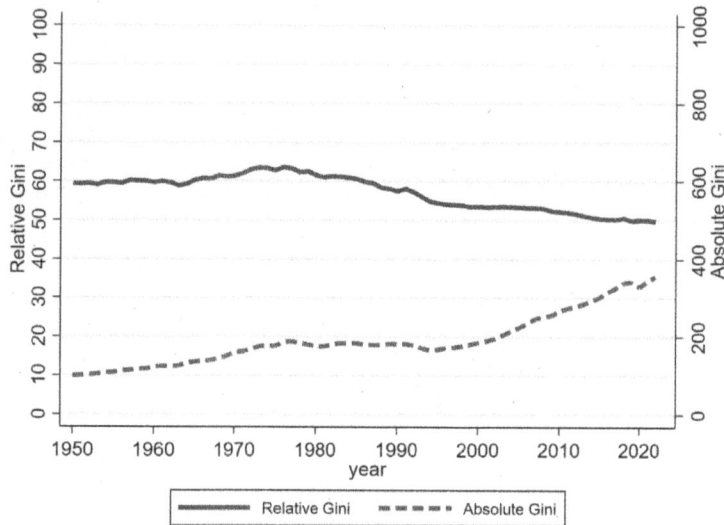

(d) Low-income countries

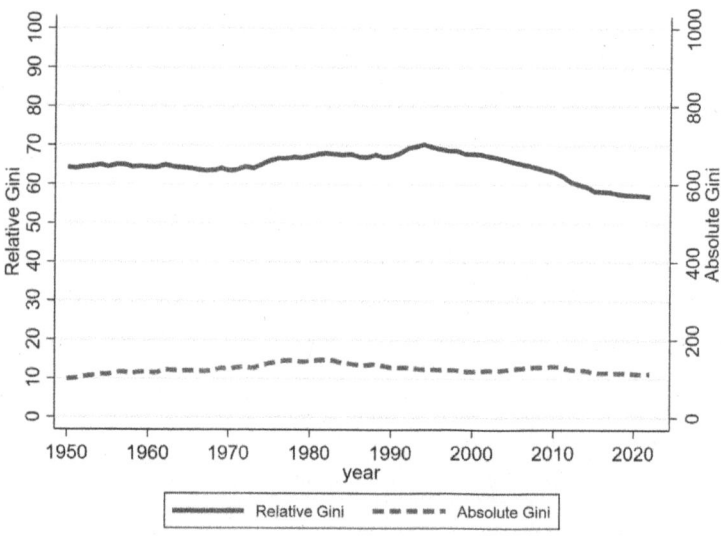

Figure 3.13 Absolute and relative Gini coefficients in countries with similar income levels, 1950–2022.

Source: Authors' illustration using World Income Inequality Database (WIID) data.

(a) East Asia and Pacific

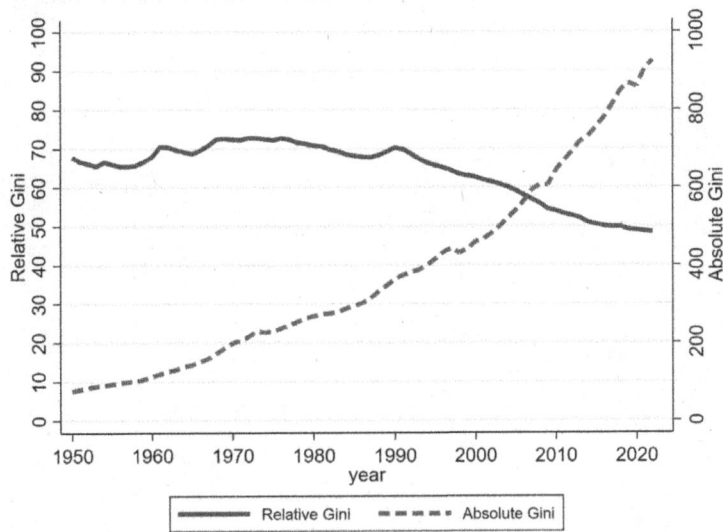

(b) South Asia

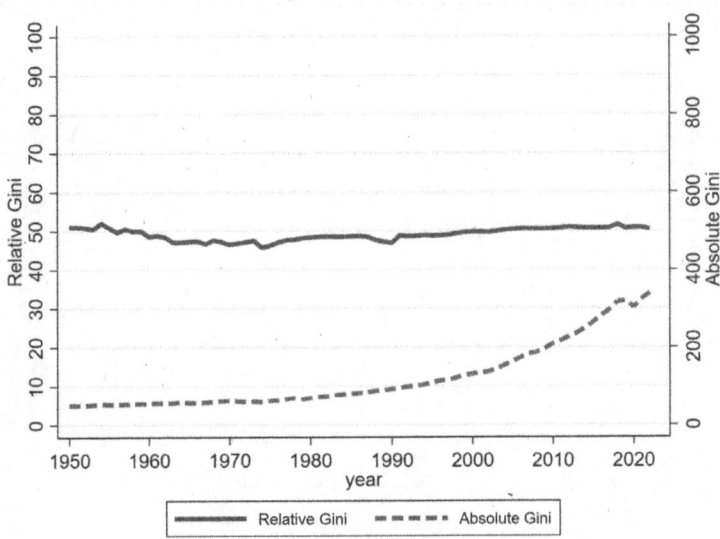

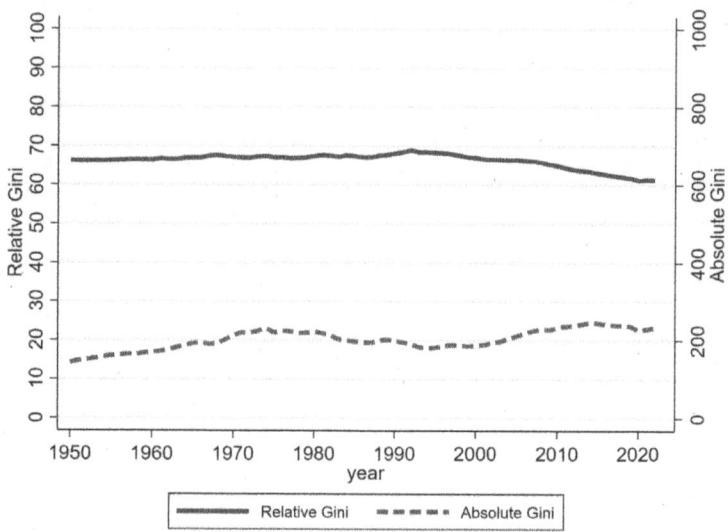

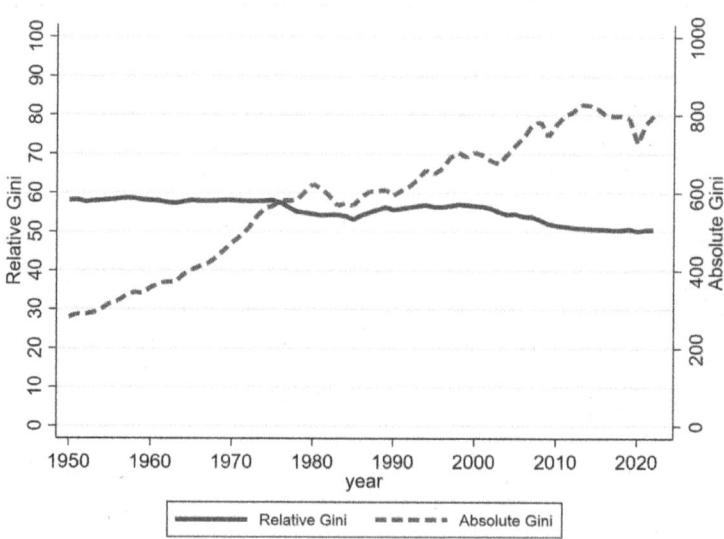

Figure 3.14 Absolute and relative Gini coefficients in different regions, 1950–2022.

Source: Authors' illustration using World Income Inequality Database (WIID) data.

(a) Colombia

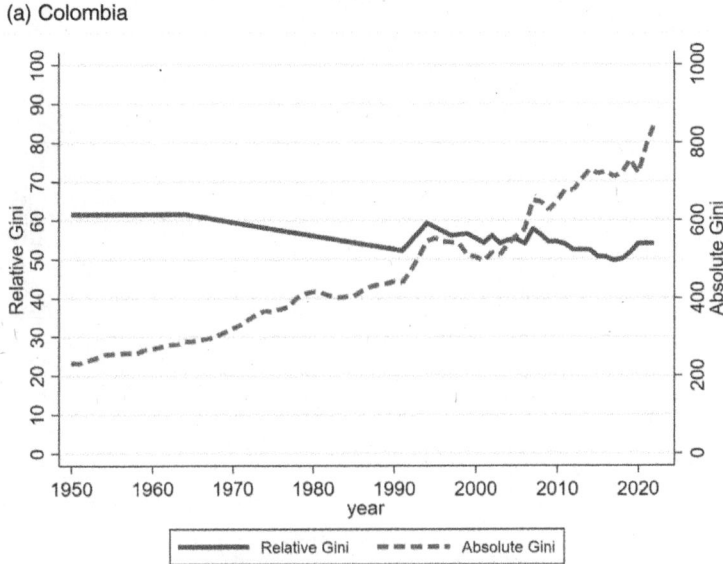

(b) Vietnam

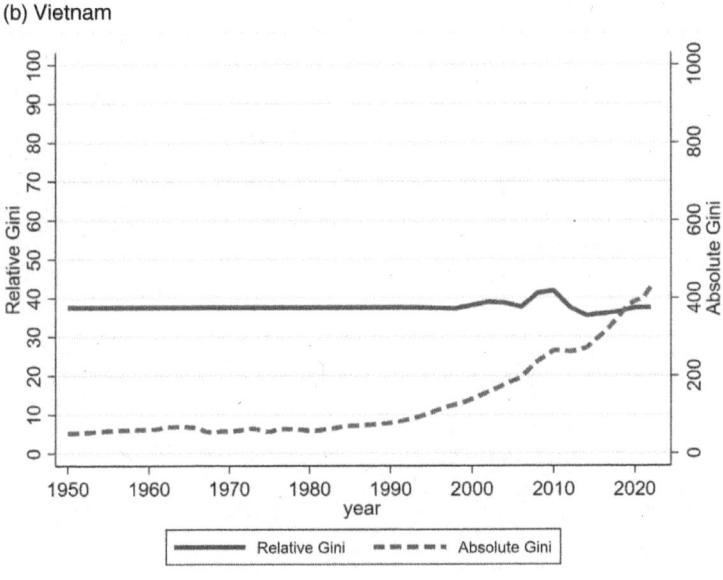

88 *Dimensions of Inequality*

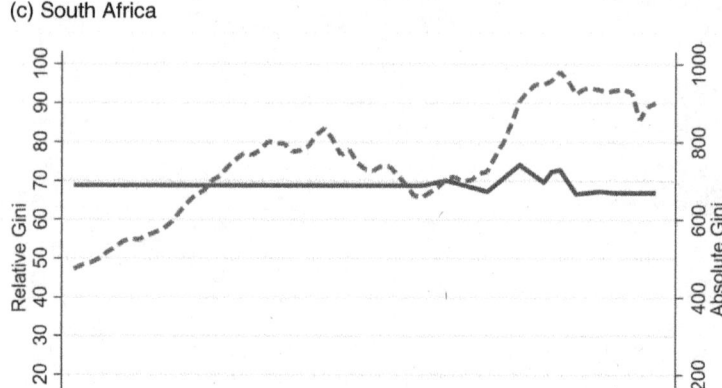

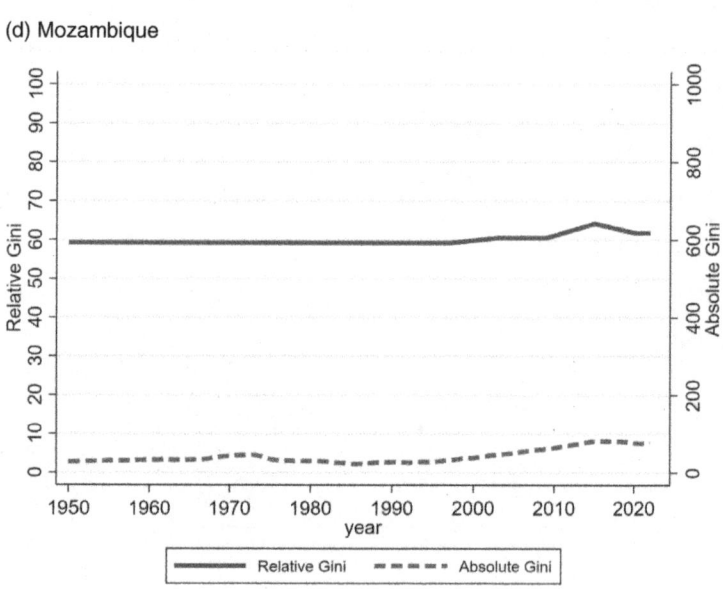

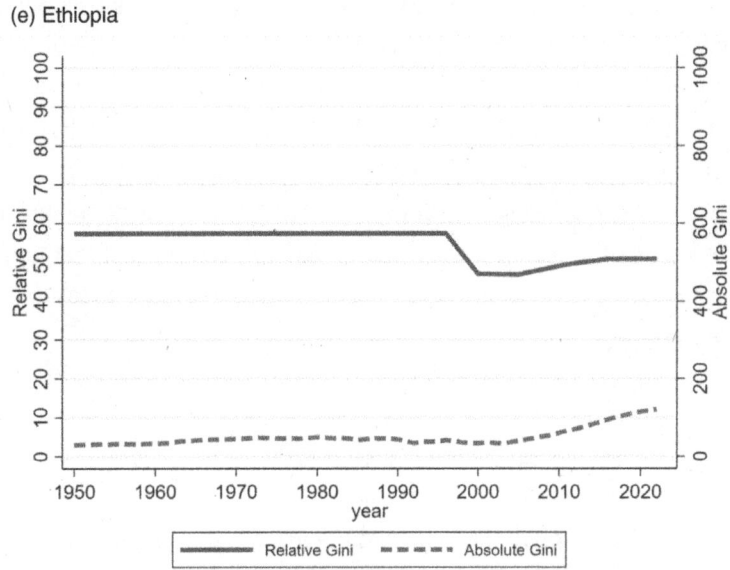

Figure 3.15 Absolute and relative Gini coefficients in our five country cases, 1950–2022.

Source: Authors' illustration using World Income Inequality Database (WIID) data.

claims about inequality can be true: inequality decreased between 1990 and 2020 in relative terms, while at the same time absolute inequality increased for the same period. While less pronounced, you can also see these differences when looking at the trends for Vietnam, where relative inequality was quite stable while absolute inequality increased. This is in line with the regional trends described above. In a similar vein, the trend of absolute and relative inequality in Mozambique[21] and Ethiopia broadly resembles the regional trends in sub-Saharan Africa. However, South Africa stands out, with little change in relative inequality, combined with a clear increase in inequality in absolute terms. These differences further illustrate the perils of considering only regional averages and the importance of also considering individual countries, given that redistributive policies are mostly done at the national level.

Overall, while relative measures seem to suggest improving trends in inequality (especially at the global level) there are clear indications of concerning trends in absolute terms. This concurs with our central argument in this book, that focusing on the relative Gini coefficient alone is insufficient to capture a comprehensive picture of inequality and that a dashboard approach that covers a variety of measures is superior.

Key takeaways

- Measuring inequality entails making many complex choices, including the unit of analysis to consider, the indicator to use and the measure to employ.
- While in relative terms inequality has decreased in the recent decades, absolute measures show instead that it has been increasing both at the global and regional levels, as well as within-country.
- Different measures reflect different normative values, and lead to different interpretations of the patterns and trends of inequality. Thus, a single measure of inequality is unlikely to capture everyone's agreement and is insufficient to inform public debates in a constructive manner.

Notes

1 For simplicity, throughout this chapter we will refer to income or consumption.

2 Equivalized incomes are income levels adjusted based on certain known attributes of the individual. This adjustment allows one to compare individuals with different attributes (Cowell and Flachaire 2021: 4-5).
3 Recall from Chapter 1 that purchasing power parity (PPP) is used to adjust for differences in the cost of living and prices across countries.
4 While we refer here to data from the WIID, consider that different data sources apply different choices in terms of data and measurement, as we discuss in more detail in the remainder of the chapter.
5 Using the national poverty line, Salvucci and Tarp (2024a, 2024b) report a consumption poverty rate of 46.1 per cent for the same period, which is still considerably above poverty rates in South Africa and Ethiopia.
6 See Atkinson and Brandolini (2009) for a comprehensive analysis of data on income inequality and the implications for the examination of the link between inequality and growth.
7 See Salvucci and Tarp (2024a, 2024b) for the importance of using prices appropriate to income groups.
8 Using the average income/consumption (which is obtained by dividing total income by the number of people in the household) leads to an under-estimation of inequality (Ravallion 2021). See Ravallion (2021) for a more technical and more comprehensive discussion (related to prices and to the role of nationality) on data concerns and biases in the estimation of inequality.
9 Recall that while we describe measurement in terms of income, the same applies to consumption or other welfare indicators.
10 See Josa and Aguado (2020) for an overview of measures of inequality. While we focus on unidimensional measures in this chapter, Chapter 2 considered several multidimensional measures.
11 For a modified approach to shared prosperity, consider Lopez-Noval et al. (2024) which proposes using inequality lines rather than the bottom 40 per cent.
12 The intuition behind the Gini is as follows. Consider that we split a certain population into pairs, and for each pair calculate the absolute difference between the two incomes. The Gini corresponds to finding half of the average of these differences, dividing by the average income of the population.

13 See Hickel (2019) (https://www.jasonhickel.org/blog/2019/5/15/how-not-to-measure-inequality), and rebuttal in Fix (2019) (https://capitalaspower.com/2019/12/are-we-measuring-inequality-the-wrong-way/).

14 As does the former United Nations assistant secretary-general for economic development in the United Nations Department of Economic and Social Affairs (DESA), Jomo Kwame Sundaram (2024), who recently stated: 'Despite some convergence among nations, many low-income countries and people are falling further behind. ... While some national-level income inequalities have fallen, North-South disparities have trended unevenly, partly due to the quantitative influence of China's and India's large economies.'

15 Milanovic (2024) divides the trends in global inequality in three periods. The first era corresponds to the period from 1820 to 1950, which was characterized by increasing between-country inequality, or divergence. It was followed by a period of high global inequality in the second half of the twentieth century, which he calls the second era of inequality. Milanovic then describes how the third era, from around the turn of the twenty-first century, is the reverse of the first era, with declining between-country inequality – that is, convergence.

16 More recent accounts also point to a less positive trend in the next decades. Kanbur, Ortiz-Juarez and Sumner (2022, 2024) argue that there will be a reversal in the declining trend of global income inequality due to changes in both the between- and the within-country components.

17 See Chancel and Piketty (2021) for a description of the trends since 1820 based on data from the WID dataset.

18 Note that the measurement of wealth inequality is still in development and data are available only for certain countries. An alternative data source is the *Global Wealth Report* hosted by UBS (https://www.ubs.com/global/en/wealth-management/insights/global-wealth-report.html).

19 We briefly clarify that we will use the terms *economic growth* and *growth* interchangeably to designate an increase in national or per capita income. National income is commonly measured as the gross national product (GNP), which is the value added of the goods and

services produced in an economy during a given period of time, or as the gross domestic product (GDP), which differs from the GNP in that it considers all output produced within the country (whether by citizens or foreign residents) and excludes the output produced by citizens living abroad. We will return to the links between inequality, poverty and growth in more detail in Chapter 5.

20 For a recent example on how conclusions may change depending on the measure and definition of inequality used, see Jenkins (2024). He finds that using an absolute rather than a relative index and using a measure that is more sensitive to the top of the distribution than the Gini index, leads to a higher chance of concluding that inequality in the UK has risen, rather than been stable, during the past 30 years.

21 For fuller consideration of the evolution of inequality in Mozambique, with consideration of absolute and relative Gini indices, as well as consumption distribution, percentiles and percentile ratios, growth incidence curves and Lorenz curves, see Barletta et al. (2024).

References

Alvaredo, F., F. Bourguignon, F. Ferreira and N. Lustig (2023). 'Seventy-Five Years of Measuring Income Inequality in Latin America', LACIR Series Working Paper 111. London: Inter-American Development Bank. https://www.lse.ac.uk/International-Inequalities/Publications/Working-Papers. Accessed: 11 September 2025.

Amiel, Y., and F. A. Cowell (1992). 'Measurement of Income Inequality: Experimental Test by Questionnaire'. *Journal of Public Economics*, 47: 3–26.

Arndt, C., S. Jones, K. Mahrt, V. Salvucci and F. Tarp (2016). 'A Review of Consumption Poverty Estimation for Mozambique', WIDER Working Paper 2016/35. Helsinki: UNU-WIDER. https://www.wider.unu.edu/sites/default/files/wp2016-35.pdf. Accessed: 11 September 2025.

Arndt, C., and K. Mahrt (2017). 'Is Inequality Underestimated in Mozambique? Accounting for Underreported Consumption', WIDER Working Paper 2017/153. Helsinki: UNU-WIDER. https://www.wider.

unu.edu/sites/default/files/Publications/Working-paper/PDF/wp2
017-153.pdf. Accessed: 11 September 2025.

Atkinson, A. B., and A. Brandolini (2009). 'On Data: A Case Study of the Evolution of Income Inequality across Time and across Countries'. *Cambridge Journal of Economics*, 33(3): 381–404. https://doi.org/10.1093/cje/bel013. Accessed: 11 September 2025.

Barletta, G., F. Castigo, E. M. Egger, M. Keller, V. Salvucci and F. Tarp (2022). 'The Impact of Covid-19 on Consumption Poverty in Mozambique'. *Journal of International Development*, 34(4): 771–802. https://doi.org/10.1002/jid.3599. Accessed: 11 September 2025.

*Barletta, G., M. Ibraimo, V. Salvucci, E. Sarmento and F. Tarp (2024). 'The Evolution of Inequality in Mozambique 1996/7–2019/20'. *Development Southern Africa*, 41(6): 1179–213. https://doi.org/10.1080/03768 35X.2024.2398545. Accessed: 11 September 2025.

Brandolini, A., and F. Carta (2016). 'Some Reflections on the Social Welfare Bases of the Measurement of Global Income Inequality'. *Journal of Globalization and Development*, 7(1): 1–15. https://doi.org/10.1515/jgd-2016-0007. Accessed: 11 September 2025.

Chancel, L., and T. Piketty (2021). 'Global Income Inequality, 1820–2020: The Persistence and Mutation of Extreme Inequality'. *Journal of the European Economic Association*, 19(6): 3025–62. https://doi.org/10.1093/jeea/jvab047. Accessed: 11 September 2025.

Cowell, F. (2016). 'Inequality and Poverty Measures'. In M. D. Adler and M. Fleurbaey (eds), *The Oxford Handbook of Well-Being and Public Policy* (pp. 82–125). New York: Oxford University Press.

Cowell, F. A., and E. Flachaire (2021). 'Inequality Measurement: Methods and Data'. In K. F. Zimmermann (ed.), *Handbook of Labor, Human Resources and Population Economics* (pp. 1–46). Online: Springer Nature.

Deaton, A. (2021). 'Covid-19 and Global Income Inequality', NBER Working Paper 28392. Cambridge, MA: National Bureau of Economic Research. http://www.nber.org/papers/w28392. Accessed: 11 September 2025.

Economist, The (2022). 'Global Inequality Is Rising Again: But the Causes of the Resurgence Are Not All Bleak'. 2 August. https://www.proquest.

com/magazines/global-inequality-is-risingagain/docview/2697466165/
se-2?accountid=13607 (accessed 29 February 2024).

Ferreira, F. H. G. (2023). 'Is There a New Consensus on Inequality?', LSE Working Paper 101. London: LSE International Inequalities Institute. https://eprints.lse.ac.uk/120113/1/III_working_paper_101.pdf. Accessed: 11 September 2025.

*Ferreira, I. A., V. Salvucci and F. Tarp (2023). 'Poverty, Inequality, and Growth: Trends, Policies, and Controversies'. In K. F. Zimmermann (ed.), *Handbook of Labor, Human Resources and Population Economics* (pp. 1–45). Online: Springer Nature.

Fix, B. (2019). 'Are We Measuring Inequality the Wrong Way?'. 9 December. https://capitalaspower.com/2019/12/are-we-measuring-inequality-the-wrong-way/ (accessed 2 December 2024).

Garcia Rojas, D. C., N. Yonzan and C. Lakner (2025). 'Global Inequality and Economic Growth: The Three Decades Before Covid-19 and Three Decades After', World Bank Policy Research Working Paper 11093. Washington, DC: World Bank. https://documents1.worldbank.org/curated/en/099928403262531089/pdf/IDU-5aad7296-6ece-49ee-a291-3acc30bac9dd.pdf. Accessed: 11 September 2025.

Gradín, C. (2024). 'Revisiting the Trends in Global Inequality'. *World Development*, 179(106607): 1–24. https://doi.org/10.1016/j.worlddev.2024.106607. Accessed: 11 September 2025.

Gradín, C., and F. Tarp (2019). 'Investigating Growing Inequality in Mozambique'. *South African Journal of Economics*, 87(2): 110–38. https://doi.org/10.1007/s10888-020-09451-w. Accessed: 11 September 2025.

Guardian, The (2023). 'Top Economists Call for Action on Runaway Global Inequality'. 17 July. https://www.theguardian.com/inequality/2023/jul/17/top-economists-call-for-action-global-inequality-rich-poor-poverty-climate-breakdown-un-world-bank. Accessed: 2 December 2024.

Hickel, J. (2019). 'How Not to Measure Inequality'. 15 May. https://www.jasonhickel.org/blog/2019/5/15/how-not-to-measure-inequality. Accessed: 2 December 2024.

Jenkins, S. P. (2024). 'Getting the Measure of Inequality'. *Oxford Open Economics*, 3: i156–i66. https://doi.org/10.1093/ooec/odad037. Accessed: 11 September 2025.

Josa, I., and A. Aguado (2020). 'Measuring Unidimensional Inequality: Practical Framework for the Choice of an Appropriate Measure'. *Social Indicators Research*, 149: 541–70. https://doi.org/10.1007/s11205-020-02268-0. Accessed: 11 September 2025.

Kanbur, R., E. Ortiz-Juarez and A. Sumner (2022). 'The Global Inequality Boomerang', WIDER Working Paper 2022/27. Helsinki: UNU-WIDER. https://doi.org/10.35188/UNU-WIDER/2022/158-7. Accessed: 11 September 2025.

Kanbur, R., E. Ortiz-Juarez and A. Sumner (2024). 'Is the Era of Declining Global Income Inequality Over?'. *Structural Change and Economic Dynamics*, 70: 45–55. https://doi.org/10.1016/j.strueco.2024.01.002. Accessed: 11 September 2025.

Lakner, C., and B. Milanovic (2016). 'Global Income Distribution: From the Fall of the Berlin Wall to the Great Recession'. *World Bank Economic Review*, 30(2): 203–32. doi:10.1093/wber/lhv039. Accessed: 11 September 2025.

***Lopez-Noval, B., M. Niño-Zarazúa, L. Roope and F. Tarp (2024). 'From the Bottom 40 to Inequality Lines: Sharing Prosperity Globally and Domestically', WIDER Working Paper 2024/77. Helsinki: UNU-WIDER. https://www.wider.unu.edu/publication/bottom-40-inequality-lines#. Accessed: 11 September 2025.**

Milanovic, B. (2020). 'Elephant Who Lost Its Trunk: Continued Growth in Asia, but the Slowdown in Top 1% Growth after the Financial Crisis', *VoxEU CEPR*. 6 October. https://cepr.org/voxeu/columns/elephant-who-lost-its-trunk-continued-growth-asia-slowdown-top-1-growth-after (accessed 2 December 2024).

Milanovic, B. (2024). 'The Three Eras of Global Inequality, 1820–2020 with the Focus on the Past Thirty Years'. *World Development*, 177 (106516): 1–24. https://doi.org/10.1016/j.worlddev.2023.106516. Accessed: 11 September 2025.

Niño-Zarazúa, M., L. Roope and F. Tarp (2017). 'Global Inequality: Relatively Lower, Absolutely Higher'. *Review of Income and Wealth*, 63(4): 661–84. 10.1111/roiw.12240.

Oxfam International (2023). *Survival of the Richest: How We Must Tax the Super-Rich Now to Fight Inequality*. Report. Oxford: Oxfam International. https://www.oxfamnovib.nl/Files/rapporten/2023/Davos_2023_full%20report_English_EMBARGOED%20(3).pdf. Accessed: 11 September 2025.

Ravallion, M. (2004). 'Competing Concepts of Inequality in the Globalization Debate', *Brookings Trade Forum 2004, Globalization, Poverty, and Inequality* (pp. 1–38). https://www.jstor.org/stable/25063189. Accessed: 11 September 2025.

Ravallion, M. (2014). 'Income Inequality in the Developing World'. *Science*, 344(6186): 851–55. 10.1126/science.1251875.

Ravallion, M. (2018). 'Inequality and Globalization: A Review Essay'. *Journal of Economic Literature*, 56(2): 620–42. https://doi.org/10.1257/jel.20171419. Accessed: 11 September 2025.

Ravallion, M. (2021). 'What Might Explain Todays Conflicting Narratives on Global Inequality?'. In C. Gradín, M. Leibbrandt and F. Tarp (eds), *Inequality in the Developing World* (pp. 17–48). Oxford: Oxford University Press.

Salvucci, V., and F. Tarp (2024a). 'Crises, Prices, and Poverty: An Analysis Based on the Mozambican Household Budget Surveys 1996/7–2019/20'. *Food Policy*, 125: 102651. https://doi.org/10.1016/j.foodpol.2024.102651. Accessed: 11 September 2024.

Salvucci, V., and F. Tarp (2024b). 'Assessing Welfare in Developing Countries Before, During, and After Covid-19 Using Actual Household Data: The Case of Mozambique'. DEEP Working Paper 24. https://doi.org/10.55158/DEEPWP24. Accessed: 11 September 2024.

Sundaram, J. K. (2024). 'World Inequality Still Rising Despite Some Convergence', *IPS Inter Press Service*, 6 November. https://www.ipsnews.net/2024/11/world-inequality-still-rising-despite-convergence (accessed 2 December 2024).

World Bank (2019). 'Yes, Global Inequality Has Fallen. No, We Shouldn't Be Complacent'. 23 October. https://www.worldbank.org/en/news/feature/2019/10/23/yes-global-inequality-has-fallen-no-we-shouldnt-be-complacent (accessed 2 December 2024).

World Bank (2024a). World Development Indicators. https://databank.worldbank.org/source/world-development-indicators (accessed 2 December 2024).

World Bank (2024b). Global Database of Shared Prosperity (13th Edition, circa 2016–21). World Bank. https://www.worldbank.org/en/topic/poverty/brief/global-database-of-shared-prosperity (accessed 3 December 2024).

UNU-WIDER (2023). World Income Inequality Database (WIID), V.28 November. https://www.wider.unu.edu/project/wiid-%E2%80%93-world-income-inequality-database (accessed 2 December 2024).

4

How do people understand, perceive and act on inequality?

This chapter considers how individual beliefs and perceptions of inequality compare with the levels and trends presented in Chapters 2 and 3. That is, we turn to the way in which individuals understand inequality, their perceptions, and the implications that those understandings and perceptions have in their preferences for acting on inequality, more specifically, in their redistributive preferences.

Our starting point is that there is variation in how people understand inequality. We begin by questioning the common use of relative measures of inequality and discussing whether people think about inequality in relative or absolute terms. Moreover, we discuss how individual behaviour may be influenced by available information as well as by how information is framed.

Moving on, we draw attention to the fact that there may be a mismatch between perceived and actual inequality. We review recent literature on individuals' 'misperceptions' of existing levels of inequality in their societies as well as their own position compared to others, highlighting how this may vary across countries and contexts, and we discuss underlying factors affecting such perceptions.

We conclude the chapter with a discussion on how individuals' perceptions, in turn, affect policy preferences – namely preferences for redistribution. We briefly review the core determinants of preferences for redistribution, focusing mainly on the role of fairness as a mediating factor. While we illustrate existing variation across diverse cultures and contexts, our discussion also points to evidence for some similarities in how people respond to perceived fair and unfair situations.

Understandings versus standard measures

Let us start by thinking about how you, our reader, understand inequality. If we ask you to think about inequality, what comes to mind? Perhaps you take as context your neighbourhood, or the country you live in or the world. Maybe you think about how your position relates to others, or alternatively you think about those who have a lot less and a lot more than you. And what is it that they have more or less than you? Is it your education level, how easily you access healthcare or how much you can influence the way in which your life is governed? Or instead, is it the assets you own or the income you earn? Then again, maybe you do not think about yourself individually but in terms of the social groups you identify with, be it in terms of gender, ethnicity and so on.

Whatever your answers are to these questions, they reflect your own understanding of what inequality is, based on your normative values and perceptions. A core idea of this book, which we introduced in more detail in Chapter 2, is that inequality is indeed a multidimensional concept. Furthermore, in Chapter 3 we illustrated that, even focusing on a single dimension, the choices made to measure inequality can lead to different interpretations of reality. In the next paragraphs we reflect more on these differences, focusing on a case where the understanding of income inequality might not match the assumptions underlying the standard measures used to describe it.[1]

Consider yourself and your neighbour.[2] Suddenly both of your incomes double. What do you think or feel about the change in inequality between you? Now imagine two different villages, each of them with a population of two individuals (just like in the example of you and your neighbour, where we did not consider anyone else). In village A, the poor person has two bars of gold, while the rich person has eight gold bars. In village B, the poor person has six bars of gold, while the rich person has twenty-four bars. Take a few seconds to think about which of the villages you think is more unequal.

If you struggled to decide between the two villages and thought that inequality was the same, you think about inequality in relative terms. As we discussed in Chapter 3, commonly used measures such as the Gini coefficient are relative, which means that they assume that if everyone's income is multiplied by a common factor, inequality remains the same (scale invariance). In our example, in both villages the rich have four times more gold than the poor. Likewise, if your income and your neighbour's income doubled, the inequality between the two of you would remain the same.

Still, you might also have thought about inequality in village B as being the most unequal. If you recall also from Chapter 3, if one thinks about inequality in absolute terms, then multiplying everyone's income by a certain factor will lead to an increase in inequality. This is because instead of being based on the scale invariance assumption, absolute measures assume that if a constant value is added to everyone's income, inequality remains unchanged.[3] In a similar manner, this would have led you to think of the doubling of incomes for you and your neighbour as an increase in inequality, unless you had the exact same income to begin with.

Expanding our reasoning to consider all individuals across the world, it is not implausible that some think in absolute rather than in relative terms. If, in the general discourse, inequality is measured and portrayed in relative terms, whereas individuals think about it in absolute terms instead, then there might be a mismatch between the individual understanding and the standard measures. Thus, we ask: how do individuals understand inequality?

Only a handful of studies have examined whether individuals think in relative or absolute terms. The early studies by Amiel and Cowell (1992, 1999) showed that 37 per cent of respondents (who were students from colleges and universities in Germany, England, Israel and the United States) supported the assumption that underlies relative measures, whereas the assumption implied by absolute measures was supported by 17 per cent. Ballano and Ruiz-Castillo (1993) and Harrison and Seidl (1994) followed this line of work and reported similar results using samples of Spanish and German respondents. A couple of decades later, Ravallion (2014, 2018) drew attention to the implications of these different understandings. Surveying his own students at Georgetown University, he repeatedly found that roughly half (and sometimes more) of his students thought about inequality in absolute terms. As we mentioned in Chapter 2, these differences in value judgements have important implications for the positions taken in policy debates (see also Ravallion 2004, 2014).

We conducted an exercise,[4] similar to our example in the beginning of this section, this time with samples of respondents in Mozambique and Vietnam (see Ferreira, Gisselquist and Tarp 2025a).[5] The results are represented in Figure 4.1. Interestingly, while in Vietnam 59 per cent think in relative terms, in Mozambique 53 per cent of respondents think in absolute terms and many (those classified as 'Other') do not agree with the underlying assumptions in either type of measures.[6] Within Vietnam, both subsamples show that participants think more in relative than in absolute terms.

These results have clear implications. Important policy decisions on redistribution (and welfare in general) are based on a specific set

(a) Mozambique and Vietnam

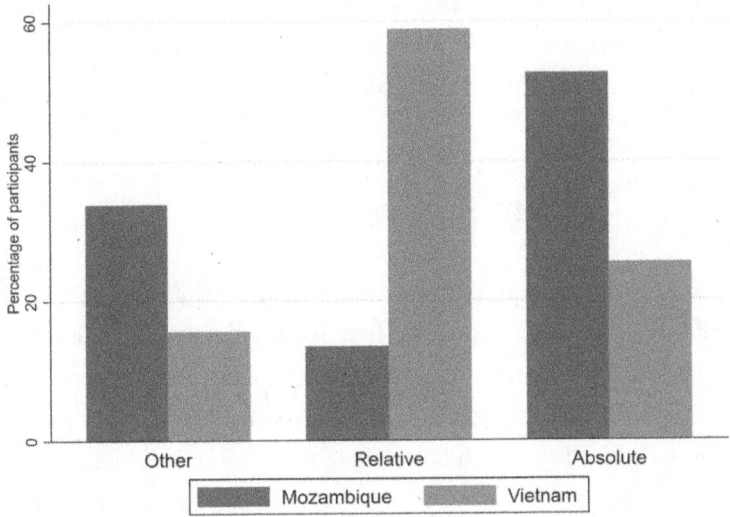

(b) Regions in Vietnam

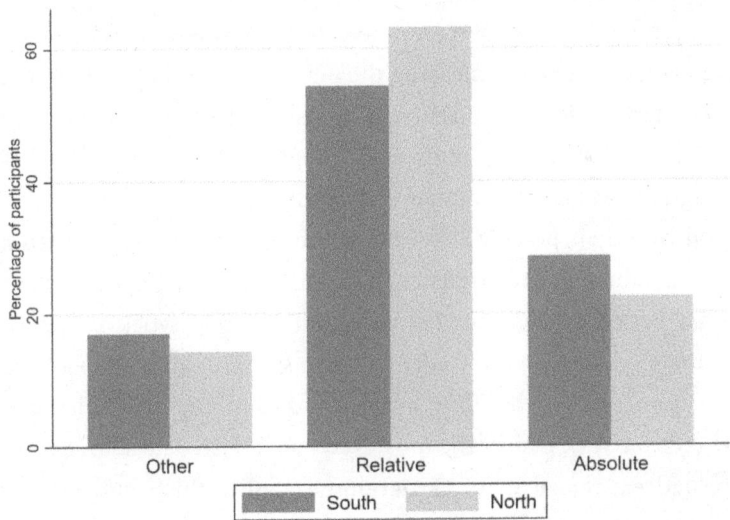

Figure 4.1 Thinking about inequality in relative versus absolute terms.

Source: Authors' illustration; see text for data details.

Note: Number of observations: 904 in Mozambique; 1681 in Vietnam; 859 in north Vietnam; 822 in south Vietnam. See more details on the data in Ferreira, Gisselquist and Tarp (2025a).

of measures which may not reflect how everyone thinks. People's different understandings may also lead to different perceptions of reality that may not match official measures and trends on inequality. We explore this further in the next section.

Perceptions versus hard numbers

Among the different drivers of demand for redistribution (or, in other words, the demand for policies that reduce inequality), the role of perceptions of inequality has received great interest. Indeed, it has been argued that perceptions, more than actual levels, shape people's views on inequality, which helps explain (at least partly) why there is lack of evidence of a link between increases in inequality and demand for redistribution (Gimpelson and Treisman 2018; Hauser and Norton 2017; Kuziemko et al. 2015; Stantcheva 2024).

How do individuals perceive inequality?[7] While several indicators have been employed to measure the perceptions of individuals, they suffer from limitations and there is no clear agreement on which one is the best (Bavetta, Li Donni and Marino 2019). Examples include asking individuals: (i) whether they think inequality is too high; (ii) to indicate their perceived values of the mean and median income in the country, and to compare these with the actual figures; (iii) to choose between diagrams that represent different types of societies that match different Gini coefficient levels; or (iv) for their perceived social position and building a perceived Gini coefficient based on that (Choi 2019). One of the most frequently used data sources is the International Social Survey Programme (ISSP), which, at the time of writing, includes five rounds focused on social inequality between 1987 and 2019 (see examples in Box 4.1).

Box 4.1: Examples of some questions by the ISSP used to obtain information about perceptions and concerns about inequality

1. [Q1, slightly adapted] From 'essential' to 'not important at all', how important do you think it is for getting ahead in life ...
   - ...how important is coming from a wealthy family?
   - ...how important is having well-educated parents?
   - ...how important is having a good education yourself?
   - ...how important is hard work?
   - ...how important is knowing the right people?
   - ...how important is having political connections?
   - ...how important is giving bribes?
   - ...how important is a person's race?
   - ...how important is a person's religion?
   - ...how important is being born a man or a woman?
2. [Q4a, slightly adapted] To what extent do you agree or disagree with the following statement? 'Differences in income in [COUNTRY] are too large.'
3. [Q15, reproduced here adapted and without diagrams included in original questionnaire] These five diagrams show different types of society. Please read the descriptions and look at the diagrams and decide which you think best describes [COUNTRY] ...

Type A	Type B	Type C	Type D	Type E
A small elite at the top, very few people in the middle, and a great mass of people at the bottom.	A society like a pyramid with a small elite at the top, more people in the middle, and most at the bottom.	A pyramid except that just a few are at the bottom.	A society with most people in the middle.	Many people near the top, and only a few near the bottom.

a. First, what type of society is [COUNTRY] today – which diagram comes closest?

b. What do you think [COUNTRY] ought to be like – which would you prefer?

c. How fair or unfair do you think the income distribution is in [COUNTRY]?

Source: Based on ISSP 2019 Questionnaire.

Existing data suggest great variation across countries in terms of the level of perceived inequality (e.g., Bavetta, Li Donni and Marino 2019; Stantcheva 2024). Choi (2019) notes some interesting patterns, namely that there is a lower level of perceived inequality in the Nordic countries, whereas the opposite is true for former socialist countries. In addition, Korea and Iceland, two countries with similar levels of actual inequality, are matched with quite different levels of perceived inequality. Underlying this variation may be differences in how people think about the concept of inequality. That is the thinking about the different dimensions of inequality (as discussed in Chapter 2) or the context – local, national, or international (as we covered in Chapter 3). However, differences may also be a result of lower overall levels of education or lack of information among the population, a point to which we return below.

The structure of the data also allows for comparisons over time. Considering the period 1992–2009, the perception in former socialist countries was that their societies were unequal during the entire period, despite an improvement in the 2000s in contrast with the rest of Europe where perceptions of inequality deteriorated around this time (Bussolo, Giolbas and Torre 2021). Figure 4.2 gives another example, comparing the evolution of inequality in Mozambique (measured with the Gini index obtained from the WIID) and the perception of inequality as a problem, using data from the Afrobarometer (2024). The latter is measured in two different ways. First, we use the answers to the question 'How well or badly would you say the current government is handling narrowing the gaps between rich and poor?' Second, we consider the shares of participants who, among different options, selected inequality as the most, the second most or the third most 'important problem facing the country that the government should address'. The line corresponding to the Gini index shows a

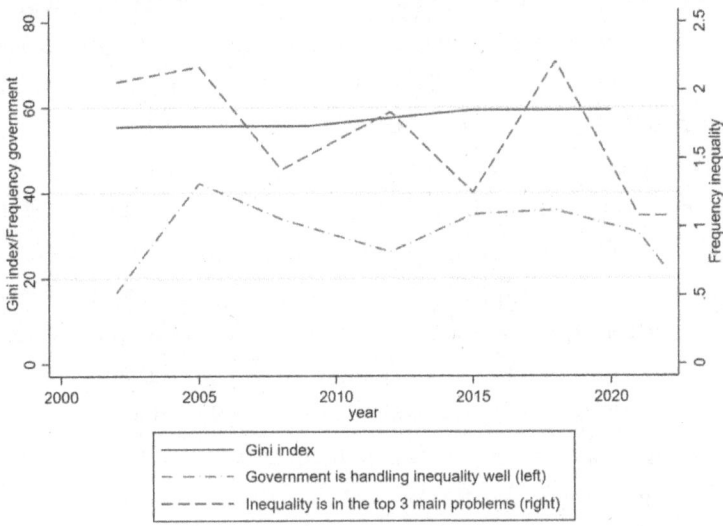

Figure 4.2 Inequality perceived as a problem versus actual level of inequality in Mozambique, 2001–22.

Source: Authors' illustration based on Afrobarometer (2024) and WIID (2023) data.

steady increase in inequality over time. The trend for thinking that the government is handling the situation well (left y-axis) deteriorated after 2005, followed by some improvement, and then a recent decline again. Surprisingly though, only a small share of participants (right y-axis) places inequality in the top three main problems affecting the country, with small variations over time.

How 'accurately' do individuals identify inequality in their societies and their own position compared to others? There is a considerable difference between perceptions and 'hard numbers'. Independent of the indicator considered, there is consensus that, on average, people do not have correct information, or *mis*perceive, current levels of inequality, how it has changed over time, and where they stand in terms of income distribution. Across different countries in the world (but mostly Western, educated, industrialized, rich, and democratic ('WEIRD') countries), individuals do not accurately identify the level and recent trend in inequality in their own country (Gimpelson and Treisman 2018).

But there is variation in these misperceptions. To illustrate, while several studies find that individuals in the United States under-estimate inequality, others found that in countries such as France and Germany, there is overestimation of inequality (Hauser and Norton 2017), whereas in Mexico, respondents' perceptions were not too different from the real levels (Campos-Vazquez et al. 2022). Moreover, we should bear in mind that similarly to what happens with measures of inequality, using different data sources to derive indicators of perceived inequality can also lead to differences in the results. While a study using a customized survey and administrative data finds that most respondents in a Swedish sample under-estimate their position in the income distribution (Karadja, Mollerstrom and Steim 2017), another study drawing on the ISSP data finds that respondents overestimate it (Bussolo, Giolbas and Torre 2021).

Relatedly, in our work, we gathered data on concerns about inequality from samples in Mozambique and Vietnam. In Figure 4.3 we present the share of participants who agreed, disagreed, or were neutral to the statement 'Inequality is too high in your country'. While the level of inequality is higher in Mozambique than in Vietnam in both samples, most participants agree that the level of inequality in their country is too high. The same is true for the UK, according to a recent review showing that around 80 per cent of people in the UK have consistently perceived income gaps to be too wide since the early 1980s until 2018 (Benson et al. 2024).

Establishing the relevance of perceptions is an important step to better understand people's redistributive preferences. A clear question emerges from this: what factors influence such perceptions?

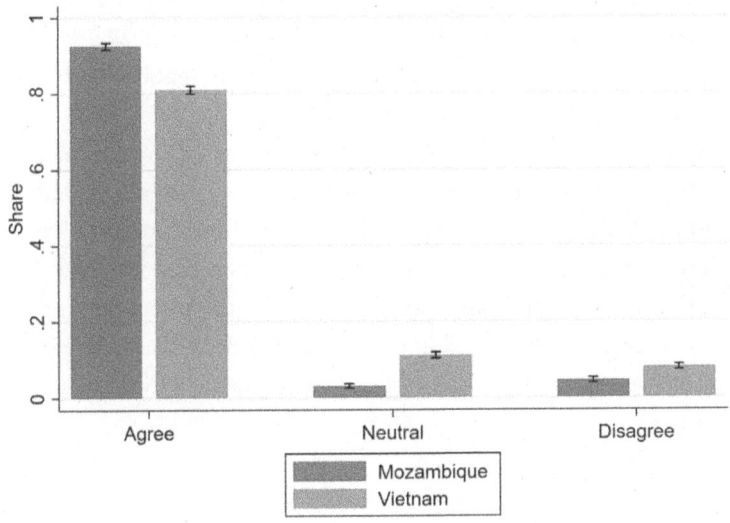

Figure 4.3 Perceptions of inequality.

Source: Authors' illustration; see text for data details. See more details on the data in Ferreira, Gisselquist and Tarp (2025b).

Note: Agreement with the statement 'Differences (in income) between rich and poor in this country are too large' does not consider 'Don't know', or missing answers. Number of observations: 886 in Mozambique; 1508 in Vietnam.

Individual views and perceptions are based on interpretations or understandings about distributional outcomes, that is, inequality, which are largely formed based on the information and time (resources) they have available (Cruces, Perez-Truglia and Tetaz 2013). Studies have advanced different sources of perceptions. At the individual level, in addition to self-interest (Easterbrook 2021), important factors include:

1. Sociodemographic characteristics, such as gender and age, as well as the vantage point of the individual in terms of income and education. Older or female individuals and those with lower levels of education and income tend to perceive higher inequality in their society (Bussolo, Giolbas and Torre 2021). Moreover,

both richer and poorer people in insulated settings are more likely to under-estimate inequality (Mijs and Hoy 2022).
2. Previous experiences of social mobility and parental wealth (Bavetta, Li Donni and Marino 2019).
3. Personal values and ideology, such as meritocratic and equal opportunity beliefs (Bobzien 2020 García-Sanchez et al. 2020), and political views (Bavetta, Li Donni and Marino 2019).
4. The (perceived) exposure to inequality in everyday life (García-Castro, Rodríguez-Bailón and Wills 2020), the places where individuals live (Minkoff and Lyons 2019), as well as exposure to information from the news and social media (Mijs and Hoy 2022).

Correcting misperceptions through information

One way of reducing the difference between perceived and actual inequality is to (attempt to) change people's understandings by providing information.[8] Indeed, several studies have found some evidence that information provision about inequality has an impact on individuals' concerns about, and perceptions of, inequality, but not on redistributive preferences (Kuziemko et al. 2015; Ciani, Fréget and Manfredi 2021). The content of the information covered, for instance, inequality levels (Trump 2018), its effects (Lobeck and Støstad 2023) and its inevitability (Pellicer, Piraino and Wegner 2019); as well as social mobility (Alesina, Stantcheva and Teso 2018) and the position of the individual in the income distribution (Cruces, Perez-Truglia and Tetaz 2013; Hoy and Mager 2021).

Focusing on the last of these aspects, participants in Argentina were given information about their relative position in the income ranking (Cruces, Perez-Truglia and Tetaz 2013). While those who under-estimated their position (i.e., who thought that they were relatively poorer than they actually were) were not affected by the information treatment, those who overestimated it increased their demand for redistribution. In contrast, based on data from ten different countries,[9] participants who had overestimated their position showed lower concern for inequality and lower support for redistribution after being informed of their actual relative position (Hoy and Mager 2021). This result was also confirmed in Sweden and explained with the fact that these participants had political preferences to the right of the spectrum and believed that effort is the main driver of success and that taxes are distortive (Karadja, Mollerstrom and Steim 2017).

Still, in a study on Mexico giving information about actual levels of inequality and social mobility did not change the chosen levels of inequality, social mobility and tax rates (Campos-Vazquez et al. 2022). In a similar vein, another study found heterogeneous responses across participants in Australia, Indonesia and Mexico (Mijs and Hoy 2022). For instance, informing participants of high levels of income inequality and low social mobility affected their belief in meritocracy in Indonesia, but not so much in Mexico.

Another aspect of providing information to affect how people perceive and act on inequality is the language used, and more specifically how information is framed.[10] To give an example, there is some evidence (though from a small group of individuals) in Germany that framing inequality as 'the advantaged group having more' rather than as 'the disadvantaged group having less' was linked to individuals perceiving inequality as less legitimate (Bruckmüller, Reese and Martiny 2017).

Moreover, relevant to our earlier discussion on the distinction between understanding inequality in absolute or relative terms, experiments in the United States and France indicated that perceptions of inequality varied depending on whether an absolute or a widely used relative indicator of salaries was used to provide information (Ziano, Lembregts and Pandelaere 2022).

We flag up here for readers to note that this literature has been heavily biased towards countries in the Global North, namely in Europe and the United States; there is increasing consensus that the same findings might not necessarily apply to countries in the Global South. In our research, we have contributed to providing evidence on similar questions from non-WEIRD contexts. We conducted a survey experiment in both Mozambique and Vietnam, where we gave information about inequality in a fictional village (see Box 4.2 and Ferreira, Gisselquist and Tarp (2025a) for more details), either in relative or in absolute terms. We then asked participants how much they would be willing to donate to building a health centre in that village. In line with some of the studies mentioned earlier, we did not find any significant difference between the way in which inequality was framed and the donation decisions of individuals. While Mozambican participants who heard the information about inequality framed in absolute terms donated slightly more than those who heard about it framed in relative terms, this difference was not statistically significant. Among Vietnamese participants the difference was even smaller (and changed depending on the amount at stake) and was not statistically significant either (Ferreira, Gisselquist and Tarp 2025a).

Box 4.2: Differences in the framing of information: An example from Vietnam

For the survey, participants were given information about a fictional village, read to them by the enumerators; at the same time a visual illustration was shown. In one room, with half of the participants, the information was framed in absolute terms and the visual was shown as follows:

'I will now give you some information about a village in Vietnam. Many people live there. As you can see in this illustration, the richest person has six gold bars more than the poorest person.'

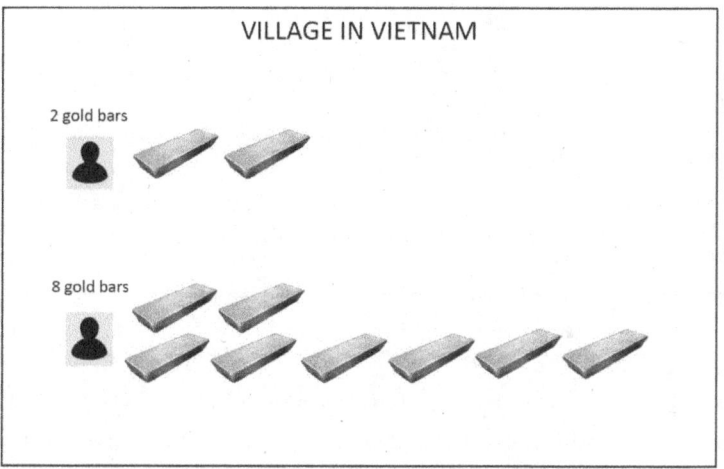

In the other room, where the other half of the participants were, we framed the information and structured the visualization in relative terms instead:

'I will now give you some information about a village in Vietnam. Many people live there. As you can see in this illustration, the richest person has four times more gold bars than the poorest person.'

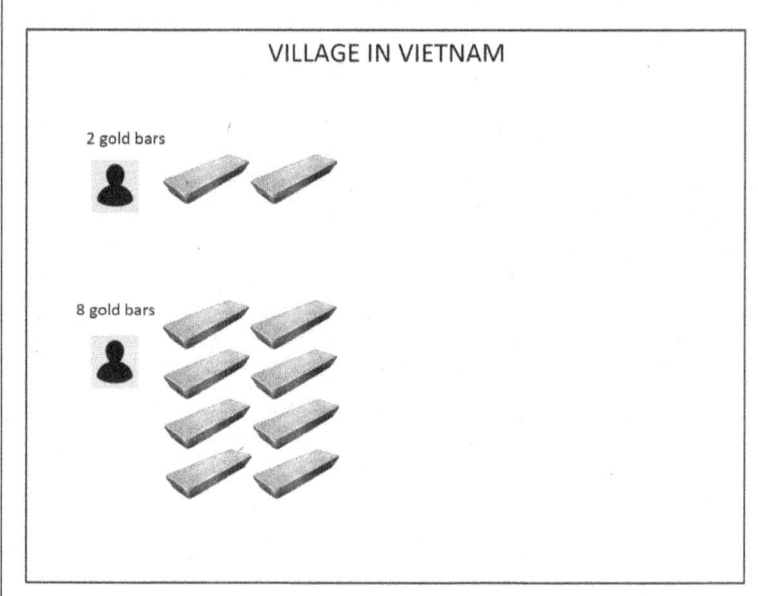

Source: Authors' illustration based on Ferreira, Gisselquist and Tarp (2025a).

Still, exploring these effects in South Africa, a recent study documented differences in fairness evaluations when presenting inequality in absolute (large-stake and small-stake units) and relative terms (percentages and multiples) (Oppel 2023). Participants were randomly allocated to one of four groups, each group corresponding to a different way of *presenting* inequality: large units (e.g., 130 units, 515 units, 999 units), small units (e.g., 0.002 units, 10 units, 20 units), percentages (e.g., 0.1 per cent, 9 per cent, 18.9 per cent) and multiples (e.g., 0.5 units, 1,900 times as much, 3,900 times as much). Participants were then presented with different distributions (with varying levels of inequality) and were asked to score them depending on how fair they considered them to be. The results suggest that individuals presented with information about inequality in absolute terms (the first two categories) consider inequality to be less fair than those who see inequality levels presented in relative terms (i.e., in percentages or multiples). We return to the role of fairness preferences in the next section.

Preferences for redistribution

Throughout the previous chapters we referred to redistribution, redistributive preferences and redistributive policies. To be clear to readers, by redistribution we mean the transfer of income and wealth in a society which can be carried out through different channels, including taxation (the most obvious), social assistance, provision of education and health services, as well as changes in the law (e.g., land reforms or inheritance laws) (Mengel and Weidenholzer 2022: 1).

Gaining insight into these preferences is critical to understanding when and why people accept these policies. An influential theoretical model developed by Meltzer and Richard (1981), building on the median voter theorem, predicted that higher inequality would lead to higher demand for redistribution (see more in Box 4.3). Based on the assumption that policymakers follow the preferences of the median voter, the higher the level of inequality, the higher would be the difference between the average income and the income of the median voter, which should then translate into higher demand for redistribution. However, the empirical evidence showed little support for this model and questioned the median voter assumption (Alesina and Giuliano 2011).

> **Box 4.3: Inequality, redistributive policy, and the median voter**
>
> The Meltzer-Richard model is an important starting point for much of the political economy literature on redistribution, connecting income inequality with the level of redistribution in democracies (Meltzer and Richard 1981). Its treatment of the 'median voter' as the decisive voter builds from earlier work by Roberts (1977), as well as Hotelling (1929) and Downs (1957).
>
> In the Meltzer-Richard model, individuals with different productivities care only about their income. This income is taxed to finance transfers from the government to individuals. The optimal tax rate then is posited to depend on the difference between the income of the median voter (i.e., the individual with the median level of income) and the mean income. This difference is, in effect, a measure of inequality. In more unequal societies, the median voter will be relatively poorer in relation to the mean income.
>
> If the government transfers (after discounting the taxes) are progressive, then the higher the level of inequality – and thus the poorer the median voter – the more the individual will benefit from taxes and transfers. Therefore, the likelihood that the median voter will vote for higher taxes and transfers is higher. The median voter theorem assumes that all individuals vote (which means that it has stronger implications for democracies) and that policymakers follow the preferences of the median voter. Thus, higher inequality will correlate with greater redistribution.
>
> Source: Authors' adaptation based on Alesina and Giuliano (2011) and Milanovic (2000).

A large academic literature (mainly in economics and economic psychology) has investigated what affects people's preferences for redistribution, that is, how do people assess and choose between different options that involve higher or lower degrees of redistribution. These studies are based on different types of data, collected from surveys, and more recently from economic experiments, carried out online or in person. A commonly used measure of preferences for redistribution is the extent to which individuals agree with the statement 'It is the responsibility of the government to reduce the differences in income between people with high incomes and those with low incomes' (ISSP 2019 Questionnaire). When we asked participants in our research in Mozambique and Vietnam, 74 per cent agreed with this statement in the former, whereas the share was 87 per cent in the latter.[11] Alternative statements include 'Taxation should be more progressive in this country' or 'The rich should pay more to help the poor' (Mengel and Weidenholzer 2022: 2).

Experiments, on the other hand, take a different approach. Instead of asking individuals about redistribution, they create a game setting where individuals make actual distribution decisions from which researchers derive their preferences. One commonly used game is a so-called dictator game played in pairs. The baseline idea is that, faced with a scenario of inequality between the individual who is deciding and one other individual (or between a pair of other individuals), the individual needs to decide how much to allocate to themselves and how much to allocate to the other individual (or how much to allocate to each of the other individuals). Based on these decisions, it can be determined how many in a group of participants prefer to keep inequality, increase/decrease inequality or equalize the outcomes. Importantly, individuals know that their decisions will lead to real payments at the end of the game, which creates a valid incentive for participants to act according to own preferences.

This is a fitting place in the discussion to share an example from our research in Mozambique and Vietnam. We created a game situation with pairs of participants, where one was allocated with three units and the other was allocated with seven units (Ferreira, Gisselquist and

Tarp 2025b). Then we asked each of them how they would like to allocate the ten units among themselves. The instructions we used are described in Box 4.4 (with each unit worth VND5,000), and Figure 4.4 shows the share of participants allocating each amount in each of the countries. While there are some differences between the two countries, in both the Mozambican and the Vietnamese samples, the most common choice was to split the ten units equally. Moreover, circa a quarter of the Mozambican participants decided to keep the initial distribution of three and seven units to the respective players, while just above 10 per cent chose this option in Vietnam, where the second most popular option was to redistribute one unit from Player B to Player A (allocation (4,6).

Box 4.4: Instructions given to participants in a modified dictator game to obtain an indicator of preferences for redistribution: Example from Vietnam

You are playing a game in pairs. You are Player A and the other player is Player B. You do not know with whom you have been paired, and Player B is not in this room. We have allocated money to you and Player B and we are going to ask you questions about how you would like to distribute that money.

We gave you VND15,000 and we gave VND35,000 to Player B. The total amount between you and Player B is VND50,000.

The question now is: 'How would you like to distribute this VND50,000 between you and Player B?'

Source: Authors' adaptation based on Ferreira, Gisselquist and Tarp (2025b).

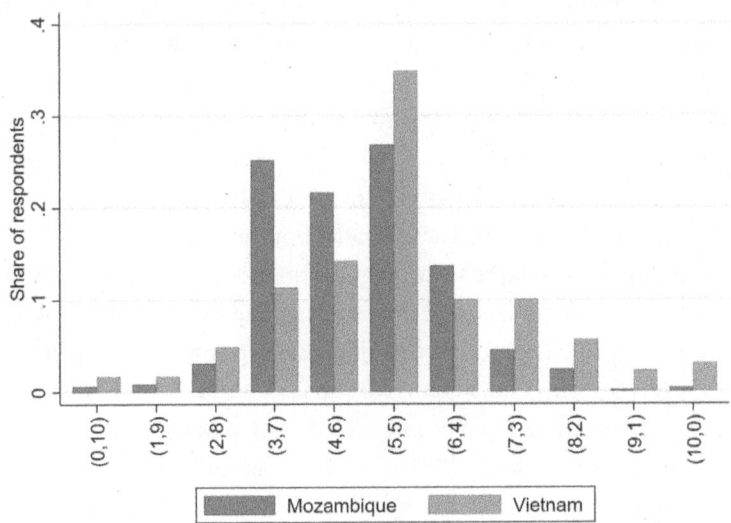

Figure 4.4 Amount allocated to the other player in a modified dictator game.

Source: Authors' illustration, based on Ferreira, Gisselquist and Tarp (2025b).

Note: Number of observations: 902 in Mozambique; 1680 in Vietnam.

Returning to our first question: what are the determinants of preferences for redistribution? Among other factors,[12] existing studies reported that redistributive preferences are affected by:

(i) Individual income and wealth (Alesina and Giuliano 2011). Still, recent evidence from a lottery in Ethiopia does not provide support for a causal effect of a windfall in wealth on preferences for redistribution. Winning a lottery did not make individuals less supportive of redistribution (Andersen et al. 2023).

(ii) The relative position of the individual in the income distribution (Cruces, Perez-Truglia and Tetaz 2013; Fehr, Mollerstrom and Perez-Truglia 2022; Hoy and Mager 2021; Hvidberg, Kreiner and Stantcheva 2023).

(iii) The belief of the individual about their future income (Alesina and La Ferrara 2005) and social mobility prospects (Alesina, Stantcheva and Teso 2018).
(iv) The level of inequality that the individual experiences or is exposed to (Roth and Wohlfart 2018; Sands 2017). Researchers conducted a field experiment in South Africa by randomly placing a high-status car in a neighbourhood and asking pedestrians walking by to sign a petition to increase taxes on the wealthy individuals, and thus, redistribute wealth (Sands and de Kadt 2020). They found that this local exposure to inequality had a positive effect on support for the tax on wealthy individuals.
(v) As we discussed earlier in the chapter, the individual perceptions of inequality, as well as of ethnic fragmentation, diversity and immigration (Stantcheva 2024). An example from Colombian undergraduate students suggests that diversity affects concerns about inequality (Londoño-Vélez 2022). A financial aid reform led to a greater share of low-income students at an elite university, which, the study shows, resulted in high-income students having more diverse social networks and supporting progressive redistribution.
(vi) Finally, there is evidence that individual considerations of what is fair affects how perceptions determine preferences for redistribution (Stantcheva 2024). We elaborate on this point in the next subsection.

Fairness as a mediating factor

Authors of a growing number of studies have argued that fairness preferences can influence how perceptions affect preferences for redistribution (e.g., Almås, Cappelen and Tungodden 2020).[13] More specifically, the evidence suggests that people prefer *fairness* over inequality, as well as fair inequality over unfair equality (Starmans et al. 2017).

Let us ponder the following:

- Bao and Mei both performed a boring task of sealing packages for 30 minutes, with each package sealed awarding participants one dollar. Bao sealed forty packages whereas Mei sealed sixty packages. In total, they sealed 100 packages corresponding to 100 dollars. How do you think they should split this amount between themselves? Would it be fair in this situation for Mei to keep more than Bao?
- Now think of a different scenario. Mei was now performing the same boring task, but this time with Lin who was born with a physical disability and therefore takes longer to seal packages. Lin sealed forty packages whereas Mei sealed sixty packages. In this situation, would it be fair for Mei to keep more than Lin?

These scenarios allude to fairness principles regarding inequality in a context where the source of inequality changes. We can think about the first example as inequality resulting from hard work or merit: Mei worked harder than Bao. In contrast, in the second example Lin sealed fewer packages than Mei due to circumstances outside of their control. Perhaps you thought that it was fair for Mei to keep the sixty dollars (resulting from the sixty sealed packages) in both examples, or you might have thought that in both cases they should split the amount equally. Or perhaps you thought of the differences in income as fair in one case but not in the other. Underlying your choices are the values that you use to judge the situation of inequality as fair or unfair.

Several studies have found that inequality resulting from differences in performance (or hard work) is more accepted than inequality due to luck or factors outside of individual control.[14] This has been termed as a *meritocratic view* of inequality. For instance, Almås, Cappelen and Tungodden (2020) reported considerable differences in views on fairness between Americans and Norwegians. Americans are more *libertarian* (i.e., accepting of inequality independent of its source) while Norwegians are more *egalitarian* (i.e., prefer equal distributions no matter the source of inequality). Expanding on this work, a recent study indicates that there is great variation across the world in terms of the sensitivity to performance (or hard work) as the source of inequality (Almås et al. 2024).

Bear in mind that most of this literature draws insights from WEIRD settings (e.g., Hvidberg, Kreiner and Stantcheva 2023 on Denmark, Benson et al. 2024 on the UK). Our aim was to fill this gap by collecting evidence in Mozambique and Vietnam. Among other questions, we asked the participants in our study whether they thought different sources of inequality were fair. In Mozambique, more than half of the participants agreed that inequality due to hard work, talent, but also luck, is fair. In Vietnam, while almost all participants agreed that hard work and talent are fair sources of inequality, a smaller proportion of just over half thought that inequality due to luck was fair (Figure 4.5). These descriptions are somehow different from those reported in Almås et al. (2024), who found that most participants in Vietnam were libertarians, with similar smaller shares (below 20 per cent) of egalitarians and meritocrats. We interpret this discrepancy as suggesting that the views on inequality and its fairness are difficult to measure and that more research is needed to unpack them.

Additionally, we conducted an economic experiment – similar to that in Almås, Cappelen and Tungodden (2020) – to better understand whether meritocratic values were also prevalent in these two countries (Ferreira, Gisselquist and Tarp 2025b). To do that, we compared the decisions of individuals in a situation of inequality (recall the example in Box 4.4) but we varied the source of inequality. Half of the participants played the game in a context where inequality was due to luck and the other half in a context where inequality was due to merit (hard work). Given that we randomly assigned our participants to one group or the other and that the only difference between the two settings is how inequality is generated, we could infer whether the source of inequality matters (see Box 4.5 for more details). To be

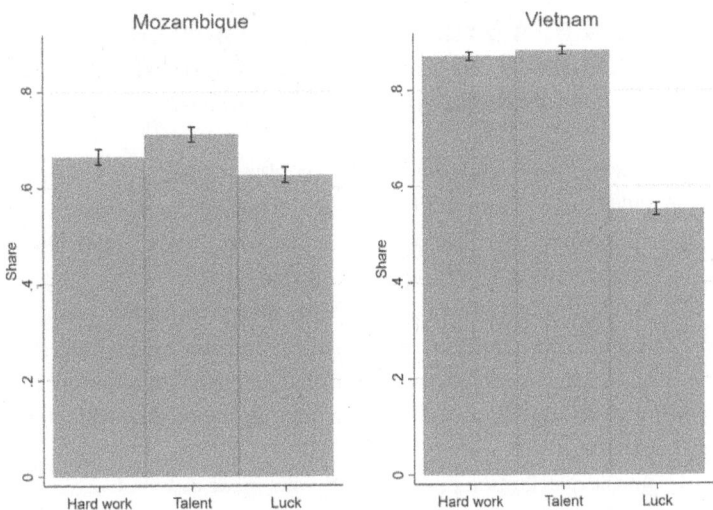

Figure 4.5 Share of participants agreeing that the source of inequality is fair.

Source: Authors' illustration, based on Ferreira, Gisselquist and Tarp (2025b).

Note: Agreement with the statement 'It is fair that source of inequality determines a person's income' where source of inequality is replaced by luck, hard work or talent and skills. Takes the value of 1 if the answer is 'Agree' and 0 if the answer is 'Neither agree nor disagree' or 'Disagree'. Does not consider 'Don't know' or missing answers. Number of observations, depending on the source of inequality: 867–878 in Mozambique; 1458–1567 in Vietnam.

clear, if we observed differences in the average choice between the two groups, this meant that merit considerations were important.

In line with previous studies, we found that our participants in both countries tolerated more inequality if it resulted from merit rather than luck (Ferreira, Gisselquist and Tarp 2025b). Still, despite these broad similarities, we also found some differences namely that the share of egalitarians was larger than the share of libertarians in the Vietnamese sample (again in contrast with Almås et al. 2024), whereas the opposite was true in the Mozambique sample.

In sum, while existing evidence points to a universal view of inequality that is in line with meritocracy, it also highlights some

> **Box 4.5: An incentivized experiment on the influence of the source of inequality on redistribution decisions**
>
> In line with Almås, Cappelen and Tungodden (2020) and Cappelen et al. (2007), our incentivized experiment involved three phases:
> (i) In the production phase, participants performed a simple task that consisted of putting crosses inside squares.
> (ii) In the allocation phase, participants were grouped into pairs, with Player A and Player B playing in different rooms. Player A was endowed with three units and Player B was endowed with seven units. Together, each pair had a total endowment of ten units.
> (iii) In the distribution phase, participants made distributive choices about these ten units between themselves and their pair (similarly to the game described in Box 4.4).
>
> To assess the importance of the source of inequality, we created two comparable groups of participants. In one of the groups (our control group), participants were split between being Players A and B randomly, based on their ID numbers (which were randomly allocated to participants in the beginning of the experiment). Participants with odd numbered IDs were Players A and participants with even numbered IDs were Players B. Thus, in this group inequality was generated by luck.
>
> In the other group (our treatment group) the split between Players A and B was based on the ranked performance in the task during the production phase. The bottom half performers were Players A whereas the top half were Players B. In this case, inequality was a result of merit.
>
> Source: Authors' elaboration, adapted from Ferreira, Gisselquist and Tarp (2025b).

differences between countries, and that the lack of evidence from the Global South undermines our knowledge of how people understand, perceive and act on inequality.

Key takeaways

- There may be a disconnect between how people think about and understand inequality and the principles underlying commonly used inequality measures. This concurs with our view that a dashboard approach is needed.
- There is broad evidence that people misperceive inequality levels and that it is challenging to change or correct these misperceptions.
- How people perceive inequality is a crucial determinant of their preferences for redistribution, and this relationship is mediated by their fairness views.

Notes

1. While we discuss multidimensional measures in more detail in Chapter 2, we focus here on the measurement of income given its prominence in policy and academic discussions.
2. We assume here that the incomes of you and your neighbour are not the same.
3. If you thought that inequality was higher in village A, this suggests that you do not consider either of the assumptions underlying absolute or relative measures. Among other reasons, this could be because you focused instead on specific parts of the distribution – in our example, the poor or the rich – which would lead you to select the village where the poorest/richest person has the lowest number of bars.
4. For further reflection on how such 'experimental' approaches can be used in the study of inequality, see Puzon and Gisselquist (2023); see also Puzon (2022).
5. We collected data from two regions in Vietnam, one in the north and the other in the south of the country. See Diaz et al. (2025) for further consideration of how attitudes towards inequality compare across regions.
6. A previous study among young people in Beira and Maputo (two provinces in Mozambique) found that some respondents thought in

absolute terms, but many did not agree with either the assumptions underlying relative and absolute measures (Barletta, Ferreira and Salvucci 2023).

7   While we focus here mainly on inequality of outcomes, perceived inequality may vary if applied to other domains, such as inequality of opportunity (Bavetta, Donni and Marino 2019).

8   In addition to correcting beliefs, information can also affect inequality beliefs by increasing salience or providing status justification (Mijs and Hoy 2022).

9   Australia, India, Mexico, Morocco, the Netherlands, Nigeria, South Africa, Spain, the UK and the United States.

10 See Easterbrook (2021) for an overview.

11 See Ferreira, Gisselquist and Tarp (2025b) for details on the data collection. The total number of observations was 884 in Mozambique and 1,552 in Vietnam.

12 For comprehensive reviews see Alesina and Giuliano (2011) and Mengel and Weidenholzer (2022).

13 Other relevant studies include Almås, Cappelen and Tungodden (2020); Cappelen et al. (2007, 2013); Durante, Putterman and van der Weele (2014); Fehr and Schmidt (1999); Mollerstrom, Reme and Sørensen (2015).

14 See references in Cappelen et al. (2022).

References

Afrobarometer (2024). Mozambique, Rounds 2–9, 2002–2023. Available online: http://www.afrobarometer.org. (accessed 4 December 2024).

Alesina, A., and E. La Ferrara (2005). 'Preferences for Redistribution in the Land of Opportunities'. *Journal of Public Economics*, 89: 897–931. 10.1016/j.jpubeco.2004.05.009. Accessed: 11 September 2025.

Alesina, A., and P. Giuliano (2011). 'Preferences for Redistribution'. In J. Benhabib, A. Bisin and M.O. Jackson (eds), *Handbook of Social Economics* (pp. 93–131). Amsterdam: North-Holland.

Alesina, A., S. Stantcheva and E. Teso (2018). 'Intergenerational Mobility and Preferences for Redistribution'. *American Economic Review*,

108(2): 521–54. https://doi.org/10.1257/aer.20162015. Accessed: 11 September 2025.

Almås, I., A. W. Cappelen and B. Tungodden (2020). 'Cutthroat Capitalism Versus Cuddly Socialism: Are Americans More Meritocratic and Efficiency-Seeking Than Scandinavians?'. *Journal of Political Economy*, 128(5): 1753–88.

Almås, I., A. W. Cappelen, E. Sørensen and B. Tungodden (2024). 'Attitudes to Inequality: Preferences and Beliefs'. *Oxford Open Economics*, 3: i64–i79. https://doi.org/10.1093/ooec/odae001. Accessed: 11 September 2025.

Amiel, Y., and F. A. Cowell (1992). 'Measurement of Income Inequality: Experimental Test by Questionnaire'. *Journal of Public Economics*, 47: 3–26.

Amiel, Y., and F. Cowell (1999). 'What Is Inequality? The Student's View'. In Y. Amiel and F. Cowell (eds), *Thinking About Inequality: Personal Judgment and Income Distributions* (pp. 31–48). Cambridge: Cambridge University Press.

Andersen, A. G., S. Franklin, T. Getahun, A. Kotsadam, V. Somville and E. Villanger (2023). 'Does Wealth Reduce Support for Redistribution? Evidence from an Ethiopian Housing Lottery'. *Journal of Public Economics*, 224(104939): 1–10. https://doi.org/10.1016/j.jpubeco.2023.104939. Accessed: 11 September 2025.

Ballano, C., and J. Ruiz-Castillo (1993). 'Searching by Questionnaire for the Meaning of Income Inequality'. *Revista Española de Economia*, 10(2): 233–59.

Barletta, G., I. A. Ferreira and V. Salvucci (2023). 'Absolute or Relative: Perceptions of Inequality among Young Adults in Mozambique', WIDER Working Paper 2023/32. Helsinki: UNU-WIDER. https://doi.org/10.35188/UNU-WIDER/2023/340-6. Accessed: 11 September 2025.

Bavetta, S., P. Li Donni and M. Marino (2019). 'An Empirical Analysis of the Determinants of Perceived Inequality'. *Review of Income and Wealth*, 65(2): 264–92. 10.1111/roiw.12351.

Benson, R., B. Duffy, R. Hesketh and K. Hewlett (2024). 'Attitudes to Inequalities'. *Oxford Open Economics*, 3: i39–i63, Dimensions of

Inequality: The IFS Deaton Review. https://doi.org/10.1093/ooec/odad069. Accessed: 11 September 2025.

Bobzien, L. (2020). 'Polarized Perceptions, Polarized Preferences? Understanding the Relationship between Inequality and Preferences for Redistribution'. *Journal of European Social Policy*, 30(2): 206–20. https://doi.org/10.1177/0958928719879282. Accessed: 11 September 2025.

Bruckmüller, S., G. Reese and S. E. Martiny (2017). 'Is Higher Inequality Less Legitimate? Depends on How You Frame It!'. *British Journal of Social Psychology*, 56: 766–81. 10.1111/bjso.12202766.

Bussolo, M., A. Giolbas and I. Torre (2021). 'I Perceive Therefore I Demand: The Formation of Inequality Perceptions and Demand for Redistribution'. *Review of Income and Wealth*, 67(4): 835–71. https://doi.org/10.1111/roiw.12497. Accessed: 11 September 2025.

Campos-Vazquez, R. M., A. Krozer, A. A. Ramírez-Álvarez, R. de la Torre and R. Velez-Grajales (2022). 'Perceptions of Inequality and Social Mobility in Mexico'. *World Development*, 151(105778): 1–13. https://doi.org/10.1016/j.worlddev.2021.105778. Accessed: 11 September 2025.

Cappelen, A. W., A. D. Hole, E. Ø. Sørensen and B. Tungodden (2007). 'The Pluralism of Fairness Ideals: An Experimental Approach'. *American Economic Review*, 97(3): 818–27.

Cappelen, A. W., J. Konow, E. Ø. Sørensen and B. Tungodden (2013). 'Just Luck: An Experimental Study of Risk-Taking and Fairness'. *American Economic Review*, 103(4): 1398–413. http://dx.doi.org/10.1257/aer.103.4.1398. Accessed: 11 September 2025.

Cappelen, A. W., J. Mollerstrom, B. A. Reme and B. Tungodden (2022). 'A Meritocratic Origin of Egalitarian Behaviour'. *Economic Journal*, 132(646): 2101–17. https://doi.org/10.1093/ej/ueac008. Accessed: 11 September 2025.

Choi, G. (2019). 'Revisiting the Redistribution Hypothesis with Perceived Inequality and Redistributive Preferences'. *European Journal of Political Economy*, 58: 220–44. https://doi.org/10.1016/j.ejpoleco.2018.12.004. Accessed: 11 September 2025.

Ciani, E., L. Fréget and T. Manfredi (2021). 'Learning About Inequality and Demand for Redistribution: A Meta-Analysis of in-Survey Informational

Experiments', Working Paper 02. Paris: OECD. Available online: https://doi.org/10.1787/8876ec48-en. (accessed 4 December 2024).

Cruces, G., R. Perez-Truglia and M. Tetaz (2013). 'Biased Perceptions of Income Distribution and Preferences for Redistribution: Evidence from a Survey Experiment'. *Journal of Public Economics*, 98: 100–12. https://doi.org/10.1016/j.jpubeco.2012.10.009. Accessed: 11 September 2025.

*Diaz, A., I. Ferreira, R. M. Gisselquist and F. Tarp (2025). 'Regional Differences in Attitudes Towards Inequality: The Case of Northern vs. Southern Vietnam', WIDER Working Paper 2025/62. Helsinki: UNU-WIDER.

Downs, A. (1957). *An Economic Theory of Democracy*. New York: Harper & Row.

Durante, R., L. Putterman and J. van der Weele (2014). 'Preferences for Redistribution and Perceptions of Fairness: An Experimental Study'. *Journal of the European Economic Association*, 12(4): 1059–86. 10.1111/jeea.12082

*Easterbrook, M. J. (2021). 'The Social Psychology of Economic Inequality', WIDER Working Paper 2021/43. Helsinki: UNU-WIDER. https://doi.org/10.35188/UNU-WIDER/2021/981-5. Accessed: 11 September 2025.

Fehr, D., J. Mollerstrom and R. Perez-Truglia (2022). 'Your Place in the World: Relative Income and Global Inequality'. *American Economic Journal: Economic Policy*, 14(4): 232–68. https://doi.org/10.1257/pol.20200343. Accessed: 11 September 2025.

Fehr, E., and Schmidt (1999). 'A Theory of Fairness, Competition, and Cooperation'. *Quarterly Journal of Economics*, 114(3): 817–68. https://www.jstor.org/stable/2586885. Accessed: 11 September 2025.

*Ferreira, I. A., R. M. Gisselquist and F. Tarp (2025a). 'Absolute Versus Relative Inequality and Social Preferences: A Comparative Study between Mozambique and Vietnam'. WIDER Working Paper 2025/24. Helsinki: UNU-WIDER. https://www.wider.unu.edu/publication/absolute-versus-relative-inequality-and-social-preferences#. Accessed: 11 September 2025.

*Ferreira, I. A., R. M. Gisselquist and F. Tarp (2025b). 'Is Inequality Always Unfair? Experimental Evidence on Preferences for Redistribution in Mozambique and Vietnam'. WIDER Working Paper 2025/11. Helsinki: UNU-WIDER. https://www.wider.unu.edu/publication/inequality-always-unfair#. Accessed: 11 September 2025.

García-Castro, J. D., R. Rodríguez-Bailón and G. B. Willis (2020). 'Perceiving Economic Inequality in Everyday Life Decreases Tolerance to Inequality'. *Journal of Experimental Social Psychology*, 90(104019): 1–10. https://doi.org/10.1016/j.jesp.2020.104019. Accessed: 11 September 2025.

García-Sanchéz, E., D. Osborne, G. B. Willis and R. Rodríguez-Bailón (2020). 'Attitudes Towards Redistribution and the Interplay Between Perceptions and Beliefs About Inequality'. *British Journal of Social Psychology*, 59: 111–36. 10.1111/bjso.12326

Gimpelson, V., and D. Treisman (2018). 'Misperceiving Inequality'. *Economics & Politics*, 30: 27–54. 10.1111/ecpo.12103

Harrison, E., and C. Seidl (1994). 'Perceptional Inequality and Preferential Judgements: An Empirical Examination of Distributional Axioms'. *Public Choice*, 79: 61–81.

Hauser, O. P., and M. I. Norton (2017). '(Mis)Perceptions of Inequality'. *Current Opinion in Psychology*, 18: 21–5. http://dx.doi.org/10.1016/j.copsyc.2017.07.024. Accessed: 11 September 2025.

Hotelling, H. (1929). 'Stability in Competition'. *The Economic Journal* 39(153): 41–57. https://doi.org/10.2307/2224214. Accessed: 11 September 2025.

Hoy, C., and F. Mager (2021). 'Why Are Relatively Poor People Not More Supportive of Redistribution? Evidence from a Randomized Survey Experiment across Ten Countries'. *American Economic Journal: Economic Policy*, **13(4): 299–328. https://doi.org/10.1257/pol.20190276. Accessed: 11 September 2025.**

Hvidberg, K. B., C. T. Kreiner and S. Stantcheva (2023). 'Social Positions and Fairness Views on Inequality'. *Review of Economic Studies*, 90: 3083–118. https://doi.org/10.1093/restud/rdad019. Accessed: 11 September 2025.

Karadja, M., J. Mollerstrom and D. Steim (2017). 'Richer (and Holier) Than Thou? The Effect of Relative Income Improvements on Demand for Redistribution'. *Review of Economics and Statistics*, 99(2): 201–12. https://www.jstor.org/stable/10.2307/26616111. Accessed: 11 September 2025.

Kuziemko, I., M. I. Norton, E. Saez and S. Stantcheva (2015). 'How Elastic Are Preferences for Redistribution? Evidence from Randomized Survey Experiments'. *American Economic Review*, 105(4): 1478–508. http://dx.doi.org/10.1257/aer.20130360. Accessed: 11 September 2025.

Lobeck, M., and M. N. Støstad (2023). 'The Consequences of Inequality: Beliefs and Redistributive Preferences'. Mimeo.

Londoño-Vélez, J. (2022). 'The Impact of Diversity on Perceptions of Income Distribution and Preferences for Redistribution'. *Journal of Public Economics*, 214(104732): 1–29. https://doi.org/10.1016/j.jpubeco.2022.104732. Accessed: 11 September 2025.

Meltzer, A. H., and S. F. Richard (1981). 'A Rational Theory of the Size of Government'. *Journal of Political Economy*, 89(5): 914–27. https://www.jstor.org/stable/1830813. Accessed: 11 September 2025.

Mengel, F., and E. Weidenholzer (2022). 'Preferences for Redistribution'. *Journal of Economic Surveys*: 1–18. https://doi.org/10.1111/joes.12519. Accessed: 11 September 2025.

Mijs, J. J. B., and C. Hoy (2022). 'How Information About Inequality Impacts Belief in Meritocracy: Evidence from a Randomized Survey Experiment in Australia, Indonesia and Mexico'. *Social Problems*, 69: 91–122. https://doi.org/10.1093/socpro/spaa059. Accessed: 11 September 2025.

Milanovic, B. (2000). 'The Median-Voter Hypothesis, Income Inequality, and Income Redistribution: An Empirical Test with the Required Data'. *European Journal of Political Economy*, 16: 367–410. https://doi.org/10.1016/S0176-2680(00)00014-8. Accessed: 11 September 2025.

Minkoff, S. L., and J. Lyons (2019). 'Living with Inequality: Neighborhood Income Diversity and Perceptions of the Income Gap'. *American Politics Research*, 47(2): 329–61. 10.1177/1532673X17733799

Mollerstrom, J., B. A. Reme and E. Sørensen (2015). 'Luck, Choice and Responsibility: an Experimental Study of Fairness Views'. *Journal* of *Public Economics*, 131: 33–40. http://dx.doi.org/10.1016/j.jpubeco.2015.08.010. Accessed: 11 September 2025.

*Oppel, A. (2023). 'Communication Matters: Sensitivity in Fairness Evaluations across Wealth Inequality Expressions and Levels', WIDER Working Paper 2023/86, Helsinki: UNU-WIDER. https://doi.org/10.35188/UNU-WIDER/2023/394-9. Accessed: 11 September 2025.

Pellicer, M., P. Piraino and E. Wegner (2019). 'Perceptions of Inevitability and Demand for Redistribution: Evidence from a Survey Experiment'. *Journal of Economic Behavior and Organization*, 159: 274–88. https://doi.org/10.1016/j.jebo.2017.12.013. Accessed: 11 September 2025.

*Puzon, K. A. M. (2022). 'Behavioural Experiments as an Impactful Tool in Sustainable Development', WIDER Background Note 2. Helsinki: UNU-WIDER.

*Puzon, K. A., and R. M. Gisselquist (2023), 'Theoretical Models of Inequality: Examples from Rational Choice Theory and Behavioral Economics'. *International Social Science Journal*, 73(248): 325–38.

Ravallion, M. (2004). 'Competing Concepts of Inequality in the Globalization Debate'. *Brookings Trade Forum, 2004, Globalization, Poverty, and Inequality*: 1–38. https://www.jstor.org/stable/25063189. Accessed: 11 September 2025.

Ravallion, M. (2014). 'Income Inequality in the Developing World'. *Science*, 344(6186): 851–55. https://doi.org/10.1126/science.1251875. Accessed: 11 September 2025.

Ravallion, M. (2018). 'Inequality and Globalization: A Review Essay'. *Journal of Economic Literature*, 56(2): 620–42. https://doi.org/10.1257/jel.20171419. Accessed: 11 September 2025.

Roberts, K. W. S (1977). 'Voting over Income Tax Schedules'. *Journal of Public Economics* 8(3): 329–40. https://doi.org/10.1016/0047-2727(77)90005-6. Accessed: 11 September 2025.

Roth, C., and J. Wohlfart (2018). 'Experienced Inequality and Preferences for Redistribution'. *Journal of Public Economics*, 167: 251–62. https://doi.org/10.1016/j.jpubeco.2018.09.012. Accessed: 11 September 2025.

Sands, M. L. (2017). 'Exposure to Inequality Affects Support for Redistribution'. *PNAS*, 114(4): 663–68. www.pnas.org/cgi/doi/10.1073/pnas.1615010113. Accessed: 11 September 2025.

Sands, M. L., and D. de Kadt (2020). 'Local exposure to inequality raises support of people of low wealth for taxing the wealthy'. *Nature*, 586(7828): 257–61.

Stantcheva, S. (2024). 'Perceptions and Preferences for Redistribution'. *Oxford Open Economics*, 3: i96–i100. https://doi.org/10.1093/ooec/odad 038. Accessed: 11 September 2025.

Starmans, C., M. Sheskin, and P. Bloom (2017). 'Why people prefer unequal societies'. *Nature Human Behaviour*, 1: article 0082. https://doi.org/10.1038/s41562-017-0082. Accessed: 11 September 2025.

Trump, K. S. (2018). 'Income Inequality Influences Perceptions of Legitimate Income Differences'. *British Journal of Social Psychology*, 48: 929–52. doi:10.1017/S0007123416000326. Accessed: 11 September 2025.

Ziano, I., C. Lembregts and M. Pandelaere (2022). 'People Weigh Salaries More Than Ratios in Judgments of Income Inequality, Fairness, and Demands for Redistribution'. *Journal of Economic Psychology*, 89: 102495. https://doi.org/10.1016/j.joep.2022.102495. Accessed: 11 September 2025.

5

Inequality, economic growth and well-being

In this chapter we loop back to some of the relationships introduced in Chapter 3 and zoom in on the link from inequality to economic development, which we explore in terms of economic growth and poverty first, and in terms of well-being later. Given that understanding the link from growth to inequality has been central in the debate on inequality, we discuss this briefly in the next section, before elaborating on the inverse relationship, that is, the impact of inequality on growth. We use income as an indicator of prosperity and focus more specifically on its growth rate (see Box 5.1 for more details). In other words, we will examine the increase in aggregate income (of a country or group of countries) over time, and how this is associated with the distribution of income. In the last section we then broaden the scope and link back to Chapter 2 where we discussed how inequalities in other dimensions – such as gender, education, health – intersect. We briefly discuss what we know about the impact of inequality on human development, with a focus on health and education outcomes, as well as about how inequality affects subjective well-being.

Box 5.1: Economic growth and its determinants

We define economic growth as the annual percentage increase in the real gross domestic product (GDP), which is the total value of all goods and services produced in an economy, with that value adjusted for the effects of inflation. National income (i.e., gross national income (GNI) refers to the income generated from production. GDP aims to capture all output produced within the country (whether by citizens or foreign residents) and excludes the output produced by citizens living abroad, whereas GNI is the GDP plus net receipts from abroad of compensation of employees, property income and net taxes less subsidies on production. Both concepts suffer from limitations (see more in Ravallion 2016: 380), including:

- Collecting data is challenging in poorer countries with weaker administrative capacity for data collection.
- Important aspects are left out, such as environmental consequences of growth.
- Information is not given about how income is distributed.

A field of study within economics has focused on understanding the determinants of growth, theoretically and empirically. The empirical studies frequently use reduced form equations, which are a simplified way of expressing complex economic models to estimate the correlations between different factors and economic growth. These correlations are the coefficients obtained from the model. For example, consider that we are estimating the link between education and growth and obtained a coefficient of 0.4. This means that, holding all other factors at a constant level, one unit of education is correlated with an increase in 0.4 units of growth.

Growth and inequality

Before we describe the different ways in which inequality affects growth, it is important to bring in the other direction of causality, that is, from growth to inequality. A key point in the literature, particularly in economics, is that inequality may be associated with growth. In fact, together with poverty, the three concepts form the poverty–growth–inequality 'iron triangle', which represents the arithmetic identity linking the growth of mean income, the change in inequality and the decrease of absolute poverty (Bourguignon 2004).

The old classical view suggested that there was a contradiction between equality and development.[1] Adam Smith[2] in his magnum opus *The Wealth of Nations* (1776) is often interpreted as arguing that inequality is a necessary trade-off to growth.[3] A more nuanced interpretation of his arguments is that inequality could potentially be beneficial: (i) through 'trickle down effects' that would make an increase in wealth eventually beneficial to the poor; (ii) by creating incentives to encourage competition and promote innovation; and (iii) to help maintain social stability by enabling different ranks in wealth to exist (Ferreira, Gisselquist and Tarp 2022: 5). Two centuries later, in *The Great Escape*, Angus Deaton (2013: 1) argued that 'Inequality is often a *consequence* of progress. Not everyone gets rich at the same time, and not everyone gets immediate access to the latest life-saving measures, whether access to clean water, to vaccines, or to new drugs for preventing heart disease.'

The well-known Kuznets curve, which portrays an inverted U-shaped relationship between mean income and inequality, concurred that inequality would in the early stage of development follow from growth.[4] While increasing mean income would lead to increased inequality first, it would ultimately reach a turning point and lead to more equality automatically as presented in the stylized Figure 5.1. Kuznets (1955) hypothesized that inequality would increase in the initial phase of the process of growth in an economy

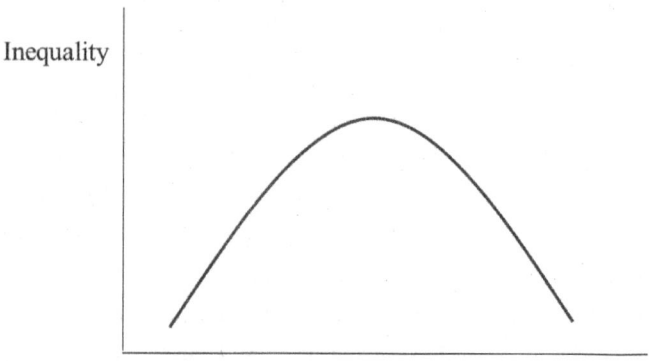

Figure 5.1 Stylized representation of the Kuznets curve.

Source: Authors' illustration; see text for details.

due to labour moving from the agriculture sector (more egalitarian with low productivity) to the industrial sector (more unequal with higher productivity), as well as from the countryside to urban areas, which would be increasingly less egalitarian (Gómez León 2020). Eventually, inequality would then decline when this process was complete at higher levels of income and with the resulting increase in political power to demand redistribution.

Let us use Brazil as an illustration of the Kuznets curve[5] to look at within-country inequality. There inequality increased until around 1950, after which it stabilized at a relatively high level (Milanovic 2016). While Brazil was one of the most unequal countries in the world in the 1970s and 1980s, inequality declined steadily from the late 1990s as a result of the economic mechanisms suggested by Kuznets, combining market-oriented reforms to enhance efficiency and growth with distributive policies (Gómez León 2020), including wider education, higher minimum wages and the introduction of social transfers targeted to the poor (Milanovic 2016: 82). According to data from the WIID based on household surveys, inequality continued decreasing until the mid-2000s, with a slight increase until 2018, then it declined marginally

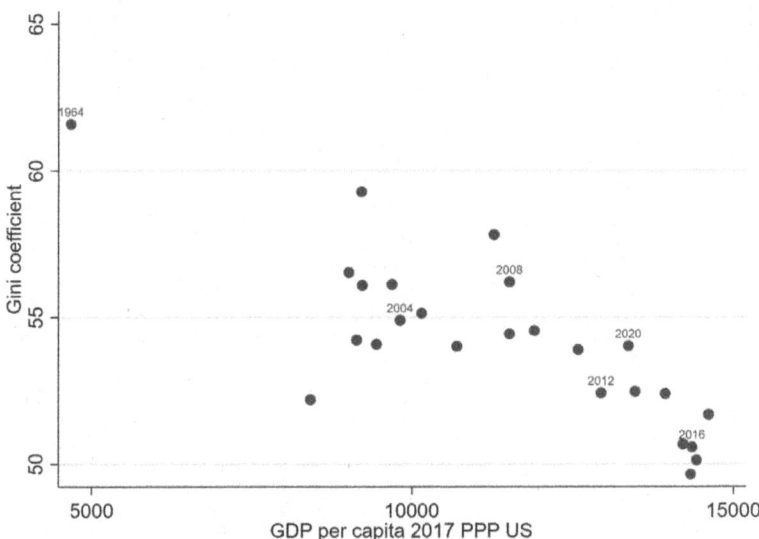

Figure 5.2 Evolution of the Gini coefficient in Colombia, 1964–2020.
Source: Authors' illustration based on UNU-WIDER (2023) data.

until 2020. The case of Brazil also highlights how macroeconomic policies can contribute to poverty reduction (Ravallion 2016: 472).

Figure 5.2 plots data for the Gini coefficient and GDP per capita and suggests that the case of Colombia is also broadly consistent with the Kuznets hypothesis (Acemoglu and Robinson 2002). Historical evidence also points to this inverted-U shape with inequality rising from the late 1930s to the mid-1960s, and then declining afterwards, as shown in the figure, due to a fundamental expansion of education (Robinson 2001: 19).

Kuznets found evidence for this inverse-U hypothesis based on a small sample of observations in the first half of the twentieth century. However, the Kuznets curve hypothesis failed to explain the latter day increase in inequality across wealthy countries which followed from the declining trend throughout most of the twentieth century – so bringing into question the curve's theoretical predictions. Moreover, the empirical findings in subsequent cross-country studies failed to confirm the Kuznets hypothesis (e.g., Deininger and Squire 1998) and showed no statistically

(a) Ethiopia, 1996–2016

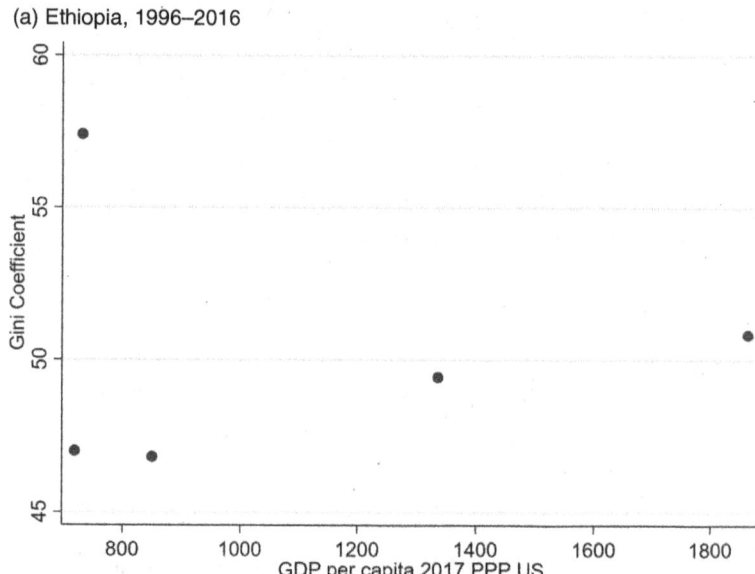

(b) South Africa, 1993–2017

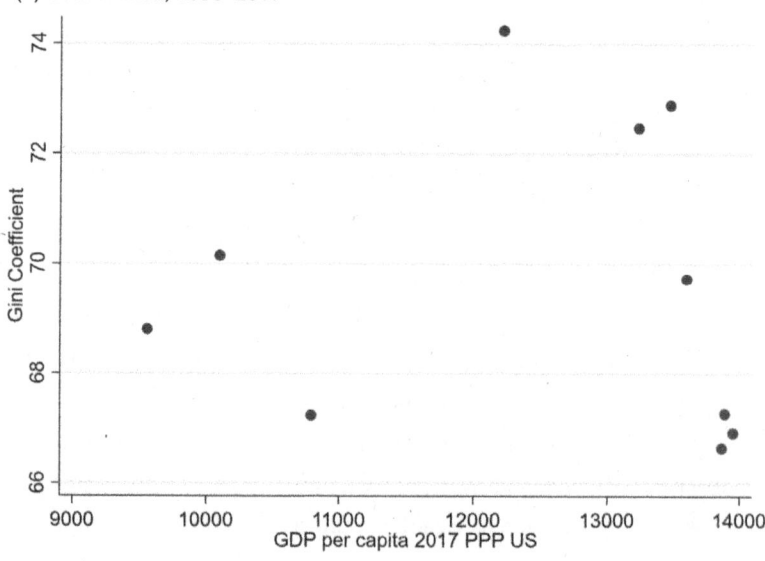

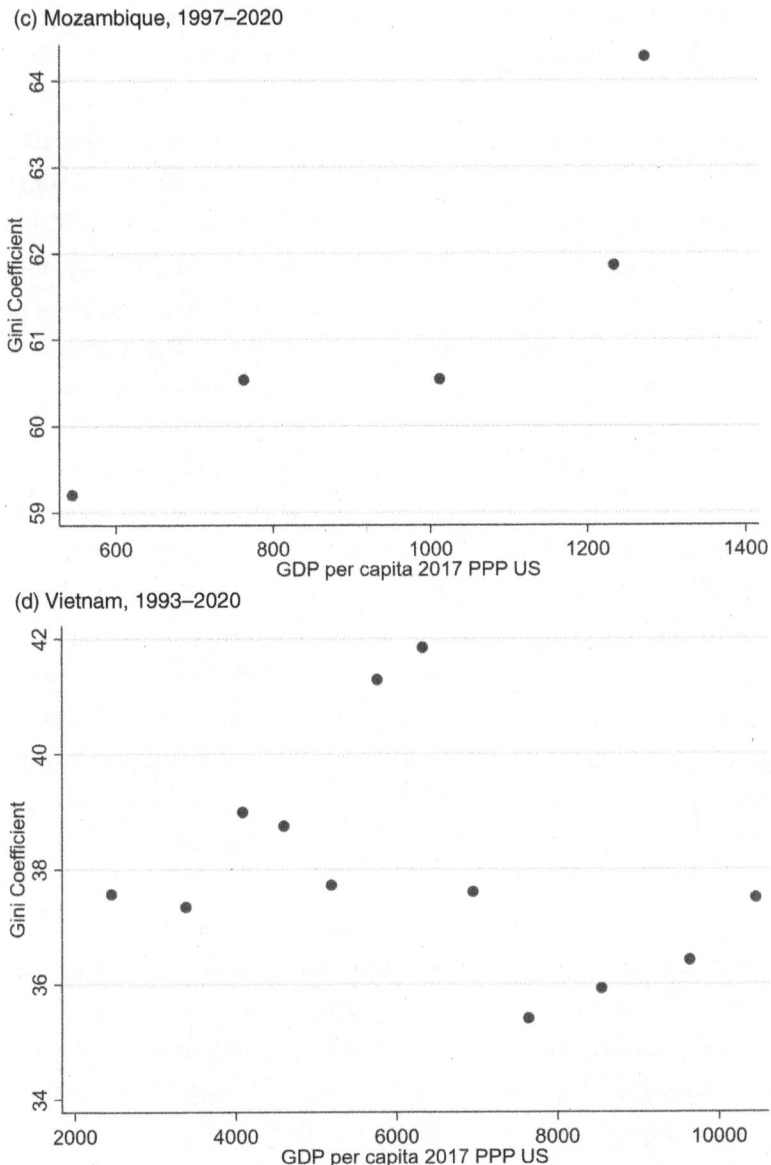

Figure 5.3 Trends in inequality and income in four countries.

Source: Authors' illustration based on UNU-WIDER (2023) data.

significant relationship between increases in mean income and changes in inequality (e.g., Ravallion and Chen 1997; Dollar and Kraay 2002).

The evidence from developing countries is even more unclear. Figure 5.3 illustrates this point by plotting the trends in inequality (measured using the relative Gini) and GDP per capita for our other countries of interest. Highlighting again the lack of data available for the African countries, the graphs show increases in inequality as income increases in Ethiopia and Mozambique, and a decrease in South Africa, despite remaining at very high levels. The patterns are harder to read for Vietnam, but seem to suggest an initial increase in inequality followed by a decline.

Some have used the success achieved by the East Asian economies to argue against the Kuznets curve (e.g., Stiglitz 1996). Between the 1960s and 1990, in what became known as the 'East Asian Miracle' (World Bank 1993), the eight economies of Hong Kong, Indonesia, Japan, the Republic of Korea, Malaysia, Singapore, Taiwan and Thailand were able to achieve rapid growth without inequality increasing. They succeeded by recognizing the limitations of markets and complementing them, for instance, through policies to ensure macroeconomic stability focused on export-promotion and through creating an environment conducive to private investment which also secured political stability (Stiglitz 1996: 156).

In particular, and in contrast with the predictions of the Kuznets hypothesis, policies that aimed at promoting equality also benefitted growth. These included initially land reforms in Korea, Japan and Taiwan, and later maintaining high and increasing wages, restricting real estate speculation and ensuring universal literacy (Stiglitz 1996). Box 5.2 gives more details on the case of Taiwan.

Moreover, this success demonstrated that not only did higher rates of growth contribute to equality, in turn the resulting increased *equality* helped to keep high growth rates.[6]

We explore the link from inequality to growth next.

> **Box 5.2: Taiwan as an example of 'growth with equity'**
>
> The period between the 1950s and the early 1960s was characterized by rapid agricultural growth and import substitution – a type of policy that defends the substitution of imports with domestic production through protective measures such as tariffs, quotas or subsidies, with the aim of reducing dependency on imports. Moreover, land reform was crucial to achieve growth and reduced inequality of income among farmers. By the mid-1960s, the government introduced policies for export promotion which contributed to decreased income inequality whereas during the 1980s and 1990s inequality started to rise again. While the share of the population receiving secondary education increased, as did unskilled wages, the initial increase was driven mainly by a reduction in the size of households.
>
> Source: Adapted from the country case example in Kanbur (2000: 808–10).

How does inequality affect growth?

In line with the classical economics thinking described earlier, similar arguments related to savings and incentives were developed throughout the 1950s and 1960s defending that inequality would benefit economic growth. At the core of this reasoning was the assumption that the rich have a higher propensity to save, and therefore higher inequality would redistribute income towards the rich, leading to higher savings and thus to higher growth through increased investment (Kaldor 1956). The second argument claimed that inequality was essential to create incentives to accumulate wealth and innovate, and hence higher redistribution would harm growth via this channel.[7] Thus, according to this line of thinking, policymakers would encounter a trade-off between promoting equality (based on social justice arguments) or growth (i.e., market efficiency).

Still, most of the subsequent theoretical work on this link suggested the opposite, that inequality has a negative effect on (i.e., is detrimental to) growth. Different strands of theory presented mechanisms that explain this relationship (see also Table 5.1). The literature is complex and mixes up several different elements, from macroeconomic channels, such as the link from inequality to growth via savings and investments, to microeconomic channels, related for instance, to household decisions to having children, and investing in education. We explore the intuition behind these channels in the next paragraphs, including references for further study.[8]

Credit market imperfections (Galor and Zeira 1993). Think about the costs of education and the circumstances of the poor in a certain society. This channel relates to the barriers in access to credit by the poorest groups in the population, which can be related to, among others, lack of information, high costs, the conditions imposed by banks to obtain credit or the regulatory environment. For instance, there were challenges in the implementation of mobile money in South Africa, where, despite 70 per cent of the population having a bank account, strict regulations to offering mobile money services created barriers to the implementation of mobile money services

Table 5.1 Schematic representation of different mechanisms through which inequality leads to lower growth

Outcomes driven by…	Mechanism	Consequence
The wealthy	Taxation and subversion of regulatory policies	Lack of protection of property rights
All/average	Less well-endowed median voter	Higher equilibrium level of taxation
	Small middle class	Structure of demand
The poor	Social discontent	Social unrest and political violence
	Imperfect credit markets	Underinvestment in human capital
	High fertility differential	

Source: Adapted from Ferreira, Gisselquist and Tarp (2022).

(FinMark Trust 2017). If the poor do not have access to credit, they may not be able to invest in education. Education is an investment in human capital, which is in turn important for growth. On aggregate, underinvestment in human capital negatively impacts growth.

Taxation and subversion of regulatory policies (Persson and Tabellini 1994; Glaeser, Scheinkman and Shleifer 2003). This mechanism is related to security over property rights, from the point of view of the share of the population with the highest income. Tax and regulatory policies affect incentives through their effects on the protection of property rights and on the capture of returns to investment, which in turn affects growth. Moreover, it can lead to subversion of the regulatory framework by the rich for their own benefit. The weaknesses in terms of rule of law and judicial independence that have characterized recent decades in Mozambique provide a useful example. Cases of members of Frelimo (the party in power), their families and high-ranking civil servants obtaining privileged access to land use and cheaper infrastructure reinforce power asymmetries (Cruz et al. 2023).

Social discontent (Alesina and Perotti 1996). Income inequality can lead to general discontent and even social unrest among the population, as well as increase the risk of political violence. In turn, this creates uncertainty over the policy environment and security of property rights. This insecurity leads to lower investment, and thus lower growth. The period of social unrest that characterized the post-2024 elections in Mozambique illustrates this channel. The main trigger was that the results of the election were contested, with several reports of irregularities – the protests were of a scale not experienced in previous elections. The leading opposition presidential candidate called for several demonstrations, demonstrations which were subsequently repressed by the police. Still, the magnitude of the unrest reflected more than just discontent with the election results. It was also rooted in dissatisfaction with the growing inequalities in the country, limited social mobility and perceived elite capture (Jones 2024), in line with that discussed relating to the previous channel.[9]

Less endowed median voter (Alesina and Rodrik 1994). Assume a tax rate that is proportional to income. Then, individuals with a lower share of capital income (relative to labour income) will choose higher taxes. Accordingly, the more unequal the distribution of income, the lower will be the endowment of the median voter (that is, the individual with the median level of income),[10] and the higher will be the equilibrium level of taxation. High taxation and redistribution discourage both savings and investment, creating a lower growth rate.

Higher fertility differential (de la Croix and Doepke 2003). Poor families may prioritize having more children rather than investing in their education, whereas rich families will give priority to investments in education and thus have a smaller number of children. This differential in the fertility between the poor and the rich leads to lower human capital accumulation (average education) which negatively affects growth.

Small middle class (Murphy, Shleifer and Vishny 1989; Zweimüller 2000). This mechanism works through the structure of demand, namely for domestic manufactures (with impact on industrialization), but also for innovation in the creation of new goods.

Furthermore, some have contended that the effects of inequality could lead to higher or lower growth depending on the time horizon, that is, short- versus long-term effects (Halter, Oechslin and Zweimüller 2014). In the short term, the classical economic arguments would apply, meaning that higher inequality would contribute to higher growth, whereas in the long term, the political economy channels would prevail and higher inequality would instead become associated with lower growth. In a similar vein, it was argued that the relationship would depend on the stages of industrialization, given that different mechanisms might operate at different phases (Galor and Moav 2004).

How does the empirical evidence compare with these theoretical predictions?[11] Initially, the studies testing the link between inequality and growth used reduced form equations (see Box 5.1) and cross-country analysis that added inequality to the growth determinants. In other words, they abstracted this relationship from the different channels through which inequality can affect growth and focused on the average effect by estimating, for a group of countries at a certain point in time, the correlation between inequality and growth.

Nevertheless, the results were inconclusive, as summarized in Table 5.2. The first group of studies in the early 1990s found that inequality hindered growth but faced serious limitations in terms of data availability. With the publication of a then new dataset by Deininger and Squire (1996), subsequent studies could draw on more, and panel (information over time for different countries) data, which enabled the application of more sophisticated analytical methods. Using these new data, studies found a positive link between inequality and growth, that is, that higher inequality was associated with higher growth, or that the effect of inequality on growth depended on other factors.[12] More recent literature reflects this lack of consensus. While the immense progress in terms of data availability has led to the emergence of new datasets, even using the same source of data, different studies find contrasting results.

Underlying this lack of consensus is also the fact that there are several challenges in determining this empirical relationship. Recall our discussion from Chapter 3 regarding the different indicators that we can use for income inequality (for example, income or consumption, pre- or post-tax, etc.) as well as the different measures available (for example, Gini coefficient, Palma ratio, among others) that require choices when analysing the data. Moreover, and as we alluded to above, there are still challenges in terms of data availability in certain places and for a consistent period that in some cases lead to the use of imputation methods (i.e., using existing values to estimate

Table 5.2 References for empirical studies on the link between inequality and growth

General finding	Reference	Data source	Data structure
Inequality *hinders* growth	Alesina and Rodrik (1994)	Jain (1975); Fields (1989)	Cross-section
	Persson and Tabellini (1994)	Paukert (1973)	Cross-section
	Clarke (1995)	United Nations Indicator of Social Development; Jain (1975); Lecaillon et al. (1984)	Cross-section
	Perotti (1996)	Jain (1975); Lecaillon et al. (1984)	Cross-section
	Cingano (2014)	OECD income distribution dataset	Panel
	Berg et al. (2018)	Standardized World Income Inequality Database (SWIID)	Panel
	Gründler and Scheuermeyer (2018)	SWIID	Panel
Inequality *promotes* growth	Li and Zou (1998)	Deininger and Squire (1996)	Panel
	Forbes (2000)	Deininger and Squire (1996)	Panel
	El-Shagi and Shao (2019)	SWIID	Panel
It depends:			
– controls	Deininger and Squire (1998)	Deininger and Squire (1996)	Cross-section
– level of income	Barro (2000)	Deininger and Squire (1996)	Panel
	Castelló-Climent (2010)	World Income Inequality Database (WIID); Luxemburg Income Study	Panel
– non-linear effects	Banerjee and Duflo (2003)	Deininger and Squire (1996)	Panel
– profile of inequality	Voitchovsky (2005)	Luxemburg Income Study	Panel
– time	Halter, Oechslin and Zweimüller (2014)	Deininger and Squire (1996); WIID	Panel

Source: Adapted from Ferreira et al. (2022: 13).

missing values).¹³ The quality of the imputations varies and we should bear in mind that their reliability depends on the actual data available, a key point to keep in mind in the Global South.¹⁴ An additional challenge relates to the methods used to estimate this relationship. They can be related, for instance, to the assumptions taken about the relationship (e.g., is it linear or quadratic like the Kuznets curve), or to the fact that, as we described in the previous section, growth also affects inequality, so it is difficult to isolate each direction of connecting effects.

You might now be wondering about the underlying mechanisms that the theorists advanced as linking inequality to growth. The evidence is much scarcer on this, but there is some support for the negative effect of inequality on growth through the channels of credit market imperfections (see related evidence from South Africa in Box 5.3), fertility and socio-political instability.

However, the link through taxation received less support and the median voter channel was rejected, whereas there is no specific evidence on the link via the structure of demand.¹⁵

Box 5.3: Inequality and household debt in South Africa

A recent study found that, considering South Africa's income levels, higher-income households borrow more than lower-income households, and a higher percentage of their debt is borrowed from formal financial institutions, which suggests that they have greater access to credit institutions.

In contrast, when considering incomes at the province level, lower-income households (relative to the richer households in the province) have higher borrowing levels and mainly from informal lenders.

Source: See Foster (2023).

While exploring the links between inequality and growth is essential, inequality also impacts other dimensions. Referring to the different mechanisms underlying this link highlighted the impact of inequality on, for instance, investment in education or aspects related to governance, such as taxation and regulatory policies, to which we return in Chapter 6.

In the next section we delve more deeply into the effects on other dimensions of human development and well-being.

The impact of inequality on human development and well-being

As we highlighted in the introduction to this chapter, inequality may be linked not only to poverty measured in economic terms, but also to well-being more broadly. This section gives an overview of literatures addressing questions such as: Does inequality affect educational outcomes? Does it affect individual health? And what about well-being and happiness in general?

Effects on education and health

What does theory say about the link between inequality and education? In our recent review (Ferreira, Gisselquist and Tarp 2022) we concluded that theory points to both beneficial and detrimental effects of inequality on education and identified two main channels: expenditure on education; school enrolment and attainment. On the one hand, higher inequality leads to fewer resources available to invest in public education as the rich favour private schools, and to higher levels of child labour (Gutiérrez and Tanaka 2009; Mayer 2001; Tanaka 2003). On the other hand, if inequality is partly a result of increased returns to schooling, it leads to incentives for children to stay in school and can positively affect educational attainment (Dabla-Norris et al. 2015).

Is there empirical support for these hypotheses? Existing evidence contrasts with theory and suggests that high inequality is correlated with higher spending for public education (Sylwester 2000). Nevertheless, different studies have shown a negative link between inequality and secondary school enrolment (see references in Ferreira, Gisselquist and Tarp 2022).

Regarding health, the theoretical hypotheses are more consensual in that inequality negatively affects health. Notably, Pickett and Wilkinson (2015) argued that inequality weakened community life and increased status competition, therefore leading to social problems and negatively affecting health. Focusing first on the effects on the health of all individuals, higher inequality can lead to (Leigh, Jencks and Smeeding 2011; O'Donnell, van Doorslaer and van Ourti 2015):

- lower public goods provision, namely public spending in health;[16]
- lower social cohesion, which affects health through decreased social and psychosocial support, access to informal insurance and diffusion of information; and
- increased levels of violent crime, which can induce stress about experiencing crime in the future and thus negatively affecting health.

However, the empirical evidence is inconclusive, with studies in public health arguing that higher inequality is linked with worse health outcomes (e.g., Pickett and Wilkinson 2015), in contrast with the caution in the economics literature which finds no evidence of this relationship (e.g., Deaton 2003).[17]

When considering the effects of health depending on income at the individual level, there are different hypotheses which place the focus on the effects of: (i) how much an additional unit of income increases health; (ii) individuals comparing their income with that of others; (iii) the extent of deprivation (i.e., the income gap);[18] and (iv) the position of individuals in the income distribution (see Wagstaff and van Doorslaer 2000, for more details). However, the existing evidence on these channels is scarce and again inconclusive.

Together with income, indicators of education and health have been aggregated in a single measure, the Human Development Index (HDI), introduced already in Chapter 2, which is often used as an aggregate indicator of well-being. Recall from Chapter 2 that the turn towards thinking about development as much more than growth in income was highly influenced by Sen's capability approach, which pointed to the need to consider human development and different dimensions of well-being. This focus was translated by the United Nations Development Programme (UNDP) into the HDI.[19] Figure 5.4 plots the correlation between HDI and inequality levels over time for our five countries. It shows that, in all five countries, there has been an improvement in the HDI over time, more pronounced in Ethiopia and in South Africa after the turn of the millennium. Except for Colombia (for which we have more data points), where the trends in HDI and inequality seem to be inverted, the graphs do not suggest a clear relationship between inequality and human development.

Not many studies have explicitly assessed the effect of inequality on the HDI. Existing work shows that the effects vary with the time horizon and the dimension of HDI. While the results point to a negative effect of inequality on HDI in the long run, in the short run higher inequality is associated with higher growth (in line with the classical view) but is at the same time harmful to educational outcomes (Castells-Quintana, Royuela and Thiel 2019), consistent with the small empirical literature on the effects on education. In follow-up work focusing on different parts of the distribution, the evidence highlighted the role of the middle class: A lower share of national income going to the middle 50 per cent corresponds to a

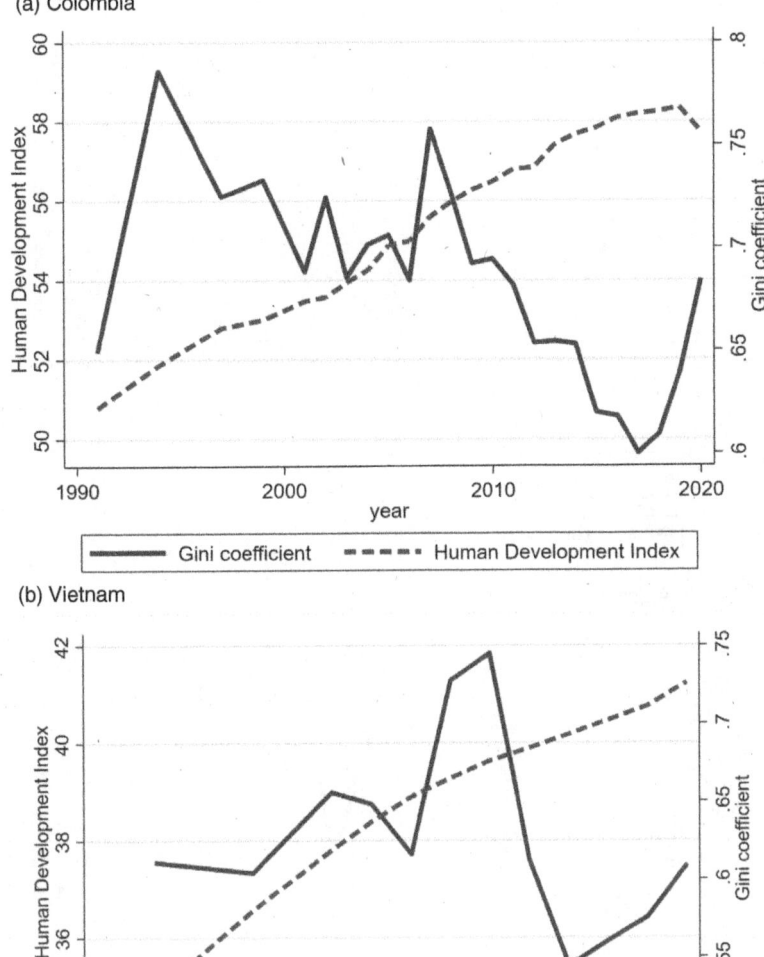

(c) Ethiopia

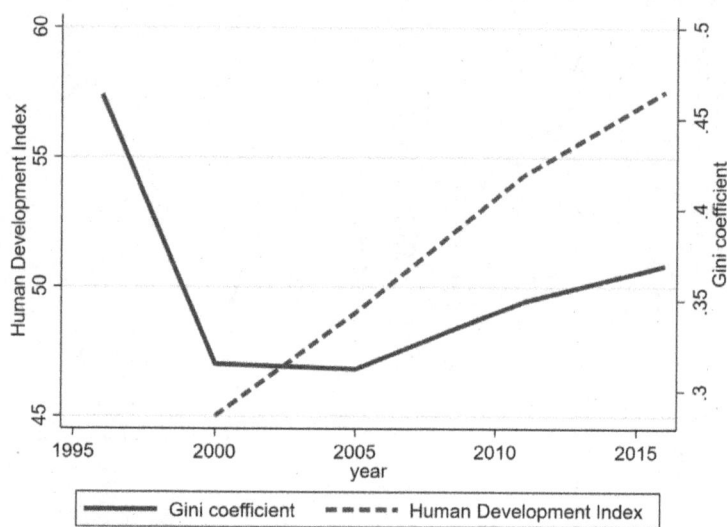

(d) South Africa

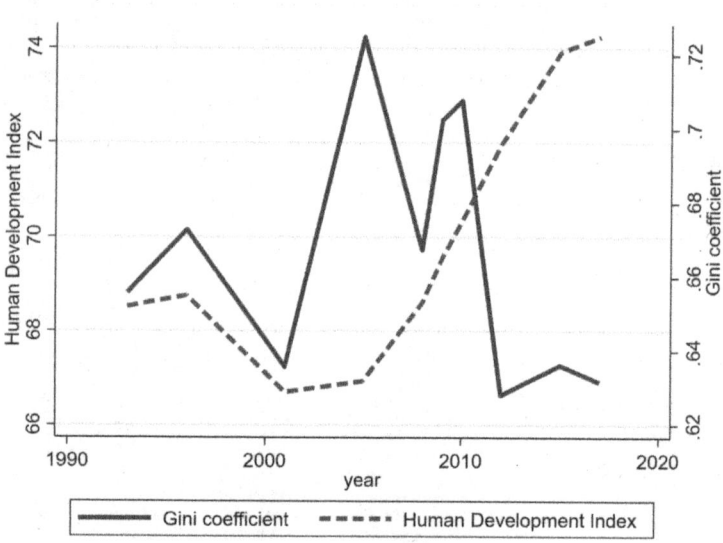

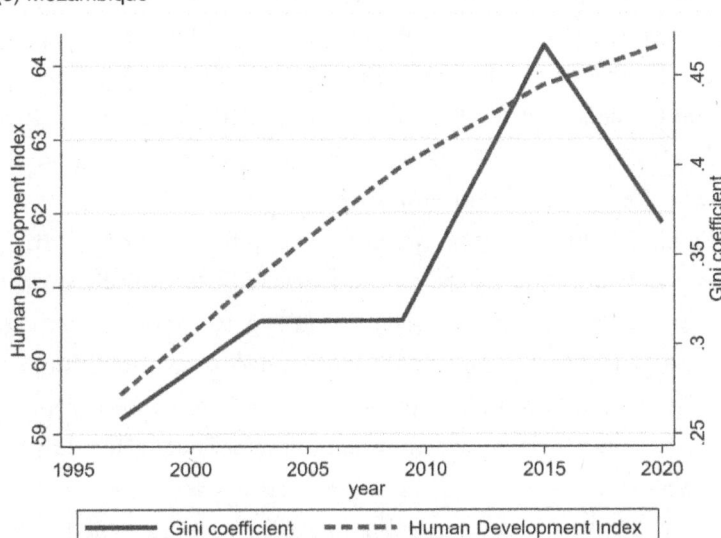

Figure 5.4 Human Development Index and the Gini coefficients over time for our five countries.

Source: Authors' illustration based on UNU-WIDER (2023) and UNDP (2024) data.

lower level of human development (Castells-Quintana, Gradín and Royuela 2025). In both studies, there are differences in the effects depending on the level of development of the country. Having focused on objective measures of well-being, we move next to subjective assessments.

Effects on subjective well-being

Health and education are among the broader set of objective dimensions that encompass what we think about as well-being. However, there is also evidence that inequality affects subjective measures of well-being or quality of life, including life satisfaction and happiness, and perceived or experienced welfare. We end this section with a brief overview of these strands of literature.

Box 5.4 gives an example of how subjective well-being is measured by the Organisation for Economic Co-operation and Development (OECD) while Figure 5.5 illustrates the trends in life satisfaction over time for four of our countries of focus.

Figure 5.5 illustrates the average scores to the question 'All things considered, how satisfied are you with your life as a whole these days?' answered on a scale from 1 (Dissatisfied) to 10 (Very satisfied). All four countries have average scores above 5 over time, with Ethiopia at the bottom and Colombia at the top as the country with the highest level of satisfaction (above 8 throughout the period). While Ethiopia and Vietnam show consistent improvement over time, especially after the 2000s, the scores for South Africa have fluctuated with a slight decline in recent years. You will notice that data availability varies between countries (a point we make throughout this book), is scarce for Ethiopia and Vietnam, and there is no data available for Mozambique. As an alternative, we reflected on the trends for Mozambique in terms of life evaluation[20] reported in the *World Happiness Report* (Helliwell et al. 2024). Since the early 2000s, the average score for Mozambique has fluctuated on a medium level between 4 and 5, on a ladder from 1 (the worst possible life) to 10 (the best possible life). Even if there was a slight increase to a score of above 5.5 in 2023 (the latest year with available data), in terms of ranking for the period 2021–3, Mozambique came in at ninetieth position out of 108 countries. Given the more recent events of violence and social unrest mentioned in this chapter, we expect this score to be reduced in the coming period.

Returning to our main question: Is there evidence linking inequality to subjective well-being? Figure 5.6 plots indicators of relative and absolute inequality and a measure of subjective well-being in Colombia. For the latter, we used the annual average answer to the question 'In

Box 5.4: Defining and measuring subjective well-being according to the OECD

The OECD argues that subjective well-being is more than happiness and defines it as: 'good mental states, including all of the various evaluations, positive and negative, that people make of their lives and the affective reactions of people to their experiences'. This definition contains the three elements we list below, together with examples of core questions to measure them, all on a scale 0–10:

(i) Life evaluation (how a person assesses their life or specific aspects of it)
- Overall, how satisfied are you with life as a whole these days? Zero means you feel 'not at all satisfied' and 10 means you feel 'completely satisfied'.
- Please imagine a ladder with steps numbered from 0 at the bottom to 10 at the top. The top of the ladder represents the best possible life for you and the bottom of the ladder represents the worst possible life for you. On which step of the ladder would you say you personally feel you stand at this time?

(ii) Affect (their feelings or emotional states at a specific point in time)
- The following questions ask about how you felt yesterday on a scale from 0 to 10. Zero means you did not experience the feeling 'at all' yesterday while 10 means you experienced the feeling 'all of the time' yesterday. I will now read out a list of ways you might have felt yesterday.
  a. How about happy?
  b. How about worried?
  c. How about depressed?

(iii) Eudaimonia (their sense of having meaning and purpose in life)
- Overall, to what extent do you feel the things you do in your life are worthwhile? Zero means you feel the things you do in your life are 'not at all worthwhile', and 10 means 'completely worthwhile'.

Notes: Adapted from questions A1–A5 and B1 in Boxes B.1 and B.2.

Source: OECD (2013).

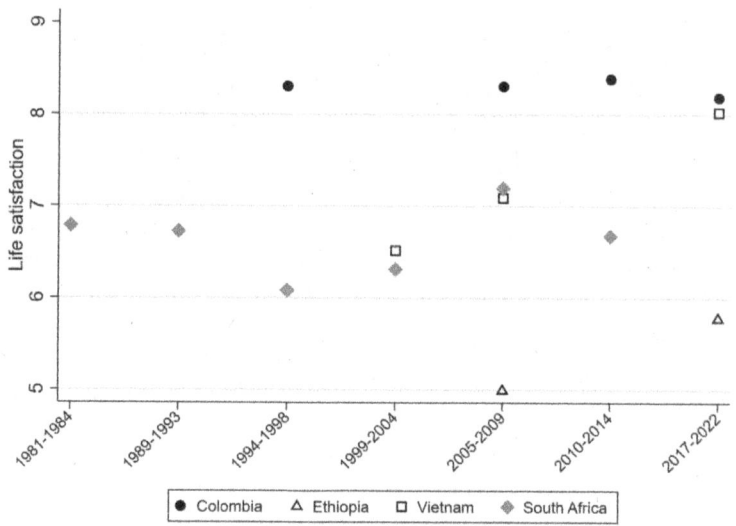

Figure 5.5 Life satisfaction over time in Colombia, Ethiopia, Vietnam and South Africa.

Source: Authors' illustration based on data from World Values Survey (Inglehart et al. 2022).

Note: Scores represent country averages to the question 'All things considered, how satisfied are you with your life as a whole these days?,' answered on a scale from 1 (Dissatisfied) to 10 (Very satisfied).

general, how satisfied do you feel with your life nowadays?' from the Government of Colombia's National Administrative Department of Statistics (DANE) survey – higher scores mean greater satisfaction. Overall, the graph shows that as inequality decreased, subjective well-being increased, whereas the later increase in inequality was in parallel with a stagnation in *perceived* well-being. However, it is important to keep in mind that there is no data available for subjective well-being for the period 2011–13 and that there was an adjustment in the scale of the answers after 2016. While we have rescaled the data in the graphs, this may have affected how individuals answered the question. Thinking again about our overall argument for the use of a dashboard approach, we included different measures of inequality in the figure. Note that the

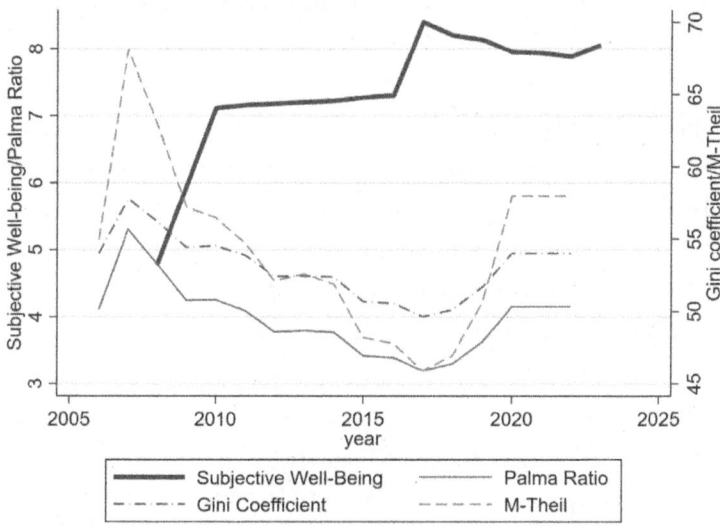

Figure 5.6 Subjective well-being and different measures of inequality over time in Colombia.

Notes: Years 2011–13 are missing for subjective well-being. Until 2016, subjective well-being was measured on a 1-4 scale, which was changed to 1-10 afterwards. We highlight that this change may have impacted how people answered. In this graph, we have rescaled data before 2016 to the 1-10 scale. Higher scores mean higher subjective well-being.

Source: Authors' illustration based on UNU-WIDER (2023) and DANE (2023) data.

Gini coefficient and the M-Theil are read from the y-axis to the right, while subjective well-being and the Palma ratio are read from the y-axis to the left in the graph. The trends portrayed by the three measures of inequality are very similar, though there are more pronounced fluctuations in the M-Theil when compared to the Gini. Recall from Chapter 3 that the M-Theil (or mean log deviation) is more sensitive to the bottom of the income distribution. Roughly speaking, the mirror relationship between the lines for subjective well-being and the Palma ratio is indicative of a negative correlation between the two concepts.

Researchers have found that individuals often dislike inequality and sought to understand exactly why.[21] It may be that individuals worry about being at the bottom of the distribution or about their prospects of social mobility, or about the negative effects of inequality (such as the ones discussed previously in this chapter), or that they care about others in society and about fairness.[22] You may have noticed the parallels with what we discussed in Chapter 4 regarding how individuals make decisions about inequality and their preferences for redistribution. In fact, the results in the happiness literature showed that there are similar patterns in the correlation between inequality and happiness, and between inequality and self-reported preferences for redistribution (Ferrer-i-Carbonell and Ramos 2021).

Still, the evidence on the link between inequality and happiness is mixed: while studies on Western societies point to a negative relationship, that is, that higher inequality is associated with lower happiness levels, studies on non-Western societies are less consistent, and, to a greater extent, the results are affected by estimation problems (Ferrer-i-Carbonell and Ramos 2014). One study on Latin America finds a negative relationship and argues that inequality is perceived as an indication of unfairness in terms of persisting advantages for the rich (and disadvantages for the poor) (Graham and Felton 2006). Concurring with these results, in a study on the quality of life of older people in rural Vietnam, Tran, Nguyen, and Van Vu (2018) documented a negative link between expenditure inequality and self-reported happiness, while highlighting the importance of individual characteristics, namely income and occupation for this relationship.

This heterogeneity in the effects across regions is well-documented in Clark and D'Ambrosio (2021). Using data from different Barometers, they conclude that more deprivation is associated with lower subjective well-being. Still, they find differences across regions in terms of how individual relative comparisons correlate with well-being. While in Europe there is a positive correlation – that is, individuals seeing themselves as better off than others correlates with higher levels of subjective well-being – it is not as strong in countries in the Global South. Again, we need to be mindful of the need to consider differences across settings when studying these relationships.

Key takeaways

- The link between inequality and growth is complex. A key point in the economics literature is that inequality tends to go along with growth in the beginning of the development process. Nonetheless, there is evidence that there are policies aimed at promoting equality that can also benefit growth.
- There are different mechanisms suggesting impacts from inequality on growth. While theory often predicts that inequality is detrimental to growth, the empirical evidence is relatively mixed.
- While there is evidence that inequality harms education, health and well-being, the results are not conclusive, and challenges remain for us to better understand these links, in particular in countries in the Global South.

Notes

1 This discussion has also been framed around a trade-off between equity and economic efficiency (underpinning economic growth) (see Thorbecke 2016), where equity refers to equality of opportunities for individuals to pursue their preferences, as well as protection from extreme deprivation; World Bank (2016: 18–19).
2 Born in Scotland into a professional middle-class family, Adam Smith is celebrated as the father of modern economics and had a profound influence on economic thought and policy. His work provided insights into how economies function and introduced key concepts such as the division of labour, free markets and the 'invisible hand' – the idea that

individuals seeking their own gain inadvertently benefit others and/or society.
3 Note there is some critique this interpretation; see, for instance, Boucoyannis (2014).
4 Note that if economic development happens according to the Lewis's (1954) two-sector dual economy model, then the inverted U-shape of the relationship between increasing income and inequality will logically follow (Tarp 1981). According to Lewis (1954), the economy was split between two sectors, modern and traditional. In the modern/urban/industrial sector, capitalists hire workers from the traditional/rural/agricultural sector (at a given wage) and reinvest the profits from production (Kanbur 2000). Under certain assumptions, this investment leads to growth, but, while the profits increase, the wages are stagnant, which increases inequality. If nothing else changes, eventually the surplus of workers in the traditional sector will end and salaries will increase, leading to a reduction in profits and consequently reducing the rate of growth; see more in Kanbur (2000).
5 Milanovic (2016) calls this a 'Kuznets wave or cycle'.
6 As a further illustration, note the results of a recent study (Bandyopadhyay and Sun 2020) that found that a growth shock increases inequality and an inequality shock reduces growth, though the effects are small and not long-lasting (based on data from the United States and China).
7 See also the analysis in Ostry, Berg and Tsangarides (2014) on how the data do not support this hypothesis using data from the Standardized World Income Inequality Database (SWIID) dataset for 153 countries between 1960 and 2010.
8 For more details, see reviews in Ferreira, Gisselquist and Tarp (2022); Neves and Silva (2014); Voitchovsky (2011).
9 We will return to this channel and elaborate on the illustration from Mozambique in Chapter 6.
10 Recall the median voter theorem we discussed in Chapter 4.
11 For more comprehensive reviews see Ferreira, Gisselquist and Tarp (2022) and Baselgia and Foellmi (2023).
12 See Atkinson and Brandolini (2009) for a discussion on the importance of data when examining the link between inequality and growth.

13 See Atkinson and Brandolini (2001, 2009) and Ferreira, Lustig and Teles (2015) for comprehensive analyses on secondary datasets on income distribution, drawing attention to issues of data quality and consistency.
14 Jenkins (2015) and Jäntti, Pirtillä and Rönkkö (2020) stress these issues when comparing the World Income Inequality Databased (WIID) and the Standardized World Income Inequality Database (SWIID).
15 For more details and references for these studies see our review paper Ferreira, Gisselquist and Tarp (2022).
16 Though it can also have the opposite effect, given that the median voter will be supportive of more spending on health.
17 See more details and references in Ferreira, Gisselquist and Tarp (2022).
18 A recent review on the relationship between inequality and health concludes that while material deprivation, especially in early life, can lead to income reductions, there is little evidence that without deprivation inequality affects health in a negative way (Currie 2024).
19 The HDI is composed of three dimensions: life expectancy at birth (measuring health and life longevity), mean years of schooling for adults 25 years old and above and expected years of schooling for children entering school age (both measuring education), and gross national income per capita (as a proxy for a decent standard of living).
20 This is the average answer to the second question under (i) in Box 5.4.
21 Comprehensive reviews are offered in Ferrer-i-Carbonell and Ramos (2014, 2021).
22 See also the discussion on how inequality matters for well-being in Graham (2014).

References

Acemoglu, D., and J. A. Robinson (2002). 'The Political Economy of the Kuznets Curve'. *Review of Development Economics*, 6(2): 183–203. https://doi.org/10.1111/1467-9361.00149. Accessed: 13 September 2025.

Alesina, A., and D. Rodrik (1994). 'Distributive Politics and Economic Growth'. *Quarterly Journal of Economics*, 109(2): 465–90. https://doi.org/10.2307/2118470. Accessed: 13 September 2025.

Alesina, A., and R. Perotti (1996). 'Income Distribution, Political Instability, and Investment'. *European Economic Review*, 40(6): 1203–28. https://doi.org/10.1016/0014-2921(95)00030-5. Accessed: 13 September 2025.

Atkinson, A. B., and A. Brandolini (2001). 'Promise and Pitfalls in the Use of 'Secondary' Data-Sets: Income Inequality in OECD Countries as a Case Study'. *Journal of Economic Literature*, 39(3): 771–99. https://doi.org/10.1257/jel.39.3.771. Accessed: 13 September 2025.

Atkinson, A. B., and A. Brandolini (2009). 'On Data: A Case Study of the Evolution of Income Inequality across Time and across Countries'. *Cambridge Journal of Economics*, 33(3): 381–404. https://doi.org/10.1093/cje/bel013. Accessed: 13 September 2025.

*Bandyopadhyay, S., and R. Sun (2020). 'Size Matters: Measuring the Effects of Inequality and Growth Shocks', WIDER Working Paper 2020/177. Helsinki: UNU-WIDER. Available online: https://doi.org/10.35188/UNU-WIDER/2020/934-1. Accessed: 13 September 2025.

Banerjee, A. V., and E. Duflo (2003). 'Inequality and Growth: What Can the Data Say?'. *Journal of Economic Growth*, 8: 267–99. https://doi.org/10.1023/A:1026205114860. Accessed: 13 September 2025.

Barro, R. J. (2000). 'Inequality and Growth in a Panel of Countries'. *Journal of Economic Growth*, 5: 5–32. https://doi.org/10.1023/A:1009850119329. Accessed: 13 September 2025.

*Baselgia, E., and R. Foellmi (2023). 'Inequality and Growth'. In K. F. Zimmermann (ed), *Handbook of Labor, Human Resources and Population Economics* (pp. 1–41). Cham: Springer. https://doi.org/10.1007/978-3-319-57365-6_332-2. Accessed: 13 September 2025.

Berg, A., J. D. Ostry, C. G. Sangarides and Y. Yakhshilikov (2018). 'Redistribution, Inequality, and Growth: New Evidence'. *Journal of Economic Growth*, 23: 259–305. https://doi.org/10.1007/s10887-017-9150-2. Accessed: 13 September 2025.

Boucoyannis, D. (2014). 'Contrary to Popular and Academic Belief, Adam Smith Did Not Accept Inequality as a Necessary Trade-Off for a More Prosperous Economy', LSE Blog. London School of Economics and Political Science.

Bourguignon, F. (2004). 'The Poverty-Growth-Inequality Triangle', Working Paper 125. New Delhi: Indian Council for Research on International Economic Relations.

Castelló-Climent, A. (2010). 'Inequality and Growth in Advanced Economies: An Empirical Investigation'. *Journal of Economic Inequality*, 8: 293–321. https://doi.org/10.1007/s10888-010-9133-4. Accessed: 13 September 2025.

*Castells-Quintana, D., C. Gradín and V. Royuela (2025). 'Concentration of Income and Human Development: The Role of the Middle Class'. *Oxford Economic Papers*, 77(3): 703–23 https://doi.org/10.1093/oep/gpae048. Accessed: 13 September 2025.

Castells-Quintana, D., V. Royuela and F. Thiel (2019). 'Inequality and Sustainable Development: Insights from an Analysis of the Human Development Index'. *Sustainable Development*, 27(3): 448–60. https://doi.org/10.1002/sd.1917. Accessed: 13 September 2025.

Cingano, F. (2014). 'Trends in Income Inequality and Its Impact on Economic Growth', OECD Social, Employment and Migration Working Paper 163. Paris: OECD. Available online: http://dx.doi.org/10.1787/5jxrjncwxv6j-en (accessed 16 November 2020).

Clark, A. E., and C. D'Ambrosio (2021). 'Economic Inequality and Subjective Wellbeing across the World'. In C. Gradín, M. Leibbrandt and F. Tarp (eds), *Inequality in the Developing World* (pp. 233–56). Oxford: Oxford University Press.

Clarke, G. R. G. (1995). 'More Evidence on Income Distribution and Growth'. *Journal of Development Economics*, 47(2): 403–27. https://doi.org/10.1016/0304-3878(94)00069-O. Accessed: 13 September 2025.

Cruz, A. S., I. A. Ferreira, J. Flentø and F. Tarp (2023). 'A Country at a Fork in the Road'. In A. S. Cruz, I. A. Ferreira, J. Flentø and F. Tarp (eds), *Mozambique at a Fork in the Road* (pp. 301–51). Cambridge: Cambridge University Press.

Currie, J. (2024). 'Health and Inequality'. *Oxford Open Economics*, 3: i549–i56. https://doi.org/10.1093/ooec/odad041. Accessed: 13 September 2025.

Dabla-Norris, E., K. Kochhar, N. Suphaphiphat, F. Ricka and E. Tsounta (2015). 'Causes and Consequences of Income Inequality: A

Global Perspective', IMF Discussion Note SDN/15/13. International Monetary Fund. https://doi.org/10.5089/9781513555188.006. Accessed: 13 September 2025.

DANE (2023). 'Encuesta De Calidad De Vida (Several Years)', Colombia. Available online: https://microdatos.dane.gov.co/index.php/catalog/186/study-description (accessed 29 November 2024).

Deaton, A. (2003). 'Health, Inequality, and Economic Development'. *Journal of Economic Literature*, 41(1): 113–58. https://doi.org/10.1257/jel.41.1.113. Accessed: 13 September 2025.

Deaton, A. (2013). *The Great Escape: Health, Wealth, and the Origins of Inequality*. Princeton: Princeton University Press.

Deininger, K., and L. Squire (1996). 'A New Data Set Measuring Income Inequality'. *World Bank Economic Review*, 10(3): 565–91. https://doi.org/10.1093/wber/10.3.565. Accessed: 13 September 2025.

Deininger, K., and L. Squire (1998). 'New Ways of Looking at Old Issues: Inequality and Growth'. *Journal of Development Economics*, 57: 259–87. https://doi.org/10.1016/S0304-3878(98)00099-6. Accessed: 13 September 2025.

De La Croix, D., and M. Doepke (2003). 'Inequality and Growth: Why Differential Fertility Matters'. *American Economic Review*, 93(4): 1091–113. https://doi.org/10.1257/000282803769206214. Accessed: 13 September 2025.

Dollar, D., and A. Kraay (2002). 'Growth Is Good for the Poor'. *Journal of Economic Growth*, 7(3): 195–225. https://www.jstor.org/stable/40216063. Accessed: 13 September 2025.

El-Shagi, M., and L. Shao (2019). 'The Impact of Inequality and Redistribution on Growth'. *Review of Income and Wealth*, 65(2): 239–63. https://doi.org/10.1111/roiw.12342. Accessed: 13 September 2025.

Ferreira, F. H. G., N. Lustig and D. Teles (2015). 'Appraising Cross-National Income Inequality Databases: An Introduction'. *Journal of Economic Inequality*, 13: 497–526. 10.1007/s10888-015-9316-0

*Ferreira, I. A., R. M. Gisselquist and F. Tarp (2022). 'On the Impact of Inequality on Growth, Human Development and Governance'.

International Studies Review, 24/1. https://doi.org/10.1093/isr/viab 058. Accessed: 13 September 2025.

Ferrer-i-Carbonell, A., and X. Ramos (2014). 'Inequality and Happiness'. *Journal of Economic Surveys*, 28(5): 1016–27. https://doi.org/10.1111/joes.12049. Accessed: 13 September 2025.

Ferrer-i-Carbonell, A., and X. Ramos (2021). 'Inequality and Happiness'. In K. F. Zimmermann (ed), *Handbook of Labor, Human Resources and Population Economics* (pp. 1–17). Cham: Springer.

Fields, G. (1989). 'A Compendium of Data on Inequality and Poverty for the Developing World'. Mimeo. Ithaca: Cornell University.

FinMark Trust (2017). *Research Report on Mobile Money in South Africa*. Midrand: FinMark Trust.

Forbes, K. J. (2000). 'A Reassessment of the Relationship between Inequality and Growth'. *American Economic Review*, 90(4): 869–87. https://doi.org/10.1257/aer.90.4.869. Accessed: 13 September 2025.

*Foster, S. (2023). 'Income Inequality and Household Debt: Examining the Impact of Relative Income on Formal and Informal Debt in South Africa', WIDER Working Paper 2023/37. Helsinki: UNU-WIDER. https://doi.org/10.35188/UNU-WIDER/2023/345-1. Accessed: 13 September 2025.

Galor, O., and J. Zeira (1993). 'Income Distribution and Macroeconomics'. *The Review of Economic Studies*, 60(1): 35–52. https://doi.org/10.2307/2297811. Accessed: 13 September 2025.

Galor, O., and O. Moav (2004). 'From Physical to Human Capital Accumulation: Inequality and the Process of Development'. *Review of Economic Studies*, 71(4): 1001–26. https://doi.org/10.1111/0034-6527.00312. Accessed: 13 September 2025.

Glaeser, E., J. Scheinkman and A. Shleifer (2003). 'The Injustice of Inequality'. *Journal of Monetary Economics*, 50(1): 199–222. https://doi.org/10.1016/S0304-3932(02)00204-0. Accessed: 13 September 2025.

Gómez León, M. (2020). 'The Kuznets Curve in Brazil, 1850-2010'. *Revista de Historia Económica/Journal of Iberian and Latin American Economic History*, 39(1): 37–61. https://doi.org/10.1017/S0212610920000166. Accessed: 13 September 2025.

Graham, C. (2014). 'Concluding Remarks. How Inequality Matters to Wellbeing'. In A.E. Clark, and C. Senik (eds), *Happiness and Economic Growth: Lessons from Developing Countries* (pp. 279–90). Oxford: Oxford University Press.

Graham, C., and A. Felton (2006). 'Inequality and Happiness: Insights from Latin America'. *Journal of Economic Inequality*, 4: 107–22. https://link.springer.com/article/10.1007/s10888-005-9009-1. Accessed: 13 September 2025.

Gründler, K., and P. Scheuermeyer (2018). 'Growth Effects of Inequality and Redistribution: What Are the Transmission Channels?'. *Journal of Macroeconomics*, 55: 293–313. https://doi.org/10.1016/j.jmacro.2017.12.001. Accessed: 13 September 2025.

Gutiérrez, C., and R. Tanaka (2009). 'Inequality and Education Decisions in Developing Countries'. *Journal of Economic Inequality*, 7: 55–81. https://doi.org/10.1007/s10888-008-9095-y. Accessed: 13 September 2025.

Halter, D., M. Oechslin and J. Zweimüller (2014). 'Inequality and Growth: The Neglected Time Dimension'. *Journal of Economic Growth*, 19: 81–104. https://doi.org/10.1007/s10887-013-9099-8. Accessed: 13 September 2025.

Helliwell, J. F., R. Layard, J. D. Sachs, J. E. De Neve, L. B. Aknin and S. Wang (eds) (2024). *World Happiness Report 2024*. Oxford: University of Oxford Wellbeing Research Centre.

Inglehart, R., C. Haerpfer, A. Moreno, C. Welzel, K. Kizilova, D. M. J., P. M. Lagos, E. P. Norris and B. Puranen (2022). World Values Survey: All Rounds: Country-Pooled Datafile Version 3.0. JD Systems Institute & WVSA Secretariat. Madrid and Vienna.

Jain, S. (1975). *The Size Distribution of Income: A Compilation of Data*. Washington, DC: World Bank.

Jäntti, M., J. Pirttilä and R. Rönkkö (2020). 'Redistribution, Inequality, and Growth Revisited: Comment on "Redistribution, Inequality, and Growth: New Evidence"', WIDER Working Paper 2020/117. Helsinki: UNU-WIDER. https://doi.org/10.35188/UNU-WIDER/2020/874-0. Accessed: 13 September 2025.

Jenkins, S. P. (2015). 'World Income Inequality Databases: An Assessment of WIID and SWIID'. *Journal of Economic Inequality*, 13: 629–71. https://doi.org/10.1007/s10888-015-9305-3. Accessed: 13 September 2025.

Jones, S. (2024). 'Mozambique in Post-Election Turmoil: Economic Policies That Could Make a Difference'. Blog post in *The Conversation*. 13 November. https://theconversation.com/mozambique-in-post-election-turmoil-economic-policies-that-could-make-a-difference-243603 (accessed 28 January 2025).

Kaldor, N. (1956). 'Theories of Distribution'. *Review of Economic Studies*, 23(2): 83–100. https://doi.org/10.2307/2296292. Accessed: 13 September 2025.

Kanbur, R. (2000). 'Income Distribution and Development'. In A. B. Atkinson, and F. Bourguignon (eds), *Handbook of Income Distribution* (Vol.1) (pp.791–841). Amsterdam: Elsevier Science B.V.

Kuznets, S. (1955). 'Economic Growth and Income Inequality'. *American Economic Review*, XLV(1): 1–28.

Lecaillon, J., F. Paukert, C. Morrison and D. Germadis (1984). *Income Distribution and Economic Development: An Analytical Survey*. Geneva: International Labour Office.

Leigh, A., C. Jencks and T. M. Smeeding (2011). 'Health and Economic Inequality'. In B. Nolan, W. Salverda, and T. M. Smeeding (eds), *Oxford Handbook of Economic Inequality* (pp. 384–405). Oxford: Oxford Handbooks Online.

Lewis, W. A. (1954). 'Economic Development with Unlimited Supplies of Labour'. *Manchester School of Economic and Social Studies*, 22(2): 139–91. https://doi.org/10.1111/j.1467-9957.1954.tb00021.x. Accessed: 13 September 2025.

Li, H., and H. F. Zou (1998). 'Income Inequality Is Not Harmful for Growth: Theory and Evidence'. *Review of Development Economics*, 2(3): 318–34. https://doi.org/10.1111/1467-9361.00045. Accessed: 13 September 2025.

Mayer, S. E. (2001). 'How Did the Increase in Economic Inequality between 1970 and 1990 Affect Children's Educational Attainment?'. *American*

Journal of Sociology, 107(1): 1–32. https://doi.org/10.1086/323149. Accessed: 13 September 2025.

Milanovic, B. (2016). 'Inequality within Countries: Introducing Kuznets Waves to Explain Long-Term Trends in Inequality'. In *Global Inequality: A New Approach for the Age of Globalization* (pp. 46–117). Boston: Harvard University Press.

Murphy, K. M., A. Shleifer and R. Vishny (1989). 'Income Distribution, Market Size and Industrialization'. *Quarterly Journal of Economics*, 104(3): 537–64. https://doi.org/10.2307/2937810. Accessed: 13 September 2025.

Neves, P. C., and S. M. T. Silva (2014). 'Inequality and Growth; Uncovering the Main Conclusions from the Empirics'. *Journal of Development Studies*, 50(1): 1–21. https://doi.org/10.1080/00220388.2013.841885. Accessed: 13 September 2025.

O'Donnell, O., E. van Doorslaer and T. van Ourti (2015). 'Health and Inequality'. In A.B. Atkinson and F. Bourguignon (eds), *Handbook of Income Distribution*, (Vol. 2b) (pp. 1419–533). Online: Elsevier.

OECD (2013). *OECD Guidelines on Measuring Subjective Wellbeing*. Paris: OECD.

Ostry, J. D., A. Berg and C. G. Tsangarides (2014). 'Redistribution, Inequality, and Growth', IMF Staff Discussion Note SDN/14/02. International Monetary Fund (IMF). https://doi.org/10.5089/9781484352076.006. Accessed: 13 September 2025.

Paukert, F. (1973). 'Income Distribution at Different Levels of Development: A Survey of the Evidence'. *International Labour Review*, 108: 97–125.

Perotti, R. (1996). 'Growth, Income Distribution, and Democracy: What the Data Say'. *Journal of Economic Growth*, 1: 149–87. https://doi.org/10.1007/BF00138861. Accessed: 13 September 2025.

Persson, T., and G. Tabellini (1994). 'Is Inequality Harmful for Growth?'. *American Economic Review*, 84(3): 600–21. https://www.jstor.org/stable/2118070. Accessed: 13 September 2025.

Pickett, K. E., and R. G. Wilkinson (2015). 'Income Inequality and Health: A Causal Review'. *Social Science & Medicine*, 128: 316–26.

https://doi.org/10.1016/j.socscimed.2014.12.031. Accessed: 13 September 2025.

Ravallion, M. (2016). 'Growth, Inequality, and Poverty'. In M. Ravallion (ed.), *The Economics of Poverty: History, Measurement, and Policy* (pp. 379–476). New York: Oxford University Press.

Ravallion, M., and S. Chen (1997). 'What Can New Survey Data Tell Us About Recent Changes in Distribution and Poverty?'. *World Bank Economic Review*, 11(2): 357–83. https://doi-org.ep.fjernadgang.kb.dk/10.1093/wber/11.2.357. Accessed: 13 September 2025.

Robinson, J. A. (2001). *Where Does Inequality Come From? Ideas and Implications for Latin America*. Paris: OECD Development Centre.

Smith, A. (1776). *An Inquiry into the Nature and Causes of the Wealth of Nations*. London: Strahan & Cadell.

Stiglitz, J. E. (1996). 'Some Lessons from the East Asian Miracle'. *World Bank Research Observer*, 11(2): 151–77. https://documents1.worldbank.org/curated/en/786661468245419348/pdf/765590JRN0WBRO00Box374378B00PUBLIC0.pdf. Accessed: 13 September 2025.

Sylwester, K. (2000). 'Income Inequality, Education Expenditures, and Growth'. *Journal of Development Economics*, 63(2): 379–98. https://doi.org/10.1016/S0304-3878(00)00113-9. Accessed: 13 September 2025.

Tanaka, R. (2003). 'Inequality as a Determinant of Child Labor'. *Economics Letters*, 80(1): 93–97. https://doi.org/10.1016/S0165-1765(03)00061-2. Accessed: 13 September 2025.

Tarp, F. (1981). 'Growth and Income Distribution in Developing Countries'. *Nationaløkonomisk Tidsskrift*, 119(1): 32–46. MPRA_paper_64174.pdf

Thorbecke, E. (2016). 'Inequality and the Trade-Off between Efficiency and Equity'. *Journal of Human Development and Capabilities*, 17(3): 460–64. https://doi.org/10.1080/19452829.2016.1203033. Accessed: 13 September 2025.

Tran, T., C. Nguyen and H. Van Vu (2018). 'Does Economic Inequality Affect the Quality of Life of Older People in Rural Vietnam?'. *Journal of Happiness Studies*, 19: 781–99. https://doi.org/10.1007/s10902-017-9851-4. Accessed: 13 September 2025.

UNDP (2024). *Human Development Report* online dataset. https://hdr.undp.org/data-center/human-development-index#/indicies/HDI (accessed 29 November 2024).

UNU-WIDER (2023). World Income Inequality Database (WIID), V. 28 November 2023.

Voitchovsky, S. (2005). 'Does the Profile of Income Inequality Matter for Economic Growth?: Distinguishing between the Effects of Inequality in Different Parts of the Income Distribution'. *Journal of Economic Growth*, 10: 273–96. https://doi.org/10.1007/s10887-005-3535-3. Accessed: 13 September 2025.

Voitchovsky, S. (2011). 'Inequality and Economic Growth'. In B. Nolan, W. Salverda, and T.M. Smeeding (eds), *Oxford Handbook of Economic Inequality* (pp. 549–74). Oxford: Oxford University Press.

Wagstaff, A., and E. van Doorslaer (2000). 'Income Inequality and Health: What Does the Literature Tell Us?'. *Annual Review of Public Health*, 21: 543–67. https://doi.org/10.1146/annurev.publhealth.21.1.543. Accessed: 13 September 2025.

World Bank (1993). *The East Asian Miracle*. New York: Oxford University Press.

World Bank (2016). *Poverty and Shared Prosperity 2016: Taking on Inequality*. Washington, DC: World Bank.

Zweimüller, J. (2000). 'Inequality, Redistribution and Economic Growth'. *Empirica*, 27: 1–20.

6

Inequality, governance and conflict

Economic inequality has potentially major impacts on numerous outcomes. In Chapter 5 we explored the impact on economic prosperity, growth and well-being. Now we turn to politics and governance, with particular attention to political polarization, social cohesion and trust, political inequality, democratic governance and transition, social mobilization and violent conflict.

These outcomes in turn also may influence, and be influenced by, economic outcomes. Inequality may lead to conflict, which may lead to the destruction of infrastructure and economic losses, and conversely economic outcomes may contribute to or mediate political harms. For instance, inequality in a time of economic regression may be more politically destabilizing than in a period of economic growth.

Economic inequality may influence political and governance outcomes via diverse channels, and we explore several such key outcomes and channels here. We begin with the linkages from inequality to political polarization, social cohesion and trust, and political inequality – which all figure prominently in popular narratives as well as in research. They are also all in themselves outcomes as well as factors that may influence other outcomes, including economic policy and growth, democratic stability and conflict.

Building on this discussion, we consider how economic inequality can be linked via these channels to democratic stability and the quality of governance. We focus on several key theories that hinge on the relationship between political elites and citizens with preferences regarding redistribution. Shifting gears, we turn to the impact of economic inequality on social mobilization and violent conflict.

Political polarization

The term 'polarization' is sometimes used to describe a situation in which groups have widely distinct characteristics or differing viewpoints (Bramson et al. 2016). Similarly, in social science research, various measures of polarization are built as a function of within-group and between-group inequality – often assessed in terms of income – and relative group size (Permanyer 2012). Jorda et al. (2023), for instance, introduce global and regional estimates of income polarization and bipolarization for the period 1960–2020, while Jorda, Niño-Zarazúa and Tejería-Martínez (2024) present new data on polarization in length of life along analogous lines. In this work, polarization can be understood as a straightforward function of inequality in the distribution of income or lifespan disparities.

But the concept of polarization also can imply more. It speaks not only to the existence of difference, but also to division, to the coalescence of 'us' versus 'them' camps with 'rigidly opposed beliefs and identities that inhibit cooperation and undermine pursuit of a common good' (Stewart et al. 2020). While inequality and polarization in this sense often go hand in hand, the relationship between the two requires more teasing out.

Polarization of views and identities within the political sphere (political polarization) is both an outcome of note in and of itself and, as we explore further below, a potentially key influence on other outcomes. Party politics are one important arena in which political polarization is observed and analysed.

Where partisan politics are fought along a traditional left–right spectrum, with positions towards economic redistribution key, the link from economic inequality to political polarization follows. In situations of high economic inequality, so expectations go, voters and the parties that represent them on the left will favour high redistributive government spending, while those on the right will oppose it. Evidence from elections in wealthy countries lends some qualified support to these expectations. For instance, using data on European national elections during 1996–2016, Gunderson (2022) finds that, under certain conditions, there is indeed a positive relationship between income inequality and party polarization on economic issues. However, this relationship does not hold when economic issues are not highly salient in elections and when partisans are not sorted by income.

The impact of rising inequality on political polarization, theory suggests, should operate especially through the positions of parties on the left. However, leftist parties in many countries over the past decades have moved towards the centre, seemingly out of alignment with popular concern over rising inequality. Such movement can be observed for instance in South Africa using data from the Comparative Manifestos Project, a project to map the salient issues in national political party manifestos across countries and elections (see Box 6.1).

Pontusson and Rueda (2008, 2010) point to several explanations. Considering the platforms of parties in ten OECD countries during 1966–2002, they show that inequality did indeed push core constituencies of left-wing parties farther to the left, but it also made some individuals less involved in politics. Moreover, in addition to trends in economic inequality, it is also important to consider the type of economic inequality (Pontusson and Rueda 2008). Parties on the left, they found, were more responsive to wage inequality, while parties on the right were more responsive to inequality in household disposable income.

Other factors, including psychological mechanisms and socialization within groups, also contribute to political polarization

(Jost, Baldassarri and Druckman 2022). Through within-group social interactions, 'new, shared social identity' is strengthened, and this in turn forms a basis for political mobilization and collective action (Smith et al. 2024).

Box 6.1: Comparative party manifestos in South Africa

Figure 6.1 shows the Comparative Manifestos Project mapping of South African party manifestos along two dimensions, left-right positioning (x-axis) and progressive-conservative (y-axis) during the 1999 elections, alongside trends from the first democratic elections in 1994. Several points are worth highlighting in this mapping. One is

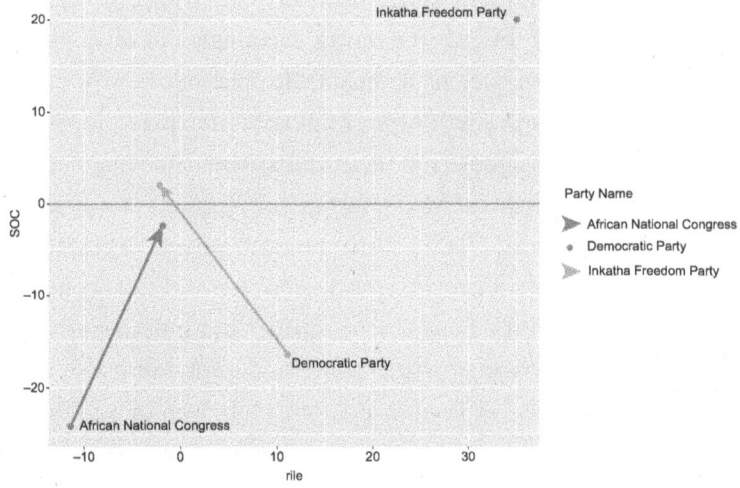

Figure 6.1 Political party positioning in South Africa, 1994–9, according to the Comparative Manifestos Project.

Inequality, Governance and Conflict 177

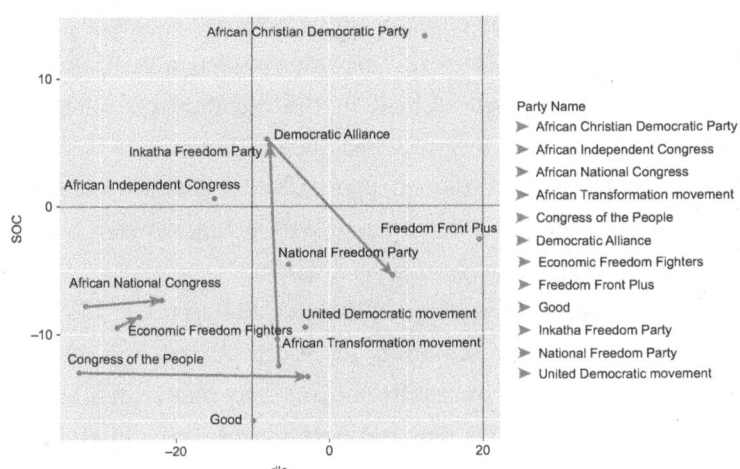

Figure 6.2 Political party positioning in South Africa 2014–19, according to the Comparative Manifestos Project.

Source: Data visualization from Manifesto Project Dataset version MPDS2024a, https://visuals.manifesto-project.wzb.eu/mpdb-shiny/cmp_dashboard_selectable/. Lehmann et al. (2024).

the observable spread on a left-right spectrum in the 1994 elections between South Africa's then two main parties, with the African National Congress clearly on the left and the Democratic Party clearly on the right. A second is the notable movement towards the centre (centre-left), with the two effectively indistinguishable on this dimension in 1999.

By the 2010s, South African party manifestos reveal a more diverse and fractionalized picture (Figure 6.2). A number of new parties have emerged, many, but not only, on the left. The ANC's positioning has moved significantly farther to the left overall when compared with the first elections after apartheid. Several parties, including the ANC, also shifted noticeably towards the centre along the left-right dimension between 2014 and 2019.

Political polarization makes governance more difficult – both enforcement of rules and engagement in collective action in support of the broader public interest. The link between polarization and political gridlock is well studied in the literature on established democracies, especially in the United States (Thurber and Yoshinaka 2015). In Global South countries – many of which have less established democratic systems, even if democracies – the link between political polarization and governance may be different.

For instance, Bornschier (2019)'s analysis of historical polarization and representation in South American countries, 1900–90, suggests that polarization can in fact play a useful role in facilitating stronger links between parties and voters in emerging democracies. Similarly, with attention to African countries, LeBas (2011) finds that polarization can contribute to stronger party organizations. Among the cases that Bornschier considers, Colombia offers important insight into how a lack of partisan polarization may be problematic for popular representation. Traditionally dominated by two elite parties, the Liberals and Conservatives, the Liberals in Colombia moved for a period to the left, appealing to the working class and other left-leaning voters (Collier and Collier 2002). But unlike in some of its neighbours (such as Uruguay) this left-right polarization was effectively dissolved after the civil war (La Violencia 1948–58), through the regime transition to democracy in 1958. Under the National Front, liberals and conservatives together held power, including alternating the presidency, excluding other parties from competing, and marginalizing the left. The collusion of the traditional oligarchic parties in this way meant that large segments of the population lacked true representation within the formal democratic system – a situation that may contribute to democratic breakdown and conflict, themes we return to more fully below.

Social cohesion and trust

Political polarization implies a lack of social cohesion, with those in the same country or community divided into opposing camps. Social cohesion conversely implies a situation characterized by trust, common identity, and cooperation for the common good (Leininger et al. 2021).

A significant body of research also points to the impact of inequality (among other factors) on trust, including evidence from both cross-country (Knack and Keefer 1997) and within-country analysis (Alesina and La Ferrara 2002; Gustavsson and Jordahl 2008). Indeed, simple comparison across countries of interpersonal trust at different levels of income inequality is suggestive of this relationship. Figure 6.3 plots inequality as measured by the Gini coefficient and interpersonal trust (as the share of people agreeing that 'most people can be trusted') drawn from the Integrated Values Surveys (2022).[1] As these data suggest, higher inequality tends to correspond with lower trust, and lower inequality with higher trust, but the relationship is far from perfect. This point is illustrated for instance through consideration of the four of our focus countries available within these data: Colombia and Vietnam follow broadly the general pattern. South Africa is a noticeable outlier with levels of trust that, while not that high, are significantly above what we might expect given the country's level of income inequality. Indeed, Ethiopia has a similar level of interpersonal trust to South Africa (both just over 20 per cent), but there is a wide gap in terms of income inequality as captured by the Gini coefficient between the two.

In linking economic inequality to lower trust and social cohesion, social networks appear to play a key role; we tend to trust those socially closer to us (Glaeser et al. 2000; Hardin 2006) in multiple ways, including in terms of income and wealth (Jordahl 2009).

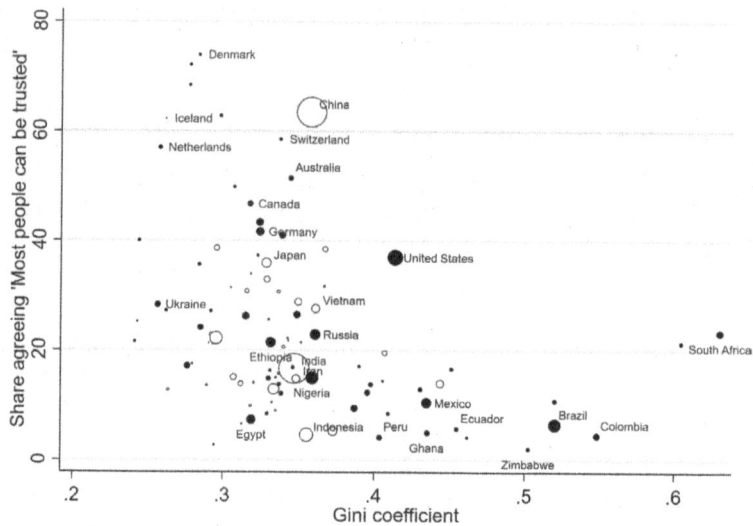

Figure 6.3 Interpersonal trust versus income inequality.

Source: Authors' illustration using data from Our World in Data (OurWorldinData.org/trust), based on original data from the Integrated Values Survey (2022) and World Bank Poverty and Inequality Platform (2024).

Notes: Trust data (share of individuals agreeing that 'most people can be trusted') corresponds to the latest survey wave for each country in the period 2009-2022. Inequality data refers to income measured after taxes and benefits, or to consumption, per capita, depending on the country and year.

Material inequality, and perceptions of inequality, may also reduce trust in other ways (Bobzien 2023). For instance, the perception by those less well-off that inequality is unfair, implying their exploitation by the rich, also may contribute to lower levels of interpersonal trust (Alesina and Angeletos 2005; Fischer and Torgler 2006; Jordahl 2009). Similarly, competition over scarce resources in situations of inequality may contribute to lower social trust (De Courson and Nettle 2021).

The impact of inequality on the erosion of trust, violence and weakened community life suggests that it harms affiliative social strategies and promotes increased status competition (Wilkinson and Pickett 2009: 508), giving rise to a variety of health and social problems, from poor health to increased crime rates. Trust too is important for governance (Braithwaite and Levi 2003). And as much as trust and social cohesion may be influenced by inequality, they may also mediate the relationship between inequality on the one hand and governance and conflict on the other (see Justino 2025). Interpersonal trust, as well as trust in government specifically, may influence the willingness of individuals to comply with government rules and demands. Trust in government also may weaken when governments behave in an untrustworthy manner (Norris 2022).

Drawing on a large-scale lab-in-the-field public goods experiment across fifty-six communes in rural Vietnam, Markussen et al. (2021) shed new light on this latter relationship. Among a small number of such studies conducted in Global South countries, their results suggest that inequality may serve to discourage voluntary cooperation, especially in environments where corruption is high. An important underlying mechanism identified is that corruption negatively influences individuals' beliefs about others' cooperation – that is, the impact of inequality is mediated by trust that others will behave pro-socially.

Political inequality and the concentration of power

Another negative implication of economic inequality is political inequality, that is, when some individuals or groups within a polity have greater (or lesser) ability to influence governance than others (see Beramendi, Besley and Levi 2024). The concept of political equality is core to democracy and implicit in democratic theory. In the work of Dahl (1971), for instance, which we introduced in Chapter 2, institutional guarantees in democracy function to provide equal access to representation and the potential to influence government policy-making, a playing field level for, and inclusive of, all players. But even in established democracies with robust institutions designed to support the free and equal exercise of political rights, political power is often unequally distributed. Political inequality, including its links with economic inequality, is a major issue of societal concern in established and high-income democracies, such as the United States and the UK (Ansell and Gingrich 2024).

In non-democratic countries, norms of political equality may be very different. In one sense, political equality is lower in all autocracies, as they are governed by an individual, or group of individuals, not chosen to lead from among and by all citizens. In this sense, inequality in political influence is an explicit feature of autocratic systems. Yet that does not mean that political equality is necessarily unimportant in non-democracies. Our research in Vietnam, for instance, underscores the attention in national government strategy to equal opportunities to public resources for all, as well as to participation and accountability at local levels.[2] The Vietnam Provincial Governance and Public Administration Performance Index (PAPI) speaks to political equality in this sense, measuring citizen experiences and perceptions of policy-making and implementation, as well as public service delivery, across Vietnam's provinces. It collects data on over a hundred indicators, including on participation at local levels, transparency in decision-making, vertical accountability and public service delivery (see Hoang et al. 2024).

Economic inequality may translate into political inequality in multiple ways (Houle 2018). On the one hand, in both democracies and non-democracies, it may do so organically, via the influence of greater economic resources on education, access to information and (non-work) time to participate actively and effectively in civic life. Studies on the United States, for example, show clear correlation between socioeconomic status and political participation, whether voting, campaigning, communal activity or interaction with public officials (Verba and Nie 1987). Studying elections across advanced industrialized countries, Solt (2008) finds that income inequality depresses participation in elections for all but the most affluent voters, but the evidence across a broader sample of countries is not strong (Stockemer and Parent 2014; Stockemer and Scruggs 2012).

Economic inequality may also translate into political inequality through more purposive efforts by the wealthy to use their economic advantages for political gain. Wealth may be translated into political influence through 'normal', legal channels such as political contributions. Research on the United States, for one, points to clear linkage between rising economic inequality and increasing concentration of political donations among the largest donors (Bonica et al. 2013). There is considerable variation across countries in political finance regulations which can help to mediate the link from economic inequality to political inequality. Such variation is illustrated in International IDEA's Political Finance Database which compiles information on bans and limits on private income, public funding, regulations on spending, and reporting, oversight and sanctions for countries around the world. These data show, for example, that many countries – including Mozambique and Ethiopia, as well as much of Africa, Asia and Europe – have no limits on the amount a donor can contribute to a political party during an election. In contrast, Colombia, along with most countries in the Americas, impose limits. South Africa also has contribution limits for both natural and legal persons, which apply during both nonelection and election periods.[3]

Likewise, the wealthy may more directly (attempt to) influence political decision-making and governance to their advantage via irregular, illegal channels such as bribes to public officials. As we saw in Chapter 5, economic inequality may give rise to greater rent-seeking activity by the wealthy, serving to weaken legal and regulatory frameworks and institutions more generally. Analysing data across 129 countries, Jong-sung and Khagram (2005) find support for the claim that income inequality increases the level of corruption, and other work demonstrates support for a causal relationship between inequality and poorer institutional quality (Chong and Gradstein 2007; Easterly 2007).

Another key channel through which economic inequality may translate into political inequality is through relationships with voters, including vote-buying, as well as other activities such as the financing of voter intimidation. Evidence suggests across diverse contexts that the poor are disproportionately more likely than the wealthy to be targets of vote-buying (Jensen and Justesen 2014; Ravanilla and Hicken 2023). While we expect vote-buying to mean weakened political representation for poor voters, Gallego, Guardado and Wantchekon (2023) argue provocatively that vote-buying in fact has limited electoral impact – based on analysis of seventeen sub-Saharan African (2000–05) and twenty Latin American (2005–10) elections. Many voters, their analysis suggests, receive electoral handouts (cash, gifts) and vote according to their preferences. In eleven of thirty-seven elections, such electoral handouts also were correlated with higher turnout.

Economic elites additionally may engage directly in politics themselves, including standing for office and forming their own parties. For instance, a recent blog on Ethiopian politics published in the IPI Global Observatory observes that 'some parties are about monetization, not representation'. One of the key factors contributing to the general ineffectiveness of Ethiopian parties, Gashaw (2024) argues, is the fact of leader-owned parties that are 'really dynasties in disguise', 'considered to be the private property of one or a few individuals who preside over the elections and position appointments within the party'.

Economic inequality can also translate into political inequality through the outsized influence of the wealthy in other spheres – from the media and sources of information to individual and corporate charitable giving (Cagé 2024). The risks of media concentration and ownership as an influence on democracy have been well studied in wealthy countries (Baker 2006) with increasing global attention (Noam and Concentration Collaboration 2016). In South Africa, one of the few Global South countries for which such analysis has been done, Angelopulo et al. (2016) document a high degree of concentration of ownership in the media, both before and after its democratic transition in 1994.

Influenced by economic inequality, political inequality in turn may shape both representation and the substance of policymaking and governance, and through that economic inequality, thus creating a looping effect (Erikson 2015; Piketty 2013). Politicians and others with political power also may reap economic benefits directly. For instance, Mozambique's ruling party Frelimo, traditionally anti-capitalist with a base in labour, 'has mobilised organizational and financial resources to actively create or recruit interests arising from the shift to a market economy' over the last several decades, thus 'to imbue private sector development with a distinctly partisan character' (Pitcher 2017: 9). Drawing on a new database on companies registered in Mozambique since independence, Jones, Schilling and Tarp (2026) present quantitative evidence that politicians reap clear benefits to their business interests from holding office.

Inequality and democracy

Economic inequality influences democracy through multiple channels. As the discussion above suggests, key channels operate on the one hand via influence on political polarization, social cohesion and trust, and political inequality. The impact of economic inequality in the discussion above is largely linear – that is, as economic inequality increases, so does its negative impact – and this in turn influences negatively the functioning and quality of democratic governance, and democratic stability. For instance, McCoy, Rahman and Somer (2018) set out three negative outcomes of polarization for democracy – 'gridlock and careening', 'democratic erosion or collapse under new elites and dominant groups' and 'democratic erosion or collapse under old elites and dominant groups'. (They also identify one possible positive outcome, 'reformed democracy'.) They provide illustration with four cases: Hungary, United States, Turkey and Venezuela. Nunn, Qian and Wen (2023) analyse the relationship between trust and political turnover in an annual panel of countries from 1951 to 2014, finding that trust tempers the impact of negative economic shocks, thus facilitating political stability in uncertain times.

More broadly, classic theories of democracy and democratic transition point to the role of distributive conflict between classes (landed aristocracy, bourgeoisie, peasantry, etc.) in influencing the nature of the political regimes that emerge (Moore 1966; Skocpol 1979). More recent work links distributive conflict explicitly with economic inequality, offering rationalist models of democratic transition and stability as a game or negotiation played out between the poor and rich, or citizens and wealthy elites, over redistribution and repression. We consider two such arguments here (see also Ansell and Samuels 2014; Houle 2009; Lizzeri and Persico 2004):

Boix (2003) explains the emergence of democracy via the interaction of three influences – economic inequality, capital mobility and the balance of power. Higher levels of economic *equality* for one, strengthen the likelihood of democracy because at higher levels of equality, popular pressures for redistribution are weaker, meaning a transition from autocracy to democracy is less costly for wealthy elites (the owners of productive assets). The costs of the repressive apparatus needed to maintain dictatorship then exceed the cost of the tax elites would bear under a democratic system with universal suffrage.

Increasing mobility of capital, through its influence on tax rates, also influences elites' willingness to accede to democratic demands.

When elites can hide their capital, or move it abroad to avoid taxation, the costs and pressure of redistributive taxation also decline – and with it elite resistance to democratic transition. Finally, the balance of power and degree of political mobilization by the poor and working classes influence political outcomes. Bringing these three factors together predicts at once the emergence of democracy (when economic inequality is moderate, or assets highly mobile and the working classes mobilized), or political violence (when inequality is high, capital is not mobile and the working classes mobilized).

A second key argument is Acemoglu and Robinson's (2006), which predicts a non-linear, inverted U-shaped relationship between economic inequality and democratic transition. When inequality is low, citizens have weak incentives to demand change in the system and elites maintain the status quo. When inequality is very high, citizens have strong incentive to demand redistribution, which will be implemented if democracy is achieved. For elites then, in a situation of high inequality, the costs of repression are less than the costs of acceding to democracy and to citizens' preferred policies of redistribution – leading to repressive non-democracy, or revolution. At mid-range inequality, however, demands for redistribution will be less and the costs of repression greater than the costs of democratic transition.

Both arguments are compelling, but whether they hold up empirically across countries is open to debate. While Boix (2003) offers empirical support for his argument in analysis of cross-country data for 1950–90 (see also Boix and Stokes 2003), Acemoglu and Robinson (2006) do not directly test their core hypothesis across countries (see Caeiro, Gisselquist and Puzon 2025). Analyses by others point to mixed support. For instance, using an original dataset of third-wave democratic transitions and reversals, Haggard and Kaufman (2012) focus on the distributive conflict mechanism posited in these theories, showing that distributive conflict is present in just over half of the cases – while substantial numbers of transitions do occur in cases with high inequality. More broadly, Barro (1999), for one, identifies a negative but only marginally significant impact for inequality on democracy, while Houle (2009) shows a weakly *positive* and insignificant relationship (see also Przeworski et al. 2000; Teorell 2012; Caeiro and Gisselquist 2025).[4]

Popular mobilization and violent conflict

Inequality is often linked to popular mobilization as both a cause and a rallying cry. In recent years the Occupy Wall Street movement is one such example of popular mobilization explicitly around inequality. Yagci (2017) analysed 398 Occupy protests in 180 countries and found inequality associated with a higher rate of protest.

The type of inequality also may matter. In a systematic review of quantitative work, Franc and Pavlović (2023) find that the literature points to sociopolitical inequality as more relevant than economic inequality for radicalization.

Economic inequality additionally may contribute to social mobilization and the emergence of violent conflict via its impact on polarization (Esteban and Schneider 2008), weak trust and social cohesion (Weipert-Fenner et al. 2024), political inequality (Justino 2025), and democratic instability and breakdown. Interestingly, the link between economic inequality and conflict overall has had only mixed support in the literature (Østby 2013). Indeed, Collier and Hoeffler (1998) analysing a dataset on civil wars 1965–99, found that inequality had no systematic effect on the risk of civil war, while Alesina and Perotti (1996)'s analysis of cross-country data for 1960–85 found a relationship between higher income inequality and higher levels of sociopolitical instability, as measured by instances of violence and political unrest.

Justino (2025) argues that two conditions influence whether economic inequality results in non-violent or violent social mobilization, and in violent conflict. In brief: 'Forms of social mobilization become violent when antagonism is the dominant form of social interaction between different social groups in unequal societies *and* when each of these social groups exhibits high levels of internal coordination.' The first condition relates to social cooperation between groups (and is closely related to political polarization as discussed here).

Thorbecke and Charumilind (2002) identify two different mechanisms through which inequality may lead to political violence. The first is the relative deprivation hypothesis. In Gurr (1968)'s terms, relative deprivation refers to an 'actor's perceptions of discrepancy between their value expectations (the goods and conditions of the life to which they believe they are justifiably entitled) and their value capabilities (the amounts of those goods and conditions that they think they are able to get and keep)'. As we have explored in Chapter 4, economic inequality is reflected through individuals' cognition and it is these perceptions, more than material 'facts', that drive behaviour. Relative deprivation in Gurr's sense links closely with perceptions of economic inequality, along with related sense of (lack of) fairness. Discontent linked with relative deprivation does not always lead to mobilization and violence; other factors would contribute, such as the legitimacy of the regime.

The second hypothesis is the resource mobilization hypothesis, which (like Justino's second condition) relates to the organizational capacity of (potential) dissident groups, including their ability to access resources necessary for their effective functioning.

Higher levels of inequality thus 'raise the probability that at least some dissident groups will be able to organize for aggressive collective action' (Muller and Seligson 1987); the authors argue that income inequality, more than agrarian inequality, matters for such mobilization. Colombia's case may be one exception. As Berry (2017) describes, one of the key contributing factors to the conflict was the heavy concentration of land within a small elite group, which contributed to grievances and a strong sense of injustice among peasants. Notably, estimates suggest only less than a quarter of current large landholdings were acquired through legitimate means. Other key factors included discriminatory economic institutions alongside political repression and, as we have discussed above, exclusion and lack of real representation in electoral politics. Raúl Reyes, second-in-command in the Revolutionary Armed Forces of Colombia (FARC), summed up the causes of the conflict thus in a 2007 interview: 'The gap between the rich and the poor grows and popular discontent grows and so does repression against those who dare to express their discontent through legal means. Often they are murdered, forced into exile, displaced by threats, or their goods are expropriated, then the number of guerrillas increases and the armed struggle grows' (Leech 2007).

Summary

Table 6.1 presents a schematic representation of some of the key mechanisms elaborated above through which inequality leads to negative political and governance outcomes. As in Chapter 5, these mechanisms might be grouped based on where in the income spectrum the key actors are located – whether they are poor, wealthy, or in between. In highly unequal systems, for instance, the weakening of institutions may come about especially through efforts by the wealthy to subvert the regulatory and legal framework towards their own ends. The poor in turn, reacting to the inequality of the system, may play a key role in driving social unrest and political violence (which in turn may have different outcomes depending

Table 6.1 Key mechanisms through which inequality impacts political and governance outcomes

Outcomes driven by…	Mechanism	Consequence
The wealthy	Subversion of regulatory and legal framework towards their own ends	Weak institutions
All/average or interaction	Less well-endowed median voter favors high redistribution	Resistance by wealthy elites to democratic governance
	Small middle class	Weak demand and mobilization for democracy
	Polarization	Weak social cohesion and trust; political gridlock
The poor	Social discontent and mobilization	Social unrest and political violence

Source: Adapted from Ferreira, Gisselquist and Tarp (2022).

on the response of political elites and the state). Other mechanisms discussed in the literature operate more through the actions of those somewhere in between (the median voter, the middle class) or the overall distribution (polarization).

Key takeaways

- Economic inequality has potentially major impacts on politics and governance. It may contribute to political polarization, lack of social cohesion and trust, and political inequality, as well to violent conflict, political instability and regime transition.
- Such impact also may influence economic outcomes, and the state of the economy may in turn impact politics, engendering political discontent and instability.
- To understand the mechanisms underlying such impact, it is useful to consider actors in different parts of the income distribution – the poor, the wealthy, and those in between. The

literature posits diverse ways in which their action and interaction may drive outcomes.

Notes

1. EVS (2022); Haerpfer et al. (2022).
2. In the terms used by the Government of Vietnam in Resolution No.136/NQ-CP on sustainable development goals, to 'create conditions for everyone and every community in society to have equal opportunities to develop, *access common resources and participate, contribute and benefit*, creating foundations-good material, knowledge and culture for future generations; leave no one behind, reach the hardest to reach first, including children, women, the elderly, the poor, people with disabilities and people in areas with poor socio-economic conditions and difficulties, border areas, islands and other vulnerable groups': (authors' italics) from Nguyen and Tarp (2024: 2).
3. The political finance landscape is evolving. This discussion is based on the 2022 database and does not reflect more recent changes. For details see https://www.idea.int.developmentzone.co/data-tools/data/political-finance-database.
4. Still other empirical analyses appear suggestive of different relationships (see, e.g., Puzon 2023 using a k-means clustering approach).

References

Acemoglu, D., and J. A Robinson (2006). *Economic origins of dictatorship and democracy.* **Cambridge: Cambridge University Press. http://www.loc.gov/catdir/toc/ecip0511/2005011262.html. Publisher description http://www.loc.gov/catdir/enhancements/fy0633/2005011262-d.html. Accessed: 13 September 2025.**

Alesina, A., and E. La Ferrara (2002). 'Who Trusts Others?'. *Journal of Public Economics*, 85(2): 207–34. https://doi.org/https://doi.org/10.1016/S0047-2727(01)00084-6. Accessed: 13 September 2025.

Alesina, A., and G. M. Angeletos (2005). 'Fairness and Redistribution'. *American Economic Review*, 95(4): 960–80. https://doi.org/10.1257/0002828054825655. Accessed: 13 September 2025.

Alesina, A., and R. Perotti (1996). 'Income Distribution, Political Instability, and Investment'. *European Economic Review*, 40(6): 1203–28. https://doi.org/https://doi.org/10.1016/0014-2921(95)00030-5. Accessed: 13 September 2025.

Angelopulo, G., P. H. Potgieter, E. Noam and P. Mutter (2016). 'Media Ownership and Concentration in South Africa'. In *Who Owns the World's Media?: Media Concentration and Ownership around the World* (pp. 986–1014). Oxford: Oxford: Oxford University Press. https://doi.org/10.1093/acprof:oso/9780199987238.003.0031. Accessed: 13 September 2025.

Ansell, B., and J. Gingrich (2024). 'Political Inequality'. *Oxford Open Economics*, 3(1): i233-61. https://doi.org/10.1093/ooec/odad043. Accessed: 13 September 2025.

Ansell, B. W., and D. J. Samuels (2014). *Inequality and Democratization: An Elite-Competition Approach*. Cambridge: Cambridge University Press.

Baker, C. E. (2006). *Media Concentration and Ownership: Why Ownership Matters*. Cambridge: Cambridge University Press.

Barro, R. J. (1999). 'Determinants of Democracy'. *Journal of Political Economy*, 107(S6): 158–83. https://doi.org/10.1086/250107. Accessed: 13 September 2025.

Beramendi, P., T. Besley and M. Levi (2024). 'Political Equality: What Is It and Why Does It Matter?'. *Oxford Open Economics*, 3(1): i262–81. https://doi.org/10.1093/ooec/odad055. Accessed: 13 September 2025.

Berry, R. A. (2017). 'Reflections on Injustice, Inequality and Land Conflict in Colombia'. *Canadian Journal of Latin American and Caribbean Studies / Revue canadienne des études latino-américaines et caraïbes*, 42(3): 277–97. https://doi.org/10.1080/08263663.2017.1378400. Accessed: 13 September 2025.

Bobzien, L. (2023). 'Income Inequality and Political Trust: Do Fairness Perceptions Matter?'. *Social Indicators Research*, 169(1): 505–528. https://doi.org/10.1007/s11205-023-03168-9. Accessed: 13 September 2025.

Boix, C. (2003). *Democracy and Redistribution*. Cambridge: Cambridge University Press.

Boix, C. and S. C. Stokes (2003). 'Endogenous Democratization'. *World Politics*, 55(4): 517.

Bonica, A., N. McCarty, K. T. Poole and H. Rosenthal (2013). 'Why Hasn't Democracy Slowed Rising Inequality?'. *Journal of Economic Perspectives*, 27(3): 103–24. https://doi.org/10.1257/jep.27.3.103. Accessed: 13 September 2025.

Bornschier, S. (2019). 'Historical Polarization and Representation in South American Party Systems, 1900–1990'. *British Journal of Political Science*, 49(1): 153–79. https://doi.org/10.1017/S0007123416000387. Accessed: 13 September 2025.

Braithwaite, V., and M. Levi (eds) (2003). *Trust and Governance*. New York: Russell Sage Foundation.

Bramson, A., P. Grim, D. J. Singer, S. Fisher, W. Berger, G. Sack, and C. Flocken, C. (2016). 'Disambiguation of social polarization concepts and measures'. *The Journal of Mathematical Sociology*, 40(2), 80–111. https://doi.org/10.1080/0022250X.2016.1147443. Accessed: 13 September 2025.

*Caeiro, R. M., and R. M. Gisselquist (2025 forthcoming). 'Democracy, Inequality and Exclusion: A Research Note'. UNU-WIDER Working Paper.

*Caeiro, R. M., R. M. Gisselquist and K. A. Puzon (2025). 'Inequality, Income, and Democracy in Perspective: Insights from Novel Data Analysis'. WIDER Working Paper 2025/32. Helsinki: UNU-WDIER.

Cagé, J. (2024). 'Political Inequality'. *Annual Review of Economics*, 16: 455–90. https://doi.org/https://doi.org/10.1146/annurev-economics-080223-040921. Accessed: 13 September 2025.

Chong, A., and M. Gradstein (2007). 'Inequality and Institutions'. *Review of Economics and Statistics*, 89(3): 454–65. https://doi.org/10.1162/rest.89.3.454. Accessed: 13 September 2025.

Collier, P., and A. Hoeffler (1998). 'On Economic Causes of Civil War'. *Oxford Economic Papers*, 50(4): 563–73. https://doi.org/10.1093/oep/50.4.563. Accessed: 13 September 2025.

Collier, R. B., and D. Collier (2002). *Sharing the Political Arena: Critical Junctures, the Labor Movement, and Regime Dynamics in Latin America*. Notre Dame: University of Notre Dame Press.

Dahl, R. A. (1971). *Polyarchy: Participation and Opposition*. New Haven: Yale University Press.

De Courson, B., and D. Nettle (2021). 'Why Do Inequality and Deprivation Produce High Crime and Low Trust?'. *Scientific Reports*, 11(1): 19–37. https://doi.org/10.1038/s41598-020-80897-8. Accessed: 13 September 2025.

Easterly, W. (2007). 'Inequality Does Cause Underdevelopment: Insights from a New Instrument'. *Journal of Development Economics*, 84(2): 755–76. https://doi.org/https://doi.org/10.1016/j.jdeveco.2006.11.002. Accessed: 13 September 2025.

Erikson, R. S. (2015). 'Income Inequality and Policy Responsiveness'. *Annual Review of Political Science*, 18: 11–29. https://doi.org/https://doi.org/10.1146/annurev-polisci-020614-094706. Accessed: 13 September 2025.

Esteban, J., and G. Schneider (2008). 'Polarization and Conflict: Theoretical and Empirical Issues', *Journal of Peace Research*, 45(2): 131–41. https://doi.org/10.1177/0022343307087168. Accessed: 13 September 2025.

EVS (2022). EVS Trend File 1981-2017. GESIS Data Archive, Cologne. ZA7503 Data file Version 3.0.0. doi:10.4232/1.14021

*Ferreira, I. A., Gisselquist, R. M. and F. Tarp (2022). 'On the Impact of Inequality on Growth, Human Development, and Governance'. *International Studies Review*, 24(1):. https://doi.org/10.1093/isr/viab 058. Accessed: 13 September 2025.

Fischer, J. A. V., and B. Torgler. (2006). 'The Effect of Relative Income Position on Social Capital'. *Economics Bulletin*, 26(4): 1–20.

Franc, R., and T. Pavlović (2023). 'Inequality and Radicalisation: Systematic Review of Quantitative Studies'. *Terrorism and Political Violence*, 35(4): 785–810. https://doi.org/10.1080/09546553.2021.1974845. Accessed: 13 September 2025.

Gallego, J., J. Guardado and L. Wantchekon (2023). 'Do Gifts Buy Votes? Evidence from Sub-Saharan Africa and Latin America'. *World*

Development, 162: 106125. https://doi.org/https://doi.org/10.1016/j.worlddev.2022.106125. Accessed: 13 September 2025.

Gashaw, T. (2024). 'In Ethiopian Politics, Some Parties Are About Monetization, Not Representation', *IPI Global Observatory*. 27 September. https://theglobalobservatory.org/2024/09/in-ethiopian-politics-some-parties-are-about-monetization-not-representation/.

Glaeser, E. L., D. I. Laibson, J. A. Scheinkman and C.L. Soutter (2000). 'Measuring Trust'. *Quarterly Journal of Economics*, 115(3): 811–46. https://doi.org/10.1162/003355300554926. Accessed: 13 September 2025.

Gunderson, J. R. (2022). 'When Does Income Inequality Cause Polarization?'. *British Journal of Political Science*, 52(3): 1315–32. https://doi.org/10.1017/S0007123421000053. Accessed: 13 September 2025.

Gurr, T. (1968). 'Urban Disorder: Perspectives From the Comparative Study of Civil Strife'. *American Behavioral Scientist*, 11(4): 50–55. https://doi.org/10.1177/000276426801100414. Accessed: 13 September 2025.

Gustavsson, M., and H. Jordahl (2008). 'Inequality and Trust in Sweden: Some Inequalities are More Harmful Than Others'. *Journal of Public Economics*, 92(1): 348–65. https://doi.org/https://doi.org/10.1016/j.jpubeco.2007.06.010. Accessed: 13 September 2025.

Haerpfer, C., R. Inglehart, A. Moreno, C. Welzel, K. Kizilova, J. Diez-Medrano, M. Lagos, P. Norris, E. Ponarin and B. Puranen (eds) (2022). World Values Survey Trend File (1981-2022) Cross-National Data-Set. Madrid and Vienna: JD Systems Institute and WVSA Secretariat. Data File Version 4.0.0, doi:10.14281/18241.27.

Haggard, S., and R. R. Kaufman (2012). 'Inequality and Regime Change: Democratic Transitions and the Stability of Democratic Rule'. *American Political Science Review*, 106(03): 495–516. https://doi.org/doi:10.1017/S0003055412000287. Accessed: 13 September 2025.

Hardin, R. (2006). *Trust*. Bristol: Polity Press.

*Hoang, T. K., K. A. M. Puzon, H. T. T. Dang and R. M. Gisselquist (2024). 'Inequality and Institutional Outcomes in Viet Nam: A Combined Principal Components and Clustering Analysis'. WIDER Working Paper 2024/38. Helsinki: UNU-WIDER

Houle, C. (2009). 'Inequality and Democracy: Why Inequality Harms Consolidation but Does Not Affect Democratization'. *World Politics*, 61(4): 589–622.

Houle, C. (2018). 'Does Economic Inequality Breed Political Inequality?'. *Democratization*, 25(8): 1500–18. https://doi.org/10.1080/13510 347.2018.1487405. Accessed: 13 September 2025.

Jensen, P. S., and M. K. Justesen (2014). 'Poverty and Vote Buying: Survey-Based Evidence from Africa'. *Electoral Studies*, 33: 220–32. https://doi.org/https://doi.org/10.1016/j.electstud.2013.07.020. Accessed: 13 September 2025.

Jones, S., F. Schilling and F. Tarp (2026). 'Politicians doing business: Evidence from Mozambique'. *Journal of Development Economics*, 178: art. 103584. https://doi.org/10.1016/j.jdeveco.2025.103584. Accessed: 17 October 2025.

Jong-sung, Y., and S. Khagram (2005). 'A Comparative Study of Inequality and Corruption'. *American Sociological Review*, 70(1): 136–57. https://doi.org/10.1177/000312240507000107. Accessed: 13 September 2025.

*Jorda, V., M. Niño-Zarazúa, L. Roope and F. Tarp (2023). 'Global Income Polarization: Relative and Absolute Perspectives'. WIDER Working Paper 2023/146. Helsinki: UNU-WIDER.

*Jorda, V., M. Niño-Zarazúa and M. Tejería-Martínez (2024). 'The Lifespan Disparity Dataset: An Open Repository on Inequality and Polarization in Length of Life (1950–2021)', *Scientific Data*, 11(1). https://doi.org/10.1038/s41597-024-03426-6. Accessed: 13 September 2025.

Jordahl, H. (2009). 'Economic Inequality'. In G. T. Svendsen and G. L. H. Svendsen (eds), *Handbook of Social Capital* (pp. 376–99). Cheltenham: Edward Elgar.

Jost, J. T., D. S. Baldassarri and J. N. Druckman, (2022). Cognitive-Motivational Mechanisms of Political Polarization in Social-Communicative Contexts'. *Nature Reviews Psychology*, 1(10): 560–76. https://doi.org/10.1038/s44159-022-00093-5. Accessed: 13 September 2025.

Justino, P. (2025). 'Revisiting the Links Between Economic Inequality and Political Violence: The Role of Social Mobilization'. *World

Development, 185: 106820. https://doi.org/https://doi.org/10.1016/j. worlddev.2024.106820. Accessed: 13 September 2025.

Knack, S., and P. Keefer (1997). 'Does Inequality Harm Growth Only in Democracies? A Replication and Extension'. *American Journal of Political Science*, 41(1): 323–32.

LeBas, A. (2011). *From Protest to Parties: Party-Building and Democratization in Africa*. Oxford: Oxford University Press.

Leech, G. (2007). 'Two Perspectives from the Colombian Left' [interview]. https://garryleech.com/2007/07/12/two-perspectives-from-the-colombian-left/. Accessed: 13 September 2025.

Lehmann, P., S. Franzmann, D. Al-Gaddooa, T. Burst, C. Ivanusch, S. Regel, F. Riethmüller, A. Volkens, B. Weßels and L. Zehnter (2024). *The Manifesto Data Collection. Manifesto Project (MRG/CMP/MARPOR). Version 2024a*. https://doi.org/https://doi.org/10.25522/manifesto. mpds.2024a. Accessed: 13 September 2025.

Leininger, J., F. Burchi, C. Fiedler, K. Mross, D. Nowack, A. von Schiller, C. Sommer, C. Strupat and S. Ziaja (2021). Social Cohesion: A New Definition and a Proposal for its Measurement in Africa', Discussion Paper 2021/31. Bonn: Deutsches Institut für Entwicklungspolitik. https://www.socialcohesion.info/library/publication/social-cohesion-africa-die-gdi. Accessed: 13 September 2025.

Lizzeri, A., and N. Persico (2004). 'Why Did the Elites Extend the Suffrage? Democracy and the Scope of Government, with an Application to Britain's "Age of Reform"'. *Quarterly Journal of Economics*, 119(2): 707–65. https://doi.org/10.1162/0033553041382175. Accessed: 13 September 2025.

*Markussen, T., S. Sharma, S. Singhal and F. Tarp (2021). 'Inequality, Institutions and Cooperation', *European Economic Review*, 138: 103842. https://doi.org/https://doi.org/10.1016/j.euroecorev.2021.103842. Accessed: 13 September 2025.

McCoy, J., T. Rahman and M. Somer (2018). 'Polarization and the Global Crisis of Democracy: Common Patterns, Dynamics, and Pernicious Consequences for Democratic Polities'. *American Behavioral Scientist*, 62(1): 16–42. https://doi.org/10.1177/0002764218759576. Accessed: 13 September 2025.

Moore, B., Jr. (1966). *Social Origins of Dictatorship and Democracy: Lord and Peasant in the Making of the Modern World* (1993 edn). Boston: Beacon Press.

Muller, E. N., and M. A. Seligson (1987). 'Inequality and Insurgency'. *American Political Science Review*, 81(2): 425–51. https://doi.org/10.2307/1961960. Accessed: 13 September 2025.

*Nguyen, C. V., and F. Tarp (2024). 'Socioeconomic Inequality in Viet Nam'. WIDER Working Paper 2024/61. Helsinki: UNU-WIDER

Noam, E. M., and The International Media Concentration Collaboration (2016). *Who Owns the World's Media?: Media Concentration and Ownership around the World*. Oxford: Oxford: Oxford University Press. https://doi.org/10.1093/acprof:oso/9780199987238.001.0001. Accessed: 13 September 2025.

Norris, P. (2022). *In Praise of Skepticism: Trust but Verify*. Oxford: Oxford University Press.

Nunn, N., N. Qian and J. Wen (2023). *Trust and Democracy: Political Stability in Times of Economic Crisis*. https://nathannunn.sites.olt.ubc.ca/files/2023/07/trust_leader_2023.2.13.pdf. Accessed: 13 September 2025.

Østby, G. (2013). 'Inequality and Political Violence: A Review of the Literature'. *International Area Studies Review*, 16(2): 206–31. https://doi.org/10.1177/2233865913490937. Accessed: 13 September 2025.

Permanyer, I. (2012). 'The Conceptualization and Measurement of Social Polarization [Journal Article]'. *The Journal of Economic Inequality*, 10(1): 45–74. https://doi.org/10.1007/s10888-010-9143-2. Accessed: 13 September 2025.

Piketty, T. (2013). *Le Capital au XXIe siècle*. Paris: Seuil.

Pitcher, M. A. (2017). 'Party System Competition and Private Sector Development in Africa'. *Journal of Development Studies*, 53(1): 1–17. https://doi.org/DOI: 10.1080/00220388.2016.117. Accessed: 13 September 2025.

Pontusson, J., and D. Rueda (2008). 'Inequality as a Source of Political Polarization: A Comparative Analysis of Twelve OECD Countries'. In P. Beramendi and C. J. Anderson (eds), *Democracy, Inequality, and Representation: A Comparative Perspective* (pp. 312–53). New York: Russell Sage Foundation.

Pontusson, J., and D. Rueda (2010). 'The Politics of Inequality: Voter Mobilization and Left Parties in Advanced Industrial States'. *Comparative Political Studies*, 43(6): 675–705. https://doi.org/10.1177/0010414009358672. Accessed: 13 September 2025.

Przeworski, A., M. Alvarez, J. Cheibub and F. Limongi. (2000). *Democracy and Development: Political Institutions and Wellbeing in the World 1950–1990*. Cambridge: Cambridge University Press.

*Puzon, K. A. M. (2023). 'Democracy Clusters and Patterns of Inequality: A k-means Approach'. WIDER Working Paper 72/2023. Helsinki: UNU-WIDER.

Ravanilla, N., and A. Hicken (2023). Poverty, Social Networks, and Clientelism'. *World Development*, 162: 106128.https://doi.org/https://doi.org/10.1016/j.worlddev.2022.106128. Accessed: 13 September 2025.

Skocpol, T. (1979). *States and Social Revolutions: A Comparative Analysis of France, Russia and China*. Cambridge: Cambridge University Press.

Smith, L. G. E., E. F. Thomas, A. M. Bliuc and C. McGarty (2024). 'Polarization is the Psychological Foundation of Collective Engagement'. *Communications Psychology*, 2(1):. https://doi.org/10.1038/s44271-024-00089-2. Accessed: 13 September 2025.

Solt, F. (2008). 'Economic Inequality and Democratic Political Engagement'. *American Journal of Political Science*, 52(1): 48–60. https://doi.org/https://doi.org/10.1111/j.1540-5907.2007.00298.x. Accessed: 13 September 2025.

Stewart, A. J., N. McCarty, and J.J. Bryson (2020). 'Polarization Under Rising Inequality and Economic Decline'. *Science Advances* 6(50): 1–9. https://doi.org/10.1126/sciadv.abd4201. Accessed: 13 September 2025.

Stockemer, D., and L. Scruggs (2012). 'Income Inequality, Development and Electoral Turnout: New Evidence on a Burgeoning Debate'. *Electoral Studies*, 31(4): 764–73. https://doi.org/https://doi.org/10.1016/j.electstud.2012.06.006. Accessed: 13 September 2025.

Stockemer, D., and S. Parent (2014). 'The Inequality Turnout Nexus: New Evidence from Presidential Elections'. *Politics and Policy*, 42(2): 221–45.

https://doi.org/https://doi.org/10.1111/polp.12067. Accessed: 13 September 2025.

Teorell, J. (2012). *Determinants of Democratization: Explaining Regime Change in the World, 1972-2006*. Cambridge: Cambridge University Press.

Thorbecke, E., and C. Charumilind (2002). 'Economic Inequality and Its Socioeconomic Impact'. *World Development*, 30(9): 1477-95. https://doi.org/https://doi.org/10.1016/S0305-750X(02)00052-9. **Accessed: 13 September 2025.**

Thurber, J. A., and A. Yoshinaka (eds) (2015). *American Gridlock: The Sources, Character, and Impact of Political Polarization*. Cambridge: Cambridge University Press.

Verba, S., and N. H. Nie. (1987 [1972]). *Participation in America: Political Democracy and Social Equality*. Chicago: University of Chicago Press.

Weipert-Fenner, I., F. M. Rossi, N. Sika and J. Wolff (2024). 'Trust and Social Movements: A New Research Agenda'. *International Journal of Comparative Sociology*, 65(4): 409-22. https://doi.org/10.1177/00207152241246216. Accessed: 13 September 2025.

Wilkinson, R. G., and K. E. Pickett (2009). 'Income Inequality and Social Dysfunction'. *Annual Review of Sociology*, 35: 493-511. https://doi.org/https://doi.org/10.1146/annurev-soc-070308-115926. **Accessed: 13 September 2025.**

Yagci, A. H. (2017). 'The Great Recession, Inequality and Occupy Protests Around the World'. *Government and Opposition*, 52(4): 640-70. https://doi.org/10.1017/gov.2016.3. Accessed: 13 September 2025.

7

What should be done? What can be done?

For many of us inequality raises deep concerns, both normative and consequential, calling for urgent, corrective action. For others inequality is less concerning, understood for instance as intrinsic to economic growth. 'Poverty bothers me,' an economist noted, 'Inequality does not. I just don't care.'[1]

In this chapter we reflect on these divergent perspectives and several others in between, asking both what should be done and what can be done to reduce inequality and to mediate its harms. We start with the question, extending from the discussion in Chapter 5: what are the possible trade-offs between attention to inequality and other key objectives? We reflect on diverse approaches, including how they fit (and do not fit) with different understandings of inequality.

We then turn to our second question: What can be done? We begin with a simple tripartite approach to the types of actions that national governments might undertake to address inequality by: (a) influencing through regulatory measures the income formation that results directly from the production process, and the distribution of it over the production factors (labour, capital); (b) changing the market-determined income distribution through taxes and transfers; and (c) building essential human capital of the poor and disadvantaged so they can reap greater return on labour efforts, which will in turn also promote growth and increase economic efficiency. We then consider several more detailed frameworks and diverse policy options.

Next, we approach the question of what can be done from a different angle: there are multiple policy options, yet also key constraints. For example, regulatory measures may be constrained in their effectiveness in institutionally weak environments and there are often limits to what can be done in practice through tax policy. Moreover, addressing inequality may involve major structural change, which can take considerable time. Effective state institutions are also important for regulating and implementing policies well. And, asking what can be done is not only a matter of identifying and evaluating policies, but also of assessing their political feasibility. What are the constraints to building the political will for adopting these policies and the institutional capacity for implementing them effectively over the long term? How might international organizations, civil society groups and individuals influence and support more inclusive policies?

Targeting inequality as a priority: Considerations and trade-offs

It is our job to glory in inequality and to see that talents and abilities are given vent and expression for the benefit of us all.
- British Prime Minister Margaret Thatcher[2]

Setting aside the lack of clarity that still undermines narratives on global inequality (as brought to light in Chapter 3), global discussions on inequality in recent years suggest broad consensus that inequality is a problem that needs addressing. But as Chapter 5 suggests, this has not always been the majority view – and there remains substantial debate over how important it should be relative to other goals, in particular economic efficiency and growth.

Historically, there has been weaker consensus around the aim of reducing inequality in comparison to that of reducing poverty, with a split between those justifying inequality as necessary for efficiency reasons and those warning about its ill-effects, including for poverty reduction.

The former position, justifying inequality, is generally in line with a more politically right-wing approach to the role of the state in market regulation and the economy more broadly. In this approach, the state should promote the functioning of private free markets, and the resulting income distribution should in general be accepted (Wade 2014: 109–10); regulations and redistribution erode the link between honest effort and its returns.

This approach has roots in classical economic thinking, which identifies a trade-off between equity and development (see Thorbecke 2016). Government intervention can result in a loss of efficiency, and inequality is needed to promote competition and to create incentives for innovation and risk-taking. The benefits of growth can then eventually 'trickle-down' to the poor and the rest of society (Wade 2014: 112).

The basic intuition underlying this trade-off was eloquently described by Okun (1975). As we illustrate in Figure 7.1, Okun compared the redistribution of money from the richer (represented on the left) to the poorer (represented on the right) to a leaky bucket transporting water, where the leaked water represented the money lost in the transfer process. This 'leak' symbolizes the losses due to

Figure 7.1 Visual representation of Okun's 'leaky bucket' metaphor.
Source: Authors' illustration.

higher tax rates on incentives to save and invest, as well as to exert effort (Baselgia and Foellmi 2022), and the costs associated with any transfer of income in a society.

We can assume a different perspective if we consider the concept of inequality of opportunities (Cerra, Lama and Loyaza 2021: 38), which we described in Chapter 2. On the one hand, like the mechanism described above, inequality of outcomes (i.e., income, consumption) may be needed to create incentives and may be perceived as fair when it rewards effort,[3] which concurs to the view that there is a trade-off between inequality and efficiency. On the other hand, inequality of opportunities will impede the poor and marginalized from contributing to growth and may also have efficiency costs as the economy does not benefit from the skills and contributions of all. It may further lead to social discontent, which speaks against a trade-off between equality of opportunity and growth. For instance, in Mozambique, roots of the social unrest that marked the period after its 2024 presidential election can be seen in a widespread sentiment among the population of not having access to opportunities to advance (Jones 2024).

Inequality reduction versus poverty reduction

The ideologies described in Chapter 5 provided arguments against the urgency of reducing inequality in poorer countries (Gradín, Leibbrandt and Tarp 2021: 3–4). According to the Kuznets inverted U-shaped curve, a reduction in inequality would eventually follow with the increases in income reaching a turning-point from a low level, and based on the classical arguments, it was essential to provide incentives and boost innovation efforts. Additionally, it was argued that pursuing inequality reductions could not be concomitant with promoting growth and achieving poverty reduction. We focus on the latter in the following paragraphs.

In simple mathematical terms, the relationship between poverty, growth and inequality (the 'iron triangle') means that changes in poverty levels are correlated with changes in levels of income and inequality *ceteris paribus*[4] – see Cerra, Lama and Loyaza (2021) for a review. This relationship implies that changes in inequality are decomposable into two effects: (i) a growth effect, which represents a proportional increase of all income with no changes in the distribution; and (ii) a distributional effect, which represents a change in the distribution of relative income (Bourguignon 2004). From this follows the stylized fact that higher levels of inequality require higher rates of growth to achieve a certain (proportionate) rate of reduction in poverty (Ferreira and Ravallion 2008: 20).

The trends in Ethiopia provide an illustrative example of this relationship. If we assume that higher growth rates will also lead to higher inequality, these two effects offset each other in terms of poverty reduction. Between 2011 and 2016 (the latest period with available data), inequality increased from a Gini index of 0.30 to 0.33 whereas the poverty rate based on the national poverty line reduced from 29.6 per cent to 23.5 per cent.

The 'Datt-Ravallion decomposition' technique is a method that breaks down the change in poverty into a change in average consumption (the growth effect) and a change in the distribution of consumption (or redistribution effect). Using this technique, we can see that, given the increase in inequality in Ethiopia during 2011–16, it was the growth component that led to the reduction in poverty (Table 7.1). Considering this period, the growth effect was -7.3, and thus poverty reducing, while the redistribution effect was 1.2, and therefore poverty increasing and counterweighted part of the poverty reduction effect from growth. The observed effect is a reduction of the poverty rate of six percentage points. If inequality had remained the same throughout the period, poverty would have decreased by over seven percentage points instead (World Bank Group 2020: 49).

Table 7.1 Datt-Ravallion decomposition: illustration from Ethiopia, 2011–16

Growth effect (changes in average consumption)	−7.3
Redistribution effect (changes in inequality)	+1.2
Poverty rate, national poverty line	*−6.1*

Source: Based on World Bank (2020: 49).

Ferreira (2010: 8) summarized three messages from empirical work on this relationship based on data from the 1980s to the early 2000s. First, while there is no correlation between growth and changes in inequality, inequality is a mediator in the relationship between growth and poverty. Second, as growth increases poverty declines, and third, the higher the initial level of inequality, the higher is the growth rate required to achieve the same amount of poverty reduction.

Thus, achieving similar levels of poverty reduction during periods of slower growth requires decreasing inequality, especially when considering relative poverty[5] (Ravallion 2016: 435). To illustrate, Lakner et al. (2022) present different simulations of global extreme poverty until 2030 considering different scenarios for the evolution of inequality and growth in each country. Under certain assumptions about the growth rate and with no changes in inequality, they predict that the global poverty rate will continue at around 7.4 per cent in 2030. Still, if inequality decreased by 1 per cent per year, the global poverty rate would fall to 6.3 per cent (Lakner et al. 2022: 560). The importance of increasing growth when compared with reducing inequality is further illustrated by their simulation showing that this 1 per cent decrease in inequality per year has a greater effect on global poverty than an increase in each country's annual growth rate that is 1 percentage point above the World Bank forecasts (Lakner et al. 2022: 560).[6]

Let us also think back to the discussion in Chapter 4 on how individuals may have different ways of thinking about inequality, namely in absolute or in relative terms. In contrast with the message that there is no robust evidence of a statistically significant link between growth and inequality, changes in income are directly linked to changes in absolute inequality, which increases with growth (and decreases with economic contraction). Thus, growth will at the same time lead to reduced poverty and to increased absolute inequality, which means that there may be a trade-off between the two goals (Ravallion 2016).

Returning to our question at the beginning of the section: Are there trade-offs between inequality and growth? The example from Vietnam, described in more detail in Box 7.1, is illustrative of how high levels of economic growth can be sustained together with stable inequality levels, and highlights the role of pro-poor policies to achieve that.

Box 7.1: Vietnam's growth-with-equity strategy

After peace and reunification in 1975, Vietnam pursued a national strategy inspired by communist central planning. However, in the mid-1980s the country gradually opened to more market-based approaches and started implementing an economic reform package (*Doi Moi*) in 1986. These reforms included the introduction of land tenure rights, market-based prices and competition, reform of the financial sector and laws promoting the development of the private sector (Arndt et al. 2012).

Since then, Vietnam's development is regarded as one of success. Starting from the position of one of the poorest countries in the world and with a population heavily reliant on small-farmer agriculture, the country has improved impressively. In the following decades, Vietnam experienced high annual growth rates of around 6 per cent (Nguyen and Tarp 2024) and graduated from being a low-income country to lower-*middle*-income status, and also experienced a noticeable reduction in poverty levels – from 58 per cent in 1993 to 19 per cent in 2004, and 14 per cent in 2008 (Nguyen and Pham 2018).

The growth with equity strategy implemented by the Vietnamese government in the 2000s has been broadly successful. This strategy included the launch of several poverty reduction programmes, supported by substantial amounts of official development assistance (Nguyen and Pham 2018). In addition to the considerable improvements in terms of poverty reduction, inequality levels remained low and stable over time and growth benefited the poor proportionally more than the rich during the 2000s (Nguyen and Pham 2018; Nguyen and Tarp 2024).

Note: For an historical perspective, see Tarp (2018). And for a more detailed account on the growth trajectory in Vietnam, see Tarp (2017).

Source: Arndt et al. (2012); Nguyen and Pham (2018); Nguyen and Tarp (2024).

Our reading of the extensive literature on this topic is that there may be some underlying trade-offs in terms of incentives, which are necessary to inspire behaviour that leads to growth (Cerra, Lama and Loyaza 2021). Still, even if inequality rises with growth, its pernicious effects can and should be countered by well-designed policies that remove barriers to access to markets and public goods, such as healthcare, education and justice (Stewart 2016; Cerra, Lama and Loyaza 2021). Moreover, redistributive policies can as already noted be growth- and efficiency-enhancing (Aghion, Caroli and García-Peñalosa 1999; World Bank 2016).

National policies to address inequality

Governments can seek to address economic inequality in three broad ways. First, they may influence market-based distributional outcomes, especially through regulation. Second, they can try to change the income distribution, via taxes and transfers. And third, they can build human capital, thus promoting the assets of poor and vulnerable people and their income generating capacity, which can support growth and increase the efficiency of the economy. Within each of these areas, policymakers face no shortage of potential policy tools to consider – strategies which might work and/or have worked in some contexts.

With focus on wealthy countries, Blanchard and Rodrik (2021) offer one useful framework for mapping the policy options. Their 'taxonomy' maps policies along two dimensions. First, at what stage of the economic production process does the intervention take place? They identify three stages (pre-production, production, and post-production) which correspond roughly, but not perfectly, to the three areas of policy outlined above. Second, which parts of the income distribution will the intervention impact (bottom, middle, top)? Their typology set out, for instance, how policies affecting the bottom of the income spectrum may intervene in the economy during the pre-production (e.g., endowment policies), production (minimum wages), or post-production stages (social transfers). By contrast, policies influencing inequality through their impact on the wealthy include inheritance/estate taxes (influencing pre-production endowments), regulations and antitrust laws (the production phase) and wealth taxes (post-production).

In Table 7.2 we bring together Blanchard and Rodrik's taxonomy with the approach to types of policies that we outlined at the start of this section.

The second dimension of this framework provides useful linkage to our discussion in Chapters 5 and 6 about the channels through which economic inequality may contribute to negative socio-political and economic outcomes. For instance, the influence of economic inequality on social discontent – among the poor – is a core mechanism identified in the literature through which inequality

Table 7.2 Policies affecting inequality: a framework of options

		Types of policies		
		Market-based	**Taxes and transfers**	**Human capital**
What kind of inequality do we care about?	Bottom	Minimum wage; job guarantees; full-employment	Social transfers (e.g., Earned Income Tax Credit); universal basic income	Endowment policies (health care, education)
	Middle	'Good jobs' policies; industrial relations and labour laws; sectoral wage boards; trade agreements; innovation policies; employee ownership	Safety nets; social insurance policies	Public spending on higher education
	Top	Regulations; antitrust laws	Inheritance/estate taxes; wealth taxes	

Source: Adapted from Blanchard and Rodrik (2021: xix).

impacts not only conflict but also economic growth and poor governance. The post-election conflicts in Mozambique in 2024 mentioned above are a concrete example. To mediate the harms of this mechanism, policymakers would be well advised to consider carefully interventions influencing inequality at the bottom end of spectrum – whether in labour, education, social protection or fiscal policy. Overall, Blanchard and Rodrik (2021) argue, 'no specific proposal will do the job by itself', that is, multiple policies are needed to address inequality in all parts of the income distribution and the various stages of its formation.

Moreover, there is no one-size-fits-all solution that works across every context. For high-income countries, they identify some 'low-hanging fruit': expanding tax credits to low-income households, increasing funding for early childhood education and tertiary education, redirecting subsidies to employment-friendly innovation, greater tax progressivity and policies to help workers organise unions. In extending this framework for consideration in low- and middle-income countries, differences in institutional capacity to implement such policies are important to consider.

They further underscore that which types of interventions to prioritize and which specific policies are most promising are not technical or economic questions alone, but also normative ones. Indeed as Drèze (2020) eloquently argues, effective policy-making relies not only on good evidence but also on sound understanding, value judgments and deliberation addressing differences in understanding and value judgments.

Jorda and Alonso (2020) present another useful framework for mapping diverse interventions to address income inequality and the research evidence on their impact. Their framework highlights policies in the same four broad areas: labour, education, social protection and fiscal policy.

As they outline, labour policies – such as minimum wage laws, training programmes and trade union legislation – directly influence labour demand and supply and, through this, earnings inequality. The overall effects of labour market policies on income inequality – whether positive or negative – however may be ambiguous. An increase in the minimum wage, for instance, increases earnings for affected workers, with a dampening effect on inequality, while at the same time may reduce labour demand. The net effect of new minimum wage policy on income inequality thus will depend on the wage elasticity of labour supply (in other words, how a change in the net wage affects labour supply) and the level of unemployment benefits. Moreover, the impact of labour policies will be dampened in contexts with a large informal economy and non-wage-earning labour force – as in many low and middle-income countries. State capacity to ensure compliance with labour policies also matters. For instance, in discussions around the introduction of South Africa's national minimum wage, implemented for the first time only in 2019, high non-compliance was among the key factors highlighted as having a dampening effect on the potential impact on poverty and inequality (Bhorat, Lilenstein and Stanwix 2020).

While there is a large literature on the impact of labour policies such as minimum wage laws in countries in the Global North, the literature on Global South countries is more limited. In terms of minimum wage laws, the former seems to suggest overall only a modest effect on inequality (Atkinson et al. 2017), while the latter points to potentially larger effects. For instance, Bogliacino and Rojas (2017) study the determinants of inequality in seventeen Latin American countries, including fiscal and labour market variables, and find that only the minimum wage is correlated with reductions in the Gini coefficient. Policies with respect to unions and resulting influence on unionization, appear arguably more promising based on the literature overall. Stronger unions may reduce inequality by reducing within-firm earnings differences, as well as by asserting more influence on policy-making that favours lower-income populations. On the other hand, unions may also contribute to inequalities between labour market 'insiders' and 'outsiders' (Lindbeck and Snower 2001). Nevertheless, the evidence base for developing countries is not robust; Jorda and Alonso's review identified only eleven studies in this area, and only one focused on developing countries.

Passive labour market policies may also potentially influence inequality. Unemployment benefits for instance may reduce incentives for workers to accept low-paid employment, while unemployment benefits may not fully equate with lost wages, thus resulting in increased inequality. The evidence for such potential impacts however does not appear to be robust (see Rueda 2015), and indeed Jorda and Alonso's review identifies no relevant studies on developing countries.

Second, education policies also may significantly affect inequality as the distribution of education affects the income distribution. Therefore, better educational provision or more compulsory years of schooling can have a mitigating impact on inequality by affecting the income-earning capacity of people on the left tail of the distribution (Brunello, Fort and Weber 2009).

On the other hand, other education policies, such as subsidies for higher education, can have ambiguous effects: more people will have access to higher paying jobs, which increases inequality, but if high-skilled job supply outstrips demand, this will have a mitigating effect on inequality. However, in developing countries, higher education seems to decrease the wage gap between higher and lower paying jobs (Shimeles and Nabassaga 2017).

Other research suggests that the relationship between education and inequality might not be linear – that is, investment into education has an equalising effect first, and after a certain point increases inequality (Josifidis and Supic 2019). Indeed, education inequality itself is also a driver of income inequality, especially in developing countries (Coady and Dizioli 2018). Likewise, improving education is often highlighted as important for addressing inequality in Global South countries. For instance, in work on Mozambique, Gradin and Tarp (2019) identify educational disparities as fundamental to increases in consumption inequality in recent decades, concluding with the need – if Mozambique is to meet its SDG targets – to accelerate the expansion of education, to the least developed rural communities.

One point of debate in the literature is over how governments might best allocate their resources across education levels. For instance, Su (2004) argues that developing countries should focus on investing heavily on primary education, 'the only way out of polarization and low aggregate efficiency'. This approach is contrary to the policies pursued in many Global South countries.

Third, social benefit policies may serve to redistribute resources from wealthier to poorer households, decreasing inequality by increasing the disposable income of households at the lower end of the income distribution. But social benefits may also influence incentives to participate in the labour market, for instance. Redistribution via social protection has been studied at length (generally with focus on relative inequality measures). Anderson et al. (2017)'s systematic review found that higher government spending is associated with lower income inequality in low- and middle-income countries. However, Yi and Woo (2015)'s review of the data suggested that the impact in least-developed countries is not large enough to mitigate inequality.

Public spending on different areas of social welfare also has different effects on inequality. Anderson et al. (2017)'s review suggests that spending on health and education has a significant but small effect, as middle-income households profit most from these measures. Likewise, the design of social policy, including the targeting approach, influences its effectiveness in reducing inequality. Among the many types of social programmes, conditional cash transfer programmes have received particular attention. Multiple studies document how such programmes have contributed to reducing inequality (Gertel, Giuliodori and Rodríguez 2008; Debowicz and Golan 2014; Flachsbarth et al. 2018).

Finally, fiscal policy and direct taxation are key means to redistribution among those in formal employment but also may have second-round effects via the labour market, education and skill premium that move in the opposite direction. In addition, direct taxation tends to be comparatively limited in lower income Global South countries which, when compared to wealthy countries, have comparatively lower income levels and smaller tax bases due to informality. Indirect taxes play a more significant role. While such taxes tend to be less distorting of labour markets, they are also often considered to be regressive, meaning that they increase (relative) inequality, though this depends on the extent of the informal sector.

Illustrative proposals

Beyond such frameworks outlining policy options, there is no shortage of more specific proposals, many with an eye to anticipating and responding to global trends with worrying potential to exacerbate inequality. One important example is Atkinson (2015)'s *Inequality: What Can be Done?* which sets out fifteen proposals for addressing inequality in wealthy countries, with attention to five core areas: technology, employment, social security, the sharing of capital and taxation. Proposal 1 relates to the direction of technological change and the trend of machines taking over more and more jobs, with potential ramifications for inequality. This direction should be an explicit concern of policymakers, Atkinson argued.

Atkinson's proposals speak directly to some of the core mechanisms identified in Chapters 5 and 6 through which inequality may influence economic and socio-political outcomes. For instance, his second proposal addresses the impact of economic inequality on political inequality and the concentration of power. With elements cross-cutting the frameworks outlined above, Atkinson highlights the value of establishing competition policy with a distributional dimension, strengthening labour union rights, and establishing social and economic councils involving social partners and non-governmental bodies.

Atkinson notes that, while his fifteen proposals are not necessarily a package, they do have interdependencies, meaning that they are more effective when implemented together, though their relative importance is not always entirely clear.

Wealth taxes – which have gained increasing attention in recent years – are not among Atkinson's core proposals, although he does identify them among a handful of key possibilities for further consideration. In this area, Zucman (2024) in particular has argued for an internationally coordinated wealth tax for ultra-high-net-worth individuals. A minimum tax of 2 per cent of the wealth from about 3,000 individuals, Zucman finds, would raise about US$200–250 billion per year globally. Figures would be higher if the tax were extended to centi-millionaires.

Another area spotlighted in more recent proposals is the need for policy responses to technological advancement, and the long-term tension between such advancement, and poverty and inequality. In their book *Power and Progress,* Acemoglu and Johnson (2023), like Atkinson, caution against current trends in technological advancement. History shows us that technology can contribute to shared prosperity, they argue, but also that this is not automatic. The predominant narrative today is 'even more blindly optimistic and more elitist about technology than in the times of Jeremy Bentham, Adam Smith, and Edmund Burke' (p. 8). It enriches a narrow elite of entrepreneurs and investors, and social power will need to change for more inclusive technology to emerge.

Drawing lessons from the contemporary environmental movement, they identify three stages of change. First, a change in narrative was essential. In the environmental movement, this shift can be linked with both the production of new narratives by individuals, such as Rachel Carson's *Silent Spring* (1962), and campaign activities by organizations like Greenpeace. Second, a more organized environmental political movement emerged, including electorally viable Green political parties and organized social protests, which put pressure on the corporate sector. In the third stage technical and policy solutions emerged, identifying carbon taxes, research subsidies, and regulations as core policy levers for change. Analogous recommendations can be drawn for redirecting technological change.

In addressing inequality in the Global South, development cooperation also has an important role to play. Indeed, Atkinson's fifteenth proposal is for wealthy countries to raise their official development assistance (ODA) target to 1 per cent of GNI, that is, above the current international target of 0.7 per cent which only a handful of countries have reached since its adoption by the UN General Assembly. Aid does not always work of course, and a large literature raised several critiques – but on balance, as Ravallion (2014: 982) so aptly sums up: 'we do not have to live under an illusion that aid can solve the problem of global poverty to think that aid can help, and even help greatly'. This is consistent with the best recent evidence available.

How feasibly can structures be changed? What can be done politically?

We began this book by noting the broad contemporary global agreement that inequality matters, underscored in the UN Sustainable Development Goals, both in SDG10 and in the central promise of

'Leave No One Behind'. This attention to inequality in the SDGs was one key way in which the SDGs departed significantly from the Millenium Development Goals (2000–15) (Fukuda-Parr 2016).[7]

In contemporary UN discussions there is little question that addressing inequality is a shared goal. The work is in achieving it through coordination and concerted action at all levels.

UN documents lay out comprehensive targets and indicators, as well as frameworks for action across the UN system. The report of the United Nations Chief Executives Board for Coordination (2017) documents a framework for policies and support programmes. 'Rising inequalities', it notes, 'are not inevitable; they are the product of the policies, laws, regulations, institutions, cultural practices, structural barriers, democratic deficits, and concentrations of wealth and power; indeed, they are the rules of the game that shape the economy and political and social systems' (p. 41). The UN CEB maps diverse policy measures to be undertaken at three core levels: national, regional and global. Additionally, these measures should be supported by a system-wide approach to the analysis and monitoring of inequalities and their causes.

The policy frameworks reviewed above suggest no shortage of policy tools that governments might adopt and adapt, yet this is not what regularly happens in practice. Indeed, this is a key entry point for Blanchard and Rodrik (2021)'s volume: 'we have the tools to address inequality', they note, yet why are these tools not used?

This is a puzzle considering the rational economic voting models so central to many of the theories we explored in Chapters 5 and 6: when inequality is high, so these arguments go, the median voter will favour redistribution and vote in leaders who will implement it (see Meltzer and Richard 1981). Clearly this has not happened in many countries, and review of empirical research studies on the relationship between economic inequality and redistribution also points to a decidedly mixed picture (Vaccaro 2025).

The above discussion hints at some key answers and why they may be somewhat different for Global South countries compared to wealthy countries.

A first answer is politics and interests – also emphasized in Blanchard and Rodrik's volume with reference to wealthy countries. Addressing inequality may be overall in the public interest, but it is naïve to expect elites benefiting from current, less-inclusive systems to straightforwardly give up their advantages – regardless of discursive commitments in global forums. Arguably, there seem to be many similarities here between wealthy and poorer nations.

Acemoglu and Johnson (2023)'s reflections on the societal and political changes needed for the emergence of more inclusive technology point to some ways that momentum for change may shift in practice – through change in narratives, political mobilization and the emergence of new technical and policy solutions. Drawing lessons for addressing inequality, we are arguably in stage two. The global narrative has shifted, and a slew of policy solutions are on the table. There have been protests and organizing efforts, but much more remains to be done. Mozambique's 2024 post-election troubles provide a telling example. Cruz et al. (2023: 348) noted in their final reflections 'the implications of increasing inequality, fragmentation, and conflict, which are already visible, serve as a strong warning sign and incentive to act in the national interest'. The need for promoting a reinvigorated social contract to be pursued vigorously by all parties stands out as essential in this and other cases studied here.

In this context, it must be kept in mind that the role of interest groups and political mobilization may play out quite differently in Global South countries when compared to wealthy democracies. For non-democracies, or in countries where democratic institutions are weak, a model of policy change like Acemoglu and Johnson's does not necessarily apply. Indeed, thinking back to Chapter 6, theories of democratic transition – through the interaction of those at the top, middle and bottom end of the income distribution – may be more useful in thinking about redistributive policy change in many Global South countries. For instance, as Boix (2003) argued, at higher levels of inequality, popular pressures for redistribution may be stronger, meaning that wealthy elites have stronger incentives to resist popular government. When inequality and redistributive pressure are highest, elites may dig in their heels deeply – when and where they can. That this may undermine the overall development process is a significant risk. Furthermore, the role of external actors in domestic politics – donors and others – in many Global South countries adds an additional layer of complexity.

Second, the toolkit available in many Global South countries may be much less sharp and more prone to breakage. Institutional capacity to implement policies and regulations is, on average, considerably weaker in the South as compared to the North. In addition, the size of the informal sector is larger and tax revenues weaker. The contribution by Cruz et al. (2023) on Mozambique is once again illustrative here.

Third, even in the best of circumstances, with governments fully committed to inclusive development and redistribution, addressing inequality can imply fundamental structural change. This can move at glacial pace, making it especially challenging to sustain political momentum. The examples from South Africa referred to across the different chapters of this volume are telling illustrations hereof, including the difficulties of impacting positively on the highly unequal distribution of income and wealth inherited from the Apartheid era.

Finally, we underscore that differences go beyond a split between the Global North and the Global South. As we have sought to illustrate throughout this book using our five country examples, there are similarities across contexts. For instance, trends in inequality in one country may align with others in the same region, many people around the world see inequality as a pressing issue that governments should tackle, and evidence links high inequality in many places to negative socio-economic outcomes – but there are also remarkable differences. Just as it is problematic to assume that we fully understand how to address inequality in low- and middle-income countries based on evidence gathered (disproportionately) in wealthy, Western countries, it is also problematic to treat all Global South countries as the same. By bringing out the nuances of inequality and its dimensions, we have argued that universal claims can be problematic, not only for our understandings, but also for informed policymaking, as they push us away from carefully crafted, tailored solutions. There is no escape from informed country-level understanding, dialogue, and engagement if policy formulation and implementation is to be effective in impacting inequality.

Key takeaways

- While there may be underlying trade-offs in terms of individual incentives, it is possible to achieve both poverty reduction and stable inequality through growth-enhancing redistribution policies and policies to mitigate the negative impacts of inequality.
- A diverse range of policy tools exist at the national level with potential to influence inequality. Policymakers can consider multiple options. Well-functioning labour markets that create jobs, prevent discrimination in all its forms and provide an enabling environment for the poorest are key to increased equality.
- Research and global policy discussion has not sufficiently considered questions of politics and political will. While we all have witnessed shifting global narratives around inequality both historically and over recent decades, there is a lot more work to be done by individuals, by citizen groups, and by policymakers in mobilizing and organizing to achieve the policy changes that can deliver more inclusive economic outcomes.

Summing up

Inequality matters. Taking a stand against inequality was once upon a time a radical position. It is no longer. Today, in endorsing the Sustainable Development Goals in 2015, 191 UN member states are committed to addressing inequality across and within countries; and a rich and fast-growing body of research and reporting centres on inequality. It measures (with ever better data) often shocking patterns and trends, reflects the lived experiences of those left behind, and documents inequality's harms – demonstrating that inequality must not be ignored.

Inequality matters because of fairness and social justice. And, as we have explored in Chapters 5 and 6 of this book, it matters also because of the implications it has had – and may have in future – for economic, social and political outcomes in many situations and contexts around the world. We should all be concerned when we observe that inequality is high or increasing – and commit to doing what we can to foster equality and to make our communities more equitable.

'Equality is a contested concept: people who praise it or disparage it disagree about what they are praising or disparaging' (Dworkin 2000: 2). We illustrated this insight in Chapters 2 and 3, as we explored various approaches to inequality. We showed that, even if we focus on economic inequality only, how we understand its patterns and trends can differ in important ways depending on the sources we rely on and the measures we use – which choice in turn reflects, implicitly or explicitly, our different values.

Inequality matters – but how so may vary across contexts. In Chapter 4, we showed how 'unequal' distributions of resources are understood and acted upon in sometimes very similar, sometimes quite different ways around the world. As we touch on in Chapter 7, addressing inequality is globally important – but how best to go about doing this concretely may vary with its local meaning and context.

We also note, there is still a yawning gap between statements and actual change. In terms of the SDGs, in particular, the global community is not on track to achieving the targets to which the UN member states committed. Many factors have contributed (including the Covid-19 pandemic). How do we move forward?

Inequality matters – but it is extremely challenging to tackle. In our assessment, the core challenge at hand is not only about building commitment to the importance of addressing inequality. It is also about deliberation and agreement among diverse constituencies and about practical action, considering messy realities. This is work for ordinary citizens as much as for experts and global policymakers. We wrote this book with the former in mind – to help provide tools to participate effectively, informed in a balanced way by research. We hope you, our reader, feel first, better equipped to contextualize your own understanding of what inequality means and how this understanding relates to current discourses; and second, motivated to engage in existing debates in a nuanced and well-informed manner, that reads beyond big claims and understands the complexity of inequality, its different dimensions, and its multifaceted impacts.

In our view, both concerted action and new thinking are needed – radical, but also considered, nuanced and practical. It is this sort of thinking that comes to grips with context, values and evidence, which will eventually inform the crafting and implementation of truly transformative policies. Our attention is often drawn to big claims and global solutions, but these are no match for the messiness and diversity of the real world. The challenge at hand goes much further. On this note, we conclude.

Notes

1 Willem Buiter, Professor of Economics at London School of Economics, *Financial Times*, 2007. Quote taken from Wade (2014: 99).
2 Quote taken from Wade (2014: 99).
3 This relates to the discussion in Chapter 4 on different attitudes towards inequality depending on whether it results from luck or from merit.
4 That is, assuming all other factors remain the same.
5 While absolute poverty focuses on whether an individual has an income/consumption level above a certain value (the poverty line), relative poverty compares individual income/consumption with a certain percentage of the median income/consumption in the country and thus focuses on comparison with peers rather than on a defined minimum standard value.
6 Bergstrom (2022) finds support for this result using a different model to predict headcount poverty.
7 Another important departure of the SDGs was in its development and perception as a North-South agenda, rather than a set of goals developed by the Global North for the Global South countries. Addressing inequality, a goal relevant to both northern and southern countries, was also important in this respect (see Fukuda-Parr and Smaavik Hegstad 2018).

References

Acemoglu, D., and S. Johnson (2023). *Power and Progress: Our Thousand-Year Struggle over Technology and Prosperity.* London: Basic Books.

Aghion, P., E. Caroli and C. García-Peñalosa (1999). 'Inequality and Economic Growth: The Perspective of the New Growth Theories'. *Journal of Economic Literature*, 37(4): 1615–60. https://doi.org/10.1257/jel.37.4.1615. Accessed: 14 September 2025.

Anderson, E., M. A. Jalles D 'Orey, M. Duvendack and L. Esposito (2017). 'Does Government Spending Affect Income Inequality? A Meta-Regression Analysis'. *Journal of Economic Surveys*, 31(4): 961–87.

Arndt, C., A. Garcia, F. Tarp and J. Thurlow (2012). 'Poverty Reduction and Economic Structure: Comparative Path Analysis for Mozambique and Vietnam'. *Review of Income and Wealth*, 58(4): 742–63. 10.1111/j.1475-4991.2011.00474.x

Atkinson, A. B. (2015). *Inequality: What can be done?*. Cambridge MA: Harvard University Press.

Atkinson, A. B., C. Leventi, B. Nolan, H. Sutherland and I. Tasseva (2017). 'Reducing Poverty and Inequality Through Tax-Benefit Reform and the Minimum Wage: The UK as a Case-Study'. *Journal of Economic Inequality*, 15: 303–23.

*Baselgia, E., and R. Foellmi (2022). 'Inequality and Growth'. In K. F. Zimmermann (ed.) *Handbook of Labor, Human Resources and Population Economics*: 1–41 Geneva: Springer Nature. https://doi.org/10.1007/978-3-319-57365-6_332-1. Accessed: 14 September 2025.

Bergstrom, K. (2022). 'The Role of Income Inequality for Poverty Reduction'. *World Bank Economic Review*. 36(3): 583–604. https://doi.org10.1093/wber/lhab026. Accessed: 21 September 2025.

Bhorat, H., A. Lilenstein and B. Stanwix (2020). *The Impact of the National Minimum wage in South Africa: Early Quantitative Evidence*. Report for the National Minimum Wage Commission. https://www.labour.gov.za/DocumentCenter/Publications/Basic%20Conditions%20of%20Employment/The%20Impact%20of%20the%20National%20Minimum%20Wage%20in%20South%20Africa,%20early%20quantitative%20evidence_.pdf. Accessed: 14 September 2025.

Blanchard, O., and D. Rodrik (2021). *Combating Inequality: Rethinking Government's Role*. Cambridge MA: MIT Press.

Bogliacino, F., and D. Rojas (2017). 'The Evolution of Inequality in Latin America in the 21st Century: Patterns, Drivers and Causal Hypotheses'. *Drivers and Causal Hypotheses*. Mimeo. 21 March.

Boix, C. (2003). *Democracy and Redistribution*. Cambridge: Cambridge University Press.

Bourguignon, F. (2004). 'The Poverty-Growth-Inequality Triangle', Indian Council for Research on International Economic Relations Working Paper 125. New Delhi: Indian Council for Research on International Economic Relations.

Brunello, G., M. Fort and G. Weber (2009). 'Changes in Compulsory Schooling, Education and the Distribution of Wages in Europe'. *The Economic Journal* 119(536): 516–39.

Cerra, V., R. Lama and N. V. Loyaza (2021). *Links between Growth, Inequality, and Poverty*. Washington, DC: World Bank.

Coady, D., and A. Dizioli (2018). 'Income Inequality and Education Revisited: Persistence, Endogeneity and Heterogeneity'. *Applied Economics*, 50(25): 2747–61.

Cruz, A., I. A. Ferreira, J. Flentø and F. Tarp (eds) (2023). ***Mozambique at a Fork in the Road: The Institutional Diagnostic Project.*** **Cambridge: Cambridge University Press.**

Debowicz, D., and J. Golan (2014). 'The Impact of Oportunidades on Human Capital and Income Distribution in Mexico: A Top-Down/Bottom-Up Approach'. *Journal of Policy Modeling* 36(1): 24–42.

Drèze, J. (2020). 'Policy beyond evidence'. *World Development*, 125: art. 104668. https://doi.org/10.1016/j.worlddev.2019.104797 (last accessed 17 September 2025).

Dworkin, R. (2000). *Sovereign Virtue: The Theory and Practice of Equality*. Cambridge MA: Harvard University Press.

Ferreira, F. H. (2010). 'Distributions in Motion: Economic Growth, Inequality, and Poverty Dynamics', World Bank Policy Research Working Paper 5424. Washington DC: World Bank. https://documents1.worldbank.org/curated/en/228561468314728723/pdf/WPS5424.pdf (accessed 29 November 2024).

Ferreira, F. H. G., and M. Ravallion (2008). *Global Poverty and Inequality: A Review of the Evidence*. Washington, DC: World Bank.

Flachsbarth, I., S. Schotte, J. Lay and A. Garrido (2018). 'Rural Structural Change, Poverty and Income Distribution: Evidence from Peru'. *Journal of Economic Inequality*, 16(4): 631–53.

Fukuda-Parr, S. (2016). 'From the Millennium Development Goals to the Sustainable Development Goals: Shifts in Purpose, Concept, and Politics of Global Goal Setting for Development'. *Gender & Development*, 24(1): 43–52. http://www.jstor.org/stable/24698089. Last accessed 21 September 2025.

Fukuda-Parr, S. and T. Smaavik Hegstad (2018). ' "Leaving No One Behind" as a Site of Contestation and Reinterpretation'. *Journal of Globalization and Development*, (9)2: art. 20180037. https://doi.org/10.1515/jgd-2018-0037 (last accessed 17 September 2025).

Gertel, H. R., R. F. Giuliodori and A. Rodríguez (2008). 'Analysis of the Short-Term Impact of the Argentine Social Assistance Program "Plan Jefes y Jefas" on Income Inequality Applying the Dagum Decomposition Analysis of the Gini Ratio', *Advances on Income Inequality and Concentration Measures*, 201–2. Abingdon: Routledge.

Gradín, C. and F. Tarp (2019). 'Investigating Growing Inequality in Mozambique'. *South African Journal of Economics*, 87(2): 110–38. https://doi.org/10.1111/saje.12215 (last accessed 17 September 2025)

Gradín, C., M. Leibbrandt and F. Tarp (2021). 'Setting the Scene'. In C. Gradín, M. Leibbrandt, and F. Tarp (eds), *Inequality in the Developing World*. pp. 3–16. Oxford: Oxford University Press.

Jones, S. (2024). 'Mozambique in Post-Election Turmoil: Economic Policies That Could Make a Difference'. *The Conversation* (13 November). https://theconversation.com/mozambique-in-post-election-turmoil-economic-policies-that-could-make-a-difference-243603

*Jorda, V., and J. M. Alonso (2020). 'What Works to Mitigate and Reduce Relative (and Absolute) Inequality?'. WIDER Working Paper 2020/152. Helsinki: UNU-WIDER.

Josifidis, K., and N. Supic (2019). 'The Uncertainty of Academic Rent and Income Inequality: The OECD Panel Evidence'. *Journal of Economic Issues*, 53(2): 394–402.

Lakner, C., D. G. Mahler, M. Negre and E. B. Prydz (2022). 'How Much Does Reducing Inequality Matter for Global Poverty?'. *Journal of Economic Inequality*. 20: 559–85. https://doi.org/10.1007/s10888-021-09510-w. Accessed: 14 September 2025.

Lindbeck, A., and D. J. Snower (2001). 'Insiders versus Outsiders'. *Journal of Economic Perspectives*, 15(1): 165–88.

Meltzer, A. H., and S. F. Richard (1981). 'A Rational Theory of the Size of Government'. *Journal of Political Economy* 89(5): 914–27.

*Nguyen, C. V., and F. Tarp (2024). 'Socioeconomic Inequality in Viet Nam'. WIDER Working Paper 2024/61. Helsinki: UNU-WIDER. https://doi.org/10.35188/UNU-WIDER/2024/524-0. Accessed: 14 September 2025.

Nguyen, C. V., and N. M. Pham (2018). 'Economic Growth, Inequality, and Poverty in Vietnam'. *Asian-Pacific Economic Literature*, 31(1): 45–58. https://doi.org/10.1111/apel.12219. Accessed: 14 September 2025.

Okun, A. M. (1975). *Equality and Efficiency: The Big Trade-off*. Washington, DC: Brookings Institution Press.

Ravallion, M. (2014). 'On the Role of Aid in The Great Escape', *Review of Income and Wealth*, 60(4): 967–84. https://www.roiw.org/2014/n4/17.pdf (last accessed 17 September 2015).

Ravallion, M. (2016). 'Growth, Inequality, and Poverty'. In *The Economics of Poverty: History, Measurement, and Policy*, 379–476. New York: Oxford University Press.

Rueda, D. (2015). 'The State of the Welfare State: Unemployment, Labor Market Policy, and Inequality in the Age of Workfare'. *Comparative Politics*, 47(3): 296–314.

Shimeles, A., and T. Nabassaga (2017). 'Why Is Inequality High in Africa?'. *Journal of African Economies*, 27(1): 108–26.

Stewart, F. (2016). 'Changing Perspectives on Inequality and Development'. *Studies in Comparative International Development*, 51: 60–80. https://doi.org/10.1007/s12116-016-9222-x. Accessed: 14 September 2025.

Su, X. (2004). 'The Allocation of Public Funds in a Hierarchical Educational System'. *Journal of Economic Dynamics and Control*, 28(12): 2485–510.

Tarp, F. (ed.) (2017). *Growth, Structural Transformation, and Rural Change in Viet Nam*. Oxford: Oxford University Press.

Tarp, F. (2018). 'Vietnam: The dragon that rose from the ashes'. WIDER Working Paper 2018/126. Helsinki: UNU-WIDER.

Thorbecke, E. (2016). 'Inequality and the Trade-Off between Efficiency and Equity'. *Journal of Human Development and Capabilities*, 17(3): 460–64. https://doi.org/10.1080/19452829.2016.1203033. Accessed: 14 September 2025.

United Nations Chief Executives Board for Coordination (2017). *Leaving No One Behind: Equality and Non-Discrimination at the Heart of Sustainable Development*. The United Nations System Shared Framework for Action. New York: United Nations

*Vaccaro, A. (2025). 'Does Higher Inequality Lead to More Redistributive Taxation in the Global South?'. Mimeo.

Wade, R. H. (2014). 'The Strange Neglect of Income Inequality in Economics and Public Policy'. In G. A. Cornia, and F. Stewart (eds), *Towards Human Development: New Approaches to Macroeconomics and Inequality* (pp. 99–121), Oxford: Oxford University Press.

World Bank (2016). *Poverty and Shared Prosperity 2016: Taking on Inequality*. Washington, DC: World Bank.

World Bank (2020). *Ethiopia Poverty Assessment: Harnessing Continued Growth for Accelerated Poverty Reduction*. Washington DC: World Bank.

Yi, D. J., and J. H. Woo (2015). 'Democracy, Policy, and Inequality: Efforts and Consequences in the Developing World'. *International Political Science Review*, 36(5): 475–92.

Zucman, G. (2024). *A Blueprint for a Coordinated Minimum Effective Taxation Standard for Ultra-High-Net-Worth Individuals*. Report commissioned by the Brazilian G20 presidency. Online: EUTAX Observatory. https://www.taxobservatory.eu/publication/a-blueprint-for-a-coordinated-minimum-effective-taxation-stand ard-for-ultra-high-net-worth-individuals/. Accessed: 14 September 2025.

Index

Note: Page numbers followed by *italics* and **bold** denote figures and tables.

absolute
   Gini coefficients *80*, 81, 82,
      83, *84–89*
   inequality 9, 84, 161, 213
Acemoglu, D. 141, 187, 191, 192, 218,
   222, 225
African National Congress 177
Afrobarometer 106
aggregation
   challenges of 34–35
   levels of 39
Alesina, A. 40, 188
Alkire-Foster multidimensional
   poverty index 35
Almas, I. 121–123, 126n13
Alonso, J. M. 213, 215
Amiel, Y. 102
Anderson, E. 216
Angelopulo, G. 185
anonymity 61
Ansell, B. 38
Argentina 110
Arndt, C. 35
Atamanov, A. 43
Atkinson, A. B. 4, 7, 70, 90n6,
   165n12, 217–219, 218, 221, 222
Atlantic, The 2
Australia 111
Auten, G. 2
Autor, D. 2

Baldwin, K. 40
Ballano, C. 102
Barro, R. J. 188
Bentham, J. 218
Berry, R. A. 190
birth registration 28, 29
Blanchard, O. 211, 213, 220, 221

Bogliacino, F. 214
Boix, C. 186, 187, 191, 192, 222, 226
Bornschier, S. 178
Bourguignon, F. 138, 211
Brazil 138, 139
Brunori, P. 43
Burke, E. 218

Canelas, C. 40
capability
   approach 152
   concept of 22
   inequality trap 41
capital 186, 187
Capital and Ideology (Piketty) 36
Capital in the Twenty-First Century
   (Piketty) 6
capital poverty trap 41
Cappelen, A. W. 121–123, 126n13
Carson, R. 219
Cerra, V. 207
Charumilind, C. 189
Chatterjee, A. 38
Chetty, R, M 38
Choi, G. 26, 30, 106
Clark, A. E. 160
coefficient of variation 63
Collier, P. 188
Colombia 139
   Colombian National Human
      Development Report 31
   education 41
   Gini coefficients **60**, 153
   Gini index in 54, *55*
   gross domestic product 14
   Human Development Index 153
   intersectional inequalities 36
   Liberals in 178

life satisfaction 156, *158*
lifespan disparities **25**
Palma ratio 63, *64*
Political Inequality Index 26, *26*, *27*
rural women 42
subjective well-being *159*
Comparative Manifestos Project 175, 176
conflict 16, 39, 40, 173, 178, 181, 186, 187
cosmopolitan view 71
Covid-19 1, 73, 75–76
Cowell, F. A. 102
credit market imperfections 144
Crenshaw, K. 36
cross-country analysis 147
Cruz, A. 221, 222
Czajka, L. 38

Dahl, R. A. 25, 181
D'Ambrosio, C. 160
dashboard approach 6–8, 35, 90, 158
'Datt-Ravallion decomposition' technique 207, 208
Deaton, A. 5, 137, 151
decomposability 61
Deininger, K. 147
demand for redistribution 104, 111, 115
democracy 1, 6, 14, 16, 25, 178, 181, 185–188
 inequality and 185–188
democratic erosion 186
developing countries 6, 37, 78, 142, 215, 216
direct taxation 217
Downs, A. 116
Dreze, J. 213
Duncan, G. J. 38

'East Asian Miracle,' 142
economic growth 4, 78, 90n19
 determinants 136
 inequality 137–142, *138–141*
economic inequality 23, 37–38, 173–175, 179, 181–185, 189, 210, 211
Economist, The 2, 72, 76
education 145, 215, 216
 impact of inequality on 150–155
elephant curve 78, 79, *79*
endowment of median voter 146
endowment policies 211
Equality of Opportunity (Roemer) 15, 21, 42–44, 210
@EQUAL project 3
Ethiopia 14, 142, 179, 207
 Gini coefficient 59, **60**, 153
 gross domestic product 13
 Human Development Index 153
 life satisfaction 156, 158, *158*, *159*
 lifespan disparities **25**
 Lorenz curves 66, *67*
 measures of inequality in 2020 **69**
ethnic inequalities 40
eudaimonia 157

fairness, as mediating factor 120–125
Ferreira. F. H. G. 36, 42, 43, 208, 212
Ferreira, I. A. 7, 12, 56, 79, 82, 102, 112, 117, 122, 124, 137, 150, 151
fertility, differential in 146
fiscal policy 217
France 108, 111
Franc, R. 188

Gallego, J. 184
Gashaw, T. 184
GDP. *see* gross domestic product (GDP)
gender
 equality 41
 intersection 36
 political inequality with 28

Index

Gender Inequality Index (GII) 41
generalized entropy (GE) indices 66
Germany 108, 111
Gethin, A. 38
Gini 3, 6–8, 28, 34, 53, 111, 104, 107, 139, 159, 179, 207, 214
   income inequality measure 66
   relative *vs.* absolute *80*, 81, 82, *83*, *84–89*
Gisselquist, R. M. 7, 12, 29, 34, 40, 102, 112, 117, 122, 124, 137, 150, 151, 187, 188
global inequality 81
   decomposition of 75, *76*
   trends 73, *74*
Global North 112, 214, 222
Global South 112, 125, 149, 160, 178, 181, 214, 216, 217, 219, 221, 222
governance 4, 12, 16, 150, 173, 178, 181, 183, 185
government policy 12, 26, 181
Gradín, C. 5, 59, 81, 158, 210, 216, 220
Great Escape, The (Deaton) 137
gross domestic product (GDP) 136, 139, 142
gross national income (GNI) 136
group-based inequalities 40–42, 43
growth
   with equity 143, 209–210
   and inequality 137–150
growth incidence curves (GICs) 78
Guardado, J. 184
Gunderson, J. R. 175
Gurr, T. 189

Haggard, S. 187
Harrison, E. 102
HDI. *see* Human Development Index (HDI)
health, impact of inequality on 150–155
health inequalities 25
Hernando, M. G. 5

Hoeffler, A. 188
Hong Kong 142
horizontal inequality 40, 41
Hotelling, H. 116
Houle, C. 188
household survey data 43
Huber, J. D. 40
human development 12, 16, 30
   impact of inequality on 150–161
Human Development Index (HDI) 30, 31, *32*, 44, 152, *155*, 163n19
Hussain, M. A. 35

Iceland 106
incentivized experiment 124
Indonesia 111, 142
inequality 3, 37–38, 44, 224
   capability approach 21–22
   cause of 1, 5
   characteristics 3
   Covid-19 pandemic 1
   dashboard approach 6–11
   defined 1, 21
   and democracy 185–188
   economic 23, 54, *55*, 56–57, 173–175, 179, 181–185, 189, 210, 211
   educational opportunity 24
   evolution of *9*
   global absolute income gains *11*
   growth and 137–150
   growth incidence curve *10*
   and household debt 149
   impact on human development and well-being 150–161
   individuals and households 44
   influence on redistribution decisions 124
   levels of analysis 39
   mean income and 137
   measures of 3, 6–7
   meritocratic view of 121
   multidimensional approach 22–23, 30–32

of opportunities 15, 42–43, 206
perceptions of 104–115
policies affecting 212
political 2, 181–185
reduction 206–210
regimes 36
relative vs. absolute *80*, 81, 82, *83*, *84–89*
social class identifiers 24, 104
social factors 2
state and public services 29
understandings vs. standard measures 100–104
inequality-adjusted HDI (IHDI) 31–32
inequality measurement
    absolute measures 80–82, *81*, *83–89*, 89–90
    challenges 57–60, **60**
    coefficient of variation 63
    empirical realities 73, *74*, 75–76, *76–77*, 78–80, *79*
    generalized entropy (GE) indices 66
    Palma ratio 63, *64*, 65
    patterns and trends 72–73
    percentiles 63, *64*
    properties 61, *62*
    value judgements 67, 70–71
    variance 63
Inequality: What Can be Done? (Atkinson) 217–219
Inner Level, The (Wilkinson, Pickett) 11
Integrated Values Surveys (2022) 179
International Social Survey Programme (ISSP) 104–106
interpersonal trust 179–181
intersectionality 35–37, **36**
inverse-U hypothesis 139

Japan 142
Johnson, S. 218, 221
Jones, S. 185
Jong-sung, Y. 183
Jorda, V. 25, 174, 213, 215
Justino, P. 189

Kaufman, R. R. 187
Khagram, S. 183
Korea 106
Kuznets curve 137, 138, 142
Kuznets, S. 137–139, 206

Lakner, C. 78, 208
Lama, R. 207
Latin America 14
LeBas, A. 178
Leibbrandt, M. 5
life evaluation 157
lifespan disparity 25, **25**
Loyaza, N. V. 207

macroeconomic stability 142
Mahrt, K. 35
Malaysia 142
Markussen, T. 181
McCoy, J. 185
median voter theorem 115, 116
Meltzer, A. H. 115
Meltzer–Richard model 116
Mexico 108, 111
Michalopoulos, S. 40
Milanovic, B. 2, 4, 5, 75, 78, 79, 91n15, 140, 165n5
Millenium Development Goals 220
minimum wages 211, 214
misperceptions 110–115
Mitchell, G. 5
mobile money 144
mobilization 188–190
Morris P. A. 38
Mounk, Y. 2
Mozambique 142
    democracy 14
    evolution of inequality in 106, 107

first-order stochastic
  dominance 35
Gini coefficient **60**, 153
gross domestic product 13
Human Development Index 153
lifespan disparities **25**
perceptions of inequality 102,
  103, 108
post-election conflicts in 213
M-Theil 159
Multidimensional Inequality
  Framework (MIF) 32, **34**, 35

national income 136
national policies 210–217
Nguyen C. 160
Nigeria, ethnic group 41
Niño-Zarazúa, M. 25, 174
Nunn, N. 186

Occupy Wall Street movement 188
official development assistance
  (ODA) 219
Okun, A. M. 205
Organisation for Economic
  Co-operation and Development
  (OECD) 156, 175
Oxfam International 72

Pabón, D. 37
Palma ratio 63, *64*, 65, 159
Papaioannou, E. 40
Pavlović, T. 188
Payne, K. 4
Peragine, V. 43
perceived inequality 110
percentiles 63, *64*
  income shares and ratios 76, *77*
perceptions of inequality 15, 99,
  104–106, *109*, 110, 180, 189
Perotti, R. 188
Pickett, K. E. 4, 151
  Inner Level, The 11
Piketty, T. 2, 4, 5, 36, 37

Capital and Ideology 36
*Capital in the Twenty-First
  Century* 6
polarization 174–178
political inequality 26, 181–185
  with gender 28
  indicators 28
Political Inequality Index (PII)
  26, *26*, 30
political polarization 174–178
political power 181–185
Pontusson, J. 175
population principle 61
poverty 56, 57, 137, 204
  reduction 206–210
Power and Progress (Acemoglu and
  Johnson) 218
preferences for redistribution
  115–120
Price of Inequality, The (Stiglitz) 6
property rights 145
Public Administration Performance
  Index (PAPI) 182
public spending 216

Qian, N. 186

race 43
  intersection 36
Rahman, T. 185
Ravallion, M. 67, 82, 102, 219
redistributive policy 115–120
redistributive taxation 187
regulatory policies 145
relative deprivation 189
relative inequality 3, 73, 82, 216,
  217. *see* alo inequality
  inadequacy of 71
  in Mozambique 89
Republic of Korea 142
resource mobilization 189
Revolutionary Armed Forces of
  Colombia (FARC) 190
Richard, S. F. 115

Roberts, K. W. S 116
Robinson, J. A. 187
Rodrigues, C. 38
Rodrik, D. 211, 213, 220, 221
Roemer, J. E. 43
Rojas, D. 214
Rueda, D. 175
Ruiz-Castillo, J. 102

Saez, E. 2
Samuels, D. 38
scale invariance 61, 70, 111
Schilling, F. 185
SDGs. *see* Sustainable Development Goals (SDGs)
Seidl, C. 102
Sen, A. 21, 22, 38
    Sen's capability approach 152
serpent curve *81*
shared prosperity 65
Silent Spring (Carson) 219
Singapore 142
Smith, A. 161n2, 218
    Wealth of Nations, The 137
social
    cohesion 179–181
    discontent 145–146, 206, 211
    inequality 104, 106
    mobility 111, 146, 160
    mobilization 188, 189
    transfer 211
sociopolitical inequality 188
Solt, F. 183
Somer, M. 186
South Africa 29, 114, 142, 179
    comparative party manifestos in 176–177
    Datt-Ravallion Decomposition **212**
    ethnicity 43
    Gini coefficients **60**, 153
    Gini index and mean log deviation 67, *68*

gross domestic product 13
household debt 149
Human Development Index 153
implementation of mobile money in 144
inequality 140, 149
life satisfaction 156, 158, *158*, *159*
lifespan disparities **25**
Palma ratio 63, *64*
Political Inequality Index 26, *26–28*
political party positioning in 176, 177
spatial inequality 39
Spirit Level, The (Wilkinson, Pickett) 5, 11
Splinter, D. 2
Squire, L. 147
Stewart, F. 23, 41
Stiglitz, J. 5, 6
Sustainable Development Goals (SDGs) 1, 29, 219–220, 224, 225
Su, X. 216
Sweden 111

Taiwan 142
    growth with equity 143
Tarp, F. 5, 7, 12, 35, 42, 56, 59, 70, 79, 81, 82, 102, 112, 118, 122, 124, 137, 150, 151, 185, 206, 209, 210, 216
taxation 117, 145, 146, 149
Tejería-Martínez, M. 25, 174
Thailand 142
Therborn, G. 22, 25, 36
Thorbecke, E. 189
trade-off 205, 206, 209
Trannoy, A. 43
transfer principle 61
Tran, T. 160
trust
    interpersonal 179–181
    social cohesion and 179–181
Tungodden, B. 121–123, 126n13

UNDP's Human Development Index (HDI) 30–32, *33*
unemployment 215
United Nations Chief Executives Board for Coordination 220
United Nations Development Programme (UNDP) 152
United States 182, 183
    perceptions of inequality 108, 111
UNU-WIDER, World Income Inequality Database (WIID) 7

Van Vu, H. 160
variance 63
Vietnam 142, 179, 182
    democracy 14
    differences in framing of information 113–114
    Gini coefficients **60**, 153
    Gini index and mean log deviation 67, *68*
    gross domestic product 14
    growth with equity 209–210
    Human Development Index 153
    life satisfaction 156, 158, *158*, *159*
    lifespan disparities **25**
    perceptions of inequality 102, 103, 108
    women 42

Vietnam Provincial Governance 182
violent conflict 188–190
vote-buying 184

Wantchekon, L. 184
wealth inequality 15, 37–38
Wealth of Nations, The (Smith) 137
wealth taxes 218
well-being 16, 22, 54
    defining and measuring 157
    impact of inequality on 150–161
    inequality affects subjective 155–156
Wen, J. 186
Wilkinson, R. G. 4, 151
    Inner Level, The 11
women 41
    Colombia 42
    Vietnam 42
Woo, J. H. 216
World Bank 208
World Happiness Report 156
World Income Inequality Database (WIID) 9, 39, 56, 59, **60**, 79, 82, 106, 138

Yagci, A. H. 188
Yi, D. J. 216

Zucman, G. 2, 218